EPIC
RUNS
of the
WORLD

Explore the world's most thrilling running routes and trails

CONTENTS

© Courtesy of Big Sur Marathon | Reg Regalado

© Ian Walton for Virgin Money London Marathon

© Stefano Jeantet

Easy · Harder · Epic

INTRODUCTION

Today running is more than just exercise. Marathons are no longer just for fitness junkies, and the sport has spawned a surprisingly rabid and diverse subculture. Sure, people still run to get into shape, but these days just as many do it to meditate. Some do it for the high or just to clear their head, while others enter races as a way to make a dozen friends all at once. Many stick to pavements, though more are running off-road and into the wilderness. Regardless of how or where they do it, most runners agree that it is the great grounding constant in their life.

Most runners will also agree that moving through a landscape while also breaking a sweat has an oddly profound effect on one's sense of place. Whether you're repeating a well-worn loop close to home or exploring an exotic new land while travelling, running affords a deeper understanding of a town or city and its citizens. Unlike a walking tour, it has a way of forcing more self-reflection, while also allowing you to cover more ground in a short amount of time. In fact, one of the best, and quickest, ways to get to know an unfamiliar place is by competing in a local race, and it is perhaps the only way one can work out and go sightseeing all at once.

Indeed, running now has a surprisingly symbiotic relationship with travel itself – experienced vagabonds insist it cures jetlag, while running seems to be the one exercise we actually do when travelling, whether for a short business trip or during a round-the-world adventure. There is nothing easier than stuffing a pair of running shoes into our luggage, and those running shoes can now take us to places such as Everest Base Camp, the Australian Outback and even to the North Pole. As more and more people seek out running travel adventures, organised races are popping up in the most extreme corners of the globe. And not only marathons – ultra-distance events are booming.

And this is perhaps the most remarkable thing to happen in the world of running in the past decade: those of us who used to run a few miles after work now run 10Ks; those who used to run 10Ks now run marathons; and those who have run a couple of marathons now have their eyes on ultramarathons.

In this book are 200 of the greatest runs on the planet, in some 60 countries across all seven continents. The 50 featured runs are first-hand accounts, written by people who are not only passionate about running – some even do it for a living – but also about the idea that to have run somewhere is to know it. These are stories that will convince you there are times when a run is the way to see a place.

You'll learn why the 120-year-old Boston Marathon has become a symbol of pride for America's oldest major city, and how a simple run from Bondi to Coogee beaches allows you to become one of Sydney's fitness-mad beach bums (if only for an hour). You'll understand why a stage race like the Sahara's brutal 156-mile (250km) Marathon des Sables sears its way into your psyche, and how a quick run around Québec in winter reveals the city's beauty.

HOW TO USE THIS BOOK
Each of the five chapters in this book includes a special collection of runs from that particular region, from easy-access park runs and city loops to iconic marathons and epic ultras. A colour-coded key on the contents page will help you identify which are easy, which require serious fitness and fortitude, and which fall somewhere in between (based almost entirely on distance and elevation gain). Accompanying each main story is some practical information to help you follow in the author's footsteps. The authors have also included three extra routes or races that have a similar character to their featured run, but may be closer to home or more accessible.

It's important to point out that there are a handful of insanely difficult runs in this book that only a few of us will ever be able to do. In many cases, the people who have written about them are professional runners, paid to train on a daily basis. But the armchair adventure value of these tales cannot be overstated. You will no doubt become parched just reading about Death Valley's Badwater 135 and become dizzy reading about the notoriously disorienting Barkley Marathons. These are stories that will inspire you to kick things up a notch, to train for something bold and, perhaps, someday sign up for a race you never thought possible.

Whichever runs you decide to add to your bucket list, take the time to source and study your own detailed maps and to gear up properly for any routes that might take you off the beaten path. Be kind to your fellow runners and even kinder to the wild landscapes you travel through. Be prepared for a few weird looks from locals and, most importantly, never forget to pack your running shoes.

Clockwise from left: pounding New Zealand's Kepler Track; running the Great Ocean Road in Australia; Positano, a picturesque pit-stop on Italy's Amalfi Coast. Previous page: negotiating tricky terrain on Australia's Larapinta Trail

Opening spread, clockwise from left: experience ancient Angkor Wat and the sunshine of California's Big Sur on foot; Alpine fancy dress on Italy's Arrancabirra; the classic London Marathon

THE SAFARICOM HALF MARATHON

Who needs a Land Rover when you can race across the Kenya's grasslands on foot, in the name of conservation?

The night before the race, I started to freak out. A few nerves are normal, I know, but this was different. In my past as a very amateur competitive runner, I'd climb into bed on the eve of a race and fret about whether I'd set the alarm for pm, not am; whether it would even go off; where I'd go for breakfast after the run. But here I was, lying on a cot in a canvas tent in northern Kenya, hours before the start of a half marathon, worrying about lions. Or, more specifically: about being eaten by one.

Last summer, my husband, four friends and I had travelled from San Francisco via Frankfurt, arriving late in Nairobi to spend the night before flying out the next morning in a little plane to land at Lewa Wildlife Conservancy. In other words, we were not in tiptop marathon shape – even half-marathon shape. And this was not your average, or easiest, course. Rather, it's said to be one of the world's toughest. At 5500ft (1670m) elevation, Lewa was hot, dry and dusty. It suddenly dawned on me: maybe I should have trained for this.

Team Gazelle – as we'd optimistically christened ourselves – had come to take part in the Safaricom Marathon, a meticulously orchestrated event co-hosted by Lewa, in partnership with the nonprofit Tusk, to raise funds for wildlife conservation, education and community development across Kenya. A 62,000-acre (25,000 hectare) preserve, Lewa is home to a wide array of local wildlife, including 169 rhinos, more than a dozen cheetahs, some 400 migrating elephants, the world's single largest population of Grevy's zebras, 44 lions and – I was promised before committing to this harebrained idea – 140 armed guards standing watch in case there's any trouble. (In the marathon's

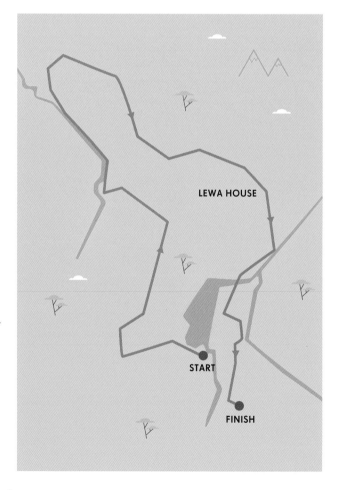

LEWA HOUSE

START

FINISH

almost two-decade existence, though, there hasn't been.)

Still, as I lay in the dark listening to screeching baboons, the possibility felt palpable. A few hours earlier, we'd gone out on a game drive and seen scores of wildlife: Cape buffalo, hyenas, black rhinos, white rhinos, so many rhinos. We even chased a cheetah. In the Land Cruiser, mind you, not on foot. For 364 days a year, safari guests aren't allowed to roam free, but race day is a different beast.

I awoke before sunrise to Kenyan pop music blaring over speakers, thumping through camp, a communal call to rise. Then came the whoosh of helicopters, revving up to ready the course. Manned by Mike Watson, longtime CEO of Lewa and a rugged bushman if ever there was one, and his colleagues, the helicopters crisscrossed the landscape, hovering overhead, gently flushing the wildlife away for the day – making way for Lewa's rarest species: humans.

Fourteen hundred runners from 20 countries – the majority from

> ## "For 364 days a year, safari guests are not allowed to roam free. Race day is a different beast"

Kenya – come together for one morning every June, in the name of conservation and inspiration. Most people opt to run the half marathon, but a hardy 200 or so, including top Kenyan runners like 2016 Olympic gold medalist Eliud Kipchoge, go for the full distance, which double-backs along the same route. There's a 5K kids' race just before it, too. Local school kids train all year in the hope of winning vouchers to the supermarket, goody bags filled with socks, pens, paper and chocolate and, to the first-place finisher, a phone.

Fuelled up on bananas and coffee and what felt like a reservoir's worth of bottled water, we laced up our sneakers and drifted down a dirt road towards the starting line, where we met up with one more member of Team Gazelle: Jacob Kanake, a Lewa driver who had worked on the preserve for years, but had never run the race before. 'I'm ready!' he said. We group-hugged. A muffled voice over the speaker beckoned everyone to the start line. The Kenyan flag waved and we were off.

It was a human stampede, 1400 runners of varying levels charging the line, a simple banner propped up by two branches, revealing a dirt path no wider than a fire-road. We squeezed onto the soft, stone-strewn path – flanked by uneven ground and prickly grasses, ensuring we didn't stray too far – and took off en masse: a scrum of sinewy Kenyans, brawny Kenyans and some barefooted Kenyans, as well as fully outfitted super-fit foreigners in dry-wick tees emblazoned with company logos, and not-as-fit foreigners, no offence to my fellow Gazelles.

And then the adrenaline-fuelled din subsided into a collective quiet, everyone instantly awed – or was it daunted? – by the

THE HILLS ARE ALIVE

The 62,000-acre Lewa Wildlife Conservancy was formed in 1995 to protect animals against extinction and poaching, and now incorporates an innovative partnership with local communities to promote awareness. It's a sanctuary for endangered and threatened species including rhino, leopard, zebra, elephant, lion and antelope. The park is in fact home to 12% of Kenya's eastern black rhino population and the world's largest congregation of Grevy's zebras.

Clockwise from top: runners from more than 20 countries traverse the Lewa Wildlife Conservancy; friends and family man aid stations; zebra lurk in the bush. Previous page: giraffes can be spotted in Lewa. Opening page: elite Kenyans often lead the pack

© TEK for the Safaricom Marathon

© Tek Production Services Ltd/Africa LEWA

vastness surrounding us, by the quest before us. Behind me was a mini-platoon of rangers running in full garb with their rifles. A helicopter hovered above keeping tabs on everyone's whereabouts as if an overly concerned parent. Soon the throngs started to split. I found my rhythm, relaxed and realised: nothing was going to maul me.

I ran. And ran. Past the odd acacia tree and lone ostrich, and a pair of giraffes in the distance, rising from the ground like elegant, blinking sculptures. Spectators were sparse – a handful at the homemade spritz station; a smattering outside Kirafu, one of nine lodges on the preserve. Uniformed, apron-clad staff waving, cheering. It might be Lewa's biggest day of the year, but the Boston Marathon this is not.

I picked up speed, crested a small hill and continued through a canopy of acacias. Soon, I found myself in lockstep with a muscular Kenyan man. We sprinted towards the finish line. We crossed together, then high-fived.

I finished the half with a respectable 1:56:28, by no stretch the fastest woman – that accolade went to local Betty Karambu, at 1:14:28. Soon enough, in strode lanky superhero Philemon Baaru, completing the full 26.2 miles in 2:22:18 – before my fellow Gazelles even finished the half.

For the rest of the trip, we were on a standard safari – tracking leopards; marvelling at lions' manes and elephant herds; aww-ing at rhino babies; bumping through the bush in the back of the Land Cruiser. And all along, I was itching to get out. **RL**

ORIENTATION

Start/End // Lewa Wildlife Conservancy
Distance // 13 miles (21km)
Getting there // Lewa is a four-hour drive, or a 45-minute flight, from Nairobi.
Where to stay // The nine lodges on Lewa usually book up long in advance with corporate groups and the like but overseas guests stay at Maridadi Camp – an 'athletes' village' with canvas tents and cots set up for runners and spectators.
More info // www.safaricommarathon.com
Things to know // Don't worry, in Lewa's two decades hosting this race, no one has ever been mauled by a lion. The starting line is kind of disorganised. Runners aren't stacked according to pace or anything like that, plus it's a fairly narrow path. So don't dawdle – weasel your way up close if you want to avoid having to trudge slowly behind the hordes until things thin out.

Opposite: during the Patagonian International Marathon in southern Chile, runners are spurred on by the stunning spires of Torres del Paine

MORE LIKE THIS
WILD RACES

BIG FIVE MARATHON, SOUTH AFRICA

Like the Safaricom races, the Big Five event also brings runners face to face with the magnificent wildlife of the African Savannah, in the name of conservation. This run is further south, in the Entabeni Safari Conservancy, which sits between Kruger National Park and Johannesburg. The June event includes traditional jeep-powered safari outings in the days leading up to the races (or after). It's a challenging race, with more ups and downs, loose rock and deep sand than other similar races. But rewards include killer views of the giant lake that sits atop the nearby plateau, as well as the possibility of spotting zebra, giraffe, antelope and lion.
Start/End // Entabeni Safari Conservancy
Distance // 13–26.2 miles (20–42km)
More info // www.big-five-marathon. com

AUSTRALIAN OUTBACK MARATHON

Just north of that famous spiritual sandstone lump known as Uluru (or Ayers Rock), is a barren stretch of remote outback with little more than a few bush trails and jeep tracks crisscrossing the vast expanse of nothingness. There is also a full 26-mile marathon course, which utilises some of those trails, but also travels totally off-trail, atop the area's ubiquitous red earth, and sometimes along slow stretches of deep sand. Held annually in late July, its course is mostly flat, with just a few dunes to climb, but there are sections with stunning views of nearby mountains, including Uluru and the peaks of Kata Tjuta (the Olgas).
Start/End // Uluru-Kata Tjuta National Park
Distance // 3.7–26.2 miles (6–42km)
More info // www. australianoutbackmarathon.com

PATAGONIAN INTERNATIONAL MARATHON, PUERTO NATALES, CHILE

Set in the Torres del Paine National Park, the Patagonian International Marathon is run on rolling gravel roads on a point-to-point course that finishes at the Hotel Rio Serrano. During the race, runners are treated to views of the park's soaring spires, glistening glaciers and golden grasslands. The first half of the race is relatively flat, but the second half is more undulating, climbing and dropping about 300ft (100m) near the 18-mile mark and concluding with a long downhill section to the finish line. There are also 10km and 21km race distances that are set on portions of the same course. To get to the race, runners fly into Punta Arenas, one of the world's southernmost cities, along the Strait of Magellan at the confluence of the Atlantic and Pacific oceans.
Start // Torres del Paine National Park
End // Hotel Rio Serrano
Distance: 6.2–26.2 miles (10–42km)
More info: www. patagonianinternationalmarathon.com

THE MARATHON
DES SABLES

*This iconic 150-mile (240km) multiday run across Morocco's unforgiving
Sahara makes for a great introduction to the world of stage racing.*

Whenever I think of Morocco I think of sensory overload. I remember street vendors selling monkeys, snakes and exotic knives. I see bags of spices in every colour imaginable and scents that are like nothing I'm familiar with back home in Virginia. But I've never fully understood why this is what I remember about Morocco – of the 40 days I've spent in the region, 99% of that time has been spent in what could only be described as Saharan sensory deprivation.

For me, Morocco is where I go to compete in the gruelling stage race known as the Marathon des Sables, a seven-day, 150-mile (240km) run across the North African desert, where average temps top out around 104°F (40°C). In the past decade, I've run the MdS twice, in 2009 and 2010, when I even finished third. After years as a sponsored ultrarunner – having also now run both the Badwater 135 and the Barkley Marathons – the MdS remains one of the hardest races I have ever attempted. But that's probably

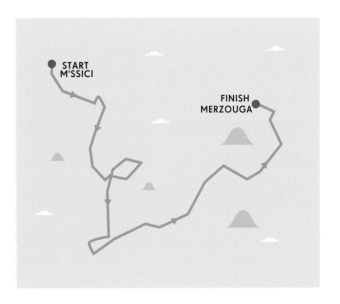

START
M'SSICI

FINISH
MERZOUGA

© Jean-Philippe Ksiazek | Getty Images

"Pre-race jitters are normal. But it doesn't help when they play AC/DC's 'Highway to Hell' over the loudspeakers at the start"

because my first experience running it in 2000 was basically as an inexperienced 'weekend warrior'. The longest run I had ever done was the JFK 50 Mile. It was a time when I still partied, and ran less than 50 miles per week – which was shorter than the longest single stage at MdS. Of course, that is the MdS that's seared into my soul.

Needless to say, I was terrified. And, while I could have just as easily experimented with multiday racing closer to home, this event, in a faraway exotic country, captivated me. The 'marathon of the sands' was founded in 1986 by Patrick Bauer, a Frenchman who hiked across the Sahara on foot and decided it was such a transformative experience that other people should do the same.

It was my first ever visit to the African continent. Pre-race jitters are part of every event I've ever competed in. But it doesn't help when the organisers like to play AC/DC's 'Highway to Hell' over the loudspeakers at the start – each and every day. Thankfully, the actual running opens 'easy' with an 18-mile (30km) day on rolling hills of hard packed dirt, with just a short section of sand dunes. Yet, as I finished that first leg – dusty, dirty, tired, hungry and exhausted – I still wondered how anyone runs the entire thing. I had made plenty of mistakes, such as miscalculating how much sand there would be, wasting a lot of time stopping and dumping out my shoes.

The camaraderie at this event was my lifeline. As I came in for a landing after that first day, I knew I could get some much-needed advice from my tentmates. Veterans were key in teaching me how

to stay cool during the day and warm at night, how to deal with limited calories, how to go to the bathroom and how to sleep in a crowded tent. The atmosphere was a little like summer camp. But conversation always seemed to come back to 'the long day'. We had three more runs before it, but if I didn't start figuring out my strategy, I wouldn't even make it that far.

The Berbers who helped setup and host the tent villages dress in such a way that makes them resemble the Sandpeople from *Star Wars*, but without the menace. They always wore big smiles and a twinkle in their eyes. Once we had bunked down for the night, the stars came out quickly and we were overwhelmed with the surreal glow from the Milky Way.

The next few days of racing can only be described as body blows. We were covering between 20 and 25 miles (32–40km) on terrain that varied from two-storey-high maize-soft sand dunes to dusty river beds known as wadies. One minute quicksand was grasping at our feet, the next jagged rocks were shredding our shoes. Distance perception was thrown off as one dune blended into the next. Nonetheless, I began to fall in love with the openness and the endless sightlines.

By day three, I was suffering as hunger became more of an issue than running. As I puked from lack of calories, a Spanish competitor yelled two simple words: '*Bebe! Come!*' I understood just enough Spanish to know he was imploring me to drink and eat.

CARRY-ON

MdS rules require you to carry everything you will use for the seven days on your back. In addition to 2000 calories of food per day, you must also carry a sleeping bag, snake bite kit and an emergency flare (which, if used, immediately disqualifies you). Thankfully, the required 9L of water per day is provided along the way, though it does involve a tightly controlled punch-card system.

From left: camps are created in the Moroccan Sahara between each stage of the MdS; the gruelling stage five run. Previous page: rough terrain during stage three of the seven-day race

ORIENTATION

Day five – the long day – is crucial. It's said that if you can get over this hump, you will likely finish. This stage is around 50 miles (80km) and athletes are given just 48 hours to complete it. It also happened to be my 25th birthday, making me the second-youngest there. Though I started off slow, I went on to have one of those perfect runs, when everything goes your way. The temperatures felt mild and the wind felt like a gentle caress. I actually led the second wave of runners and ended up finishing as the top American.

The final two stages are simple 26.2-mile/42km marathon distances over forgiving and relatively flat jeep roads. At this point, things begin to look and feel like a party. I suppose it has a lot to do with knowing you are so close and that nothing is going to stop you from reaching the finish line. As we did, we were handed ice-cold soft drinks as an orchestra played.

As I came down from my runner's high, my mind was both fuzzy and sharp. I thought of the mountains we traversed, the valleys we navigated, the shockingly white salt flats and sharp black stones that destroyed my swollen feet. Now, after so many years in this sport, having done a lot of unique races, this remains one of my favourites. Strangely, the MdS is a great beginner's stage race.

One thing I learned early in my career is that accomplishing something as huge as this makes everything else in life – whether it's a long run or any other challenge – feel a bit more attainable. It gave me a bottomless belief in my ability. **MW**

Start/End // Ouarzazate, Morocco
Distance // Approx 150–156 miles (240–250km)
Getting there // Fly into Marrakesh and then fly or drive 125 miles (200km) to Ouarzazate.
When to go // MdS is held annually in April.
Where to stay // Bivouac tents are set up at the end of each stage.
More info // www.marathondessables.com
Things to know // Mastering your gear is an artform in itself. A couple of things worth noting: you don't need a stove as it is so hot you can literally cook your meals by leaving them on a rock in the sun. With clothing, the goal is to stay cool but also covered. Always use shade wisely at every rest and after the day of running is over.

MORE LIKE THIS
EPIC STAGE RACES

RACING THE PLANET, NAMIBIA, MONGOLIA, ATACAMA, ANTARCTICA

The Racing the Planet events take place all over the world, though each race takes place in a desolate unforgiving desert of sorts. And they directly mimic the Marathon des Sables, in distance and organisation. Each 4 Deserts event – most people choose one, though some have done all four – is a seven-day, six-stage, 150-mile (240km), marked course. During the event, competitors must carry their own personal gear and the only assistance provided during the race is water. The exact location of the start and finish of each race is kept secret so that competitors cannot cache food or supplies along the route. At each location you can expect an incredibly remote, raw and beautiful landscape.
Distance // 150 miles (240km)
More info // www.racingtheplanet.com

ULTRA GOBI 400K, GOBI DESERT, CHINA

The Ultra Gobi 400K is a self-navigated, self-supported race, held in the southern Gobi Desert, on the edge of the Tibetan Plateau in Gansu province, Western China. This is a graduate-level event that requires advanced orienteering. But with the right GPS unit and the knowledge to use the device it's pretty straightforward. The challenges are deciding when to eat, what to pack for the rest stations and when – and if – to sleep. Expect lots of sand dunes, mountains, shepherds and their massive flocks, wild dogs, wolves and flies (lots of flies). Also expect temperature swings from below freezing to scorching sun and wind.
Start/End // Guazhou County, China, about 125 miles (200km) from the Mongolian border
Distance // 250 miles (400km)
More info // www.ultragobi.com

THE COASTAL CHALLENGE, COSTA RICA

The Coastal Challenge is a terrific introduction to stage racing. The six-day race has two categories: the beginner 96-mile (155km) Adventure run and the Expedition run, which is longer and more difficult. Both events showcase all that Costa Rica has to offer, including jungle waterfalls, beautiful beaches and rainforest teeming with howler monkeys, poison dart frogs, snakes and the most vibrant butterflies you've ever seen. Competitors need only bring a small running bag for each of the stages, as traditional Costa Rican food and drinks are provided along the way. You have the option of setting up your own tent or having race staff do it. Most days, the race ends near a beach.
Start // Playa del Rey
End // Drake's Bay
Distance // 96 miles (155km)
More info // www. thecoastalchallengecostarica.com

From top: the 400km Ultra Gobi in China is one of the longest stage races in the world; Costa Rica's Coastal Challenge is great for those who are new to stage racing

THE GREAT ETHIOPIAN RUN

This 'fun run' through the heart of one of East Africa's great capitals is a roving party celebrating the country's running heroes.

I am what you'd call a running nerd, and proud of it. I keep track of kilometre splits, elevation gain and loss, and heart-rate zones. I can tell you my personal bests at every distance, from 400m to a marathon. But if there is any event sure to cure a bad case of runner's OCD, it's the delightfully chaotic Great Ethiopian Run in Addis Ababa.

I have in fact done this run, held every year since 2001, twice. And I am proud to say I have absolutely no idea what my time was on either occasion – if I did know, it would have meant I'd done it all wrong. Many will tell you that the best strategy is to make it the slowest 10K of your life. You see, this isn't so much a race as it is a 10,000-metre-long party. And who wants to be the first to leave a party?

On the morning of my first GER, I had no choice but to come to terms with the lack of race information. Forget about pre-race packs, efficient bag drops, chip timing, goody bags – there's none of that here. What you will get is a single, heavy cotton T-shirt in the yellow and green of the Ethiopian flag, in a size large enough to camp under, and a vague idea of how to get to the start. I find my way by following other runners wearing the same oversized T-shirt. But while I look swamped by it, many veteran GER runners have brilliantly customised their tops, adding strategic rips or holes, and other artistic touches.

The atmosphere is electric. Addis Ababa – sometimes called "the political capital of Africa" – is a city in flux and the rate of change is phenomenal. It feels as though you could go to sleep next to a building site and wake up next to a shopping mall. Terrifyingly rickety bamboo scaffolding mushrooms up in minutes, as Chinese money pours into the economy. Yet, you might also see a herd of goats holding up traffic. It is also quite beautiful. Sure,

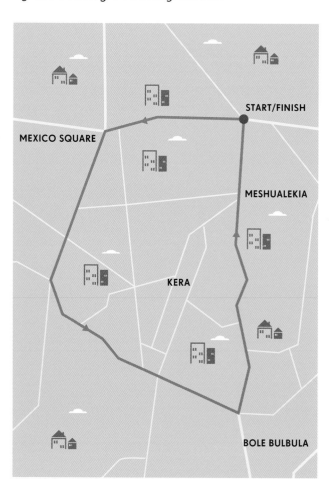

the city itself is a dusty and traffic-laden metropolis, but it sits on a verdant and lush plateau. The light is like nothing I have ever seen, a certain golden hue, diffused through a haze of heat and dust.

One thing that doesn't seem to change in Addis is a sense of pride in local heroes, and particularly athletes. When Abebe Bikila won the 1960 Olympic marathon barefoot, he inspired a nation. Running is, in fact, for Ethiopians – as for Kenyans and other East Africans – a possible route out of poverty. Role models such as Haile Gebrselassie and Kenenisa Bekele inspire devotion and respect. It's no wonder there is huge competition here, even at school level. Many young runners will get up at 3am or 4am to train in the dark before a full day's work, perhaps dreaming of a day that their faces adorn posters, as do those of Haile and Kenenisa.

It was Haile himself who started the Great Ethiopian Run, following his return from the 2000 Sydney Olympics with another gold medal in his pocket. Even in the first year, the 10,000 entries sold out in days – everyone wanted to run with Haile. He single-handedly started a mass-participation running movement. Today, the GER attracts more than 40,000 amateurs.

The vast majority of participants are locals, with a handful of European expats, many from the NGOs or embassies based in Addis. Standing at the edge of the startline is like trying to begin

"The GER was started by Haile Gebrselassie after he returned from Sydney with another gold medal"

a race in front of the bulls of Pamplona. Eager runners are being held back by a line of batoned policemen linked together. Someone sounds a non-official klaxon, the line strains to breaking point. The policemen turn and run for their lives. In the melee that ensues, a shoe flies up into the air. No one with an ounce of self-preservation is going back for it. It takes a few minutes before I'm brave enough to jump into the seemingly endless stream but about 400m later, people have already slowed to a happy walking pace.

Jogging alongside me is a man who points to my GPS watch. The strap had broken the day before and my makeshift repair isn't holding up well. Laughing, he grabs it off my wrist, waves it in front of me and then sprints off. But he stays just close enough that I might be able to catch up. We cat and mouse for a good mile, until he finally throws me my watch and disappears.

As we pass local bars, spectators nursing coldish beers jeer in good fun. I can't understand anything they are saying, but the body language couldn't be more clear: 'Why are you mad people

WORLD DOMINATION

While competitive Ethiopian runners excel at many distances, the 10,000m is their sweet spot. The combined efforts of Haile Gebrselassie, Kenenisa Bekele, Almaz Ayana and others have given the country the most golds across the Olympics and World Championships, with Ayana and Bekele currently holding both world records for the event.

From left: the colour and chaos of Addis Ababa provide a rich backdrop for the GER; Ethiopian coffee is so strong it should be a banned substance. Previous page: running is a national sport in this part of Africa

running in this heat?' A mix of Amharic tunes and cheesy Europop booms out from sound stations en route. One group of runners, all wearing jeans, has stopped to form a circle around an amateur breakdancer. Further along, two stilt walkers wearing lurid electric green trousers tower over us.

A few miles in, one thing becomes clear: absolutely no one is taking this seriously. Many are dancing under makeshift sprinklers, while others are queueing up for a bottle of Malta Guinness, the local, non-alcoholic favourite. The route itself is quite urban, with wide roads, overpasses and, of course, some spectacular potholes. And while I'm doing everything I can to take it easy, the thin air – Addis sits at 7726ft (2355m) altitude – and the dry, dusty heat are definitely taking their toll. Finally, we approach Jan Meda, the old racing ground where the race finishes.

However, passing under the finish arch is only the end of the course, not the party. The big flat green space heaves with thousands of runners, carrying on the festivities and banter. I actually somehow find my way into a 'VIP' area, where I drink Ethiopian coffee and snatch a selfie with Haile. After a few sips I think I may have discovered the true secret of Ethiopian distance domination: Ethiopian coffee is rocket fuel. If only I had had one at the start. **KC**

ORIENTATION

Start/End // Meskel Square, Addis Ababa
Distance // 6 miles (10km)
Getting there // Fly into Addis Ababa, taxi to as close to the start as you can get with road closures.
Where to stay // Race packets are collected at the official race hotel, The Hilton, which also makes a good base for your stay.
More info //www.ethiopianrun.org
Things to know // International entrants must pick up their race packs in the week before the race. Race entry fee includes the pre-race pasta party at the official race hotel, The Hilton. Haile Gebrselassie will almost certainly be there.

MORE LIKE THIS
GREAT AFRICAN RACES

SOWETO MARATHON FESTIVAL, JOHANNESBURG

The annual Soweto Marathon weekend takes place every November and offers several distances (10K, a half and the full 26.2-mile marathon). The route is designed to celebrate this Johannesburg township's rich history, passing heritage sites such as Walter Sisulu Square, the birthplace of The Freedom Charter in 1955; and The Regina Mundi Catholic Church, which became famous for its role in the anti-apartheid struggle and as the place where Archbishop Emeritus Desmond Tutu presided over the Truth and Reconciliation Commission hearings.
Start/End // FNB Stadium
Distance // 6–26.2 miles (10–42km)
More info // www.sowetomarathon.com

MARRAKESH MARATHON, MOROCCO

Now entering its 30th year, this January race has built up a reputation both for speed – the elite winning times are world class – and for offering visiting runners some midwinter sunshine. The course is flat and passes by picturesque minarets and alongside ancient ramparts and souks, with views of snow-capped mountains in the distance. Local bands play to cheer on the 8000 runners and the atmosphere is carnival-like. Perfect for those chasing good times.
Start/End // Avenue de la Menara
Distance //13–26.2 miles (20–42km)
More info // www.marathon-marrakech. com

MALAWI IMPACT MARATHON

The Malawi Marathon is part of the Impact series, a global movement that aims to change and improve communities through running, with events in Malawi, Kenya, Nepal and Guatemala. To enter the Malawi race is to throw yourself entirely into the experience for a week in May – living in the athletes' village by the shores of Lake Malawi, visiting and engaging in service projects that you have been fundraising for and then, of course, taking part in the race itself. The course – one lap for the half marathon; two for the full – carries runners over hills, through trails in the Baobab Plains and along the shores of the vast lake. It's certainly not an easy course, but it's also not a race where personal bests are a priority.
Start/End // Nkope
Distance // 13–26.2 miles (20–42km)
More info // www.impactmarathon. com/malawi

From top: Lake Malawi's Otter Point at sunset; Marrakesh's heaving public square

THE COMRADES MARATHON

At the South African grandfather of all ultramarathons, the
sense of history and tradition may get you across the finish line.

As I rounded the last corner into the cricket ground in Pietermaritzburg, I couldn't quite believe I was finally there. For the past few hours I'd been battling mind-melting levels of exhaustion, in 84°F (29°C) heat, along a nondescript road through residential suburbs. I was dragging myself to the end of a race that had begun 54 miles (87km) away in the coastal city of Durban. In total, I'd been running for almost nine hours. As crowds five people deep lined the final section, cheering and whooping, I told myself to remember this feeling in my body, remember how much it hurt – because I was worried I'd forget and find myself going through it all over again the following year.

The Comrades Marathon in South Africa – which is actually technically an 'ultramarathon' – has a way of getting inside you. In the days leading up to the race I met many people who had done it multiple times. The amount of finishes you have is even printed on your race number, with those having run 10 times or more getting a coveted green number, a badge of honour that elicits reverence from everyone else. The day before the race, I met Barry Holland, who had run the race for 44 consecutive years. 'You know, I envy you running Comrades for the first time,' he told me. 'The first time is so raw. You never forget it.'

It's raw, that's for sure. As soon as I crossed the finish line, I was

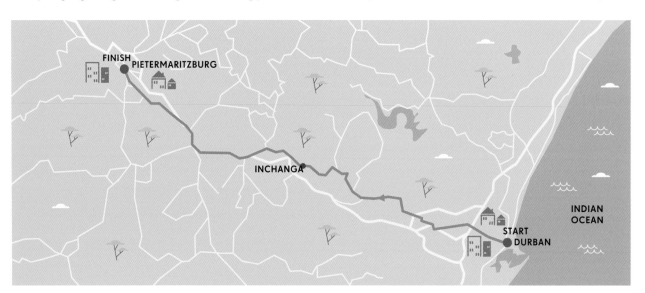

welling up. An official held my hand, looking at me kindly, intently. 'Are you OK?' she asked, looking like she expected me to hug her.

In the rest of the world, ultra running may still be a niche sport. But in South Africa ultra running is just running. It is normal. Here, marathons have always been merely warm-up events for the two big ones, the Two Oceans marathon (35 miles; 56km) and the Granddaddy of the lot, the biggest and the oldest ultramarathon in the world: Comrades. The Comrades marathon was created in 1921 by World War I veteran Vic Clapham. During the war he undertook arduous marches of hundreds of miles through East Africa with the 8th South Africa infantry, and was deeply touched by the camaraderie of his fellow soldiers, despite the suffering they endured. Feeling that this close bond with his fellow man was missing from his life after the war, he put on the first Comrades Marathon in 1921.

The bond with the other runners begins to form on the startline. I was worried, standing there among the throng at 5am, that I had been oversold the start. Too many people had told me how incredible it was, how it had given them goosebumps. It may have been early, but Durban was already rocking, 1980s power ballads blaring out across the darkened streets. No one in Durban was sleeping this morning.

With a few minutes to go, the traditional folk song 'Shosholoza' came on and soon we were all singing its deep, soulful refrains together. The words mean 'go forward' and are imbued with the pain and defiance of South Africa's turbulent past. Comrades has always been a rare melting pot in this divided nation, with the first black runner taking part in 1935 and the first woman finisher in 1923. It took until 1975 before official finisher's medals were awarded to runners from any race or gender, but even that was almost 20 years before the end of apartheid.

Then the gun went, and like that, as one heaving mass, we started to move. Almost 18,000 of us, people of all ages, shapes and sizes. This is so much more than a regular marathon. Not only the distance – which equates roughly to two marathons and a park run back-to-back – but the fact that it is mostly uphill. The journey takes us out through the grimy, concrete arteries of the city, up into the grass-covered highlands, across the baking plains. The very names of the hills, such as Inchanga and Polly Shortts, evoke fear and awe, each with its own history of triumphs and disasters.

As the sun rises and the legs weary, the bonds between the runners deepen. There are countless times out on the road when another runner helps me, handing me a drink, some food, asking my name, telling me to run with them. Along the way, hundreds of thousands of spectators line the course, singing, dancing, calling out encouragement – even massaging our legs if we need it.

In South Africa, Comrades is one of the biggest sporting events of the year with more than 12 hours of wall-to-wall television coverage. But the highest viewing figures are recorded at the very end, when after 12 hours the finish line is closed and those who haven't quite made it across are disqualified. It's a cruel tradition,

LOCAL LEGEND

In 1922 – the year of the second Comrades event – South African national rugby team-member Bill Payn was convinced to run the race after a few stiff drinks the night before. He turned up and ran it in his rugby boots, stopping along the way to eat bacon and eggs, a chicken curry and, at halfway, to drink a beer. He finished eighth overall. The next day he took part in a rugby match, but because his feet were blistered, he elected to play the match in his running shoes.

Clockwise from top: 20,000 people participate in the world's oldest ultramarathon; South African Bongmusa Mthembu is a back-to-back winner; for many, it's 12 full hours of running. Previous page: the clock ticks

"Those who have not finished in 12 hours are disqualified – it's a cruel tradition but one that ensures high drama"

© Courtesy of Comrades Marathon

© Courtesy of Comrades Marathon

but one that ensures high drama. I dragged my weary self to the main grandstand in time to catch the final action.

The music was still blaring, with the commentator still full of voice, urging the runners to make that last big effort. With just a few minutes to go, thousands of people were funnelling through. Each year, more than half the runners finish in the last hour of the race, and the majority of those in the last 10 minutes. People were arriving like the weak and wounded at the gates of heaven, throwing their arms wide, their heads back, exultant. Others were carried across the line by other runners, clinging on to their necks for dear life. The compassion and kindness had me wiping away tears again.

In the last 30 seconds, it got frantic. People were sprinting, others collapsing across the finish. And then that brutal countdown began and the officials began forming a line: 3, 2, 1 – the door closes, the music stops, the lights go out. Those who hadn't quite made it stood there, stunned, beaten. The lonely, forlorn strains of 'The Last Post' sounded, and that, ladies and gentlemen, was that.

The day after the race I found myself at a local Aches & Pains party, where runners meet in the pub to tell each other their war stories. The question they all had for me is whether I'd be back next year. I tried to remember the pain I felt during the final 20 miles. But it was already fading, being replaced by memories of the euphoria, the emotional rawness, of finishing such a great race.

'I don't think so,' I say. They all laugh.

'You will,' they reply, knowingly. 'You will.' **AF**

ORIENTATION

Start // Durban

End // Pietermaritzburg (on alternate years the start and finish points are reversed)

Distance // 54 miles (87km)

Getting there // Fly to Durban. The race starts in the city centre near the sea front.

When to go // The race takes place in May/June, at the beginning of the South African winter.

Where to stay // The race starts (or finishes) near the beach in Durban, where there are lots of hotels within easy walking distance. The Southern Sun Elangeni and the City Lodge Hotel cater to racers and have great atmosphere.

More info // www.comrades.com

Things to know // There is food along the course – boiled potatoes dipped in salt are a favourite – but you may want to carry some emergency gels. It can get hot later in the day so don't forget some good sunscreen.

*Opposite: Cape Town in South Africa
hosts the Two Oceans ultramarathon*

MORE LIKE THIS
HISTORIC ULTRAMARATHONS

TWO OCEANS MARATHON, SOUTH AFRICA

Billing itself as 'the world's most beautiful marathon', this 35-mile (56km) road ultramarathon is the closest thing you can find to Comrades, with the route taking in spectacular views of both the Atlantic and Indian oceans (hence the name) on a loop run in the shadow of Cape Town's iconic Table Mountain. The April race was originally conceived as a warm-up for Comrades, and anyone taking part will be asked endlessly if they are in fact doing the race as 'training' for Comrades. But the event has grown into itself since the first running in 1970 and is now a huge event in its own right, with a route more spectacular than Comrades. A half marathon – the biggest in South Africa – is held on the same weekend and runs along part of the same route.
Start // Newlands, Cape Town
End // University of Cape Town
Distance // 13–34.8 miles (20–56km)
More info // www.twooceansmarathon. org.za

JFK 50, MARYLAND, USA

This is the oldest and biggest ultramarathon in the US. The race began as one of a large number of 'JFK Challenges' that sprung up across the country in the winter of 1962–63, in response to President Kennedy's challenge to the US Marines to prove their fitness by hiking 50 miles in less than 20 hours. Unexpectedly, the challenge was also taken up by thousands of civilians, in a phenomenon that became known as the great '50-mile craze' of 1963. After Kennedy's assassination, all the other JFK Challenges were discontinued, except the one in Maryland, which continued to grow. The race today still has a large military presence with the prestigious Kennedy Cup presented to the best military team. In all, a field of 1250 runners take up the challenge every January to finish before the 13-hour cut-off, following a route that traverses paved roads, a long stretch of the towpath of the C&O canal, and 13 miles (21km) along the beautiful Appalachian Trail.
Start // Boonsboro, MD
End // Williamsport, MD
Distance // 50 miles (80km)
More info // www.Jfk50mile.org

DURBAN CITY MARATHON, SOUTH AFRICA

If you want a taste of running in Durban without tackling anything as big and long as Comrades, each April the Durban City Marathon, half marathon and 10km races offer the same Indian Ocean breezes and a fast, flat course passing along the city's promenade and harbour. As the full marathon is a qualifier race for Comrades – you need to run it in under five hours to qualify – you will find some of that legendary Comrades atmosphere in the air as you run. The city at the other end of the Comrades route, Pietermaritzburg, offers its own alternative big city marathon experience, the Maritzburg City Marathon, in February each year. For South Africans, these races are inextricably linked with Comrades and offer a small insight into the country's obsession with the big one.
Start/End // Moses Mabhida Stadium
Distance // 6–26.2 miles (10–42km)
More info // www.durbancitymarathon. co.za

THE BOSTON MARATHON

Qualifying for the world's oldest and most iconic marathon is a milestone in itself. Running it, however, transcends athletic accomplishment.

Hopkinton, Massachusetts is a quiet town of about 17,000, with all the hallmarks of an old New England village – historic buildings, a grassy common and a farmers market. One day every spring, however, this quiet town goes absolutely bananas. That day is the third Monday of every April. Though it happens to be Patriots' Day, commemorating the first battles of the Revolutionary War, that is not what all the commotion is about. For this is also the day that 30,000 or so runners from all over the world show up to compete in the Boston Marathon, a race that begins on Hopkinton's Main St and ends 26.2 miles later in Copley Square, Boston.

No other marathon can match Boston in terms of history. Held annually since 1897, it's the world's oldest, and few can touch it in terms of prestige. Apart from the Olympics, Boston is the only major marathon to impose qualifying times. (The toughest, for men ages 18 to 34, is 3:05, an average pace of 7:03 minutes per mile.) For many runners, a Boston qualifier, or 'BQ', is the Holy Grail.

Runners begin arriving early in the morning, in a caravan of yellow school buses. 'Welcome to Hopkinton, it all starts here' reads a large sign. It does indeed. I ran my first Boston Marathon in 1999 and when I saw that sign it hit me like 26.2 tons of bricks. Wow! This is really happening. On the morning of my ninth Boston

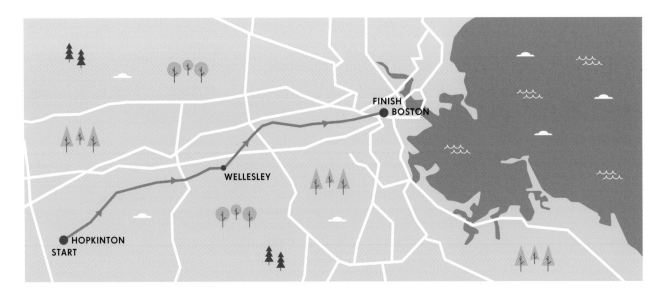

Marathon last year, that feeling hadn't changed one bit.

The first half-dozen times I ran it, Boston was, for me, all about racing. Then, the year of the bombings in 2013, in which three people were killed and 260 were injured, I was actually home on paternity leave with my newborn son. I vowed to return the following year, in solidarity and defiance. And I did. That year was transformative – I felt grateful and more connected to the race.

A couple of years later, my friend Tim, who is registered blind, asked me to guide him in the 2017 race. Afterwards, it was clear Boston had become something much bigger for me. And Tim was hooked. We agreed we would do it again the following year.

So there we were in Hopkinton in 2018, beneath that sign once again, beneath a cold, steady rain that would make this year a bone-chilling slog. 'You know,' I told Tim as we walked through puddles. 'This is not that bad.' It was that bad, of course, and would only get worse. Nonetheless, Tim – who was clearly in denial – agreed that the weather wasn't a big deal. Tim and I each grasped an end of a short elastic band as we slowly moved toward the hand-painted startline.

We cruised the first mile, a downhill stretch that's easy for adrenaline-juiced runners to take too fast. In fact, the first several miles are almost completely downhill. Seductively so. Runners who blaze these early miles hammer their quads and pay for it later. Tim and I kept cool. We enjoyed easy conversation, which included occasional cues: 'Here's a guy walking, move left to pass him... Rough road up ahead... Timing mat coming up in 3... 2...'

Here's the thing about the Boston Marathon: even your first time here, the course can feel familiar. After leaving Hopkinton, the race wends east through towns and villages that, if you've been a runner for any length of time, you'll recognise by name alone: Ashland, Framingham, Natick, Wellesley, Brookline. Same goes for the landmarks: the red-brick Newton Firehouse, its tall garage doors flung open, music blaring; the Chestnut Hill Reservoir around mile 22; the CITGO sign, looming high above Kenmore Square.

Around three miles in, Tim and I passed a golden retriever in a raincoat, sitting on a wooden box. The dog had two blue-and-gold BOSTON STRONG flags clenched in his teeth – a typical Boston spectator insofar as there is no typical Boston spectator. Everybody turns out, lining the roads, cheering their heads off.

For me, the next 9 to 10 miles, through Framingham and Natick, are all about getting to Wellesley. No offence to Framingham and Natick, which are fine towns. But Wellesley is home to the Scream Tunnel, which you can hear long before you can see it. Tim and I picked up the din a good quarter-mile away. Soon after we were passing hundreds of women leaning over steel barriers, cheering and holding signs like 'Kiss me, I'm a mathematician', and 'I won't tell your wife'.

After Wellesley, the crowds thin and the course dips into Newton Lower Falls. The Newton hills, as much as anything, have come to define Boston. Heartbreak Hill, between miles 20 and 21, gets most of the attention, but Heartbreak is actually the last in a series

TORTOISE OR HARE?

Despite its prestige and reputation, the Boston Marathon is not world-record eligible. For one, Boston's course is a net downhill, starting at 490ft (150m) elevation and ending at 10ft (3m). It's also a point-to-point, meaning a tailwind could give competitors an unfair advantage. Meanwhile, slower runners with little chance of qualifying, take heart: If you can raise at least $5000 for one of the marathon's official charities, you're guaranteed a place on the starting line.

Clockwise from top: challenging weather is the norm in Boston; George Washington statue in Boston Public Garden; the Old State House. Previous page: more than 30,000 runners participate in the historic race

"After the bombing, I vowed to return in solidarity and defiance – that race a year later was transformative"

©Boston Globe | Getty Images

© Sean Pavone | Shutterstock

of climbs. No single one is that bad —Heartbreak itself climbs just 91ft (28m) – but the fact that they come in rapid succession, and so late in the race, makes them feel like Alpine passes.

Tim and I put our heads down, grinding our way upward. The rain, perhaps sensing an opportunity to destroy what was left of our good cheer, lashed down harder than ever. The only good thing about the Newton hills is that once you're past them, it's almost entirely downhill to the finish. Still, unless you've done everything perfectly, it doesn't matter. By then, you're running on empty.

But it's Boston and things conspire to keep you moving. The crowds grow denser and louder with each stride. Nothing prepares you for that turn on to Boylston St, the grandstands full of roaring spectators, the 120-year-old finish line. In the blink of an eye, all the suffering and pain and doubt – not just from that day, but from the months or years you spent working to get there – all of it rushes up and out. Then, bliss. There was nothing but me, Tim, and the big, blue-and-yellow finish line, four-tenths of a mile away.

Many people cry at this point. I usually do, at least a little.

In 1999 I crossed that finish line for the first time, in under three hours. I crossed it with Tim in five and change. As we trudged towards the finishers' medals and space blankets, I found myself shaking uncontrollably from the cold. 'You OK?' a volunteer asked. I wasn't, but I lied. In fact, 130 runners were treated for hypothermia that year. But I'd be warm and dry soon enough. To paraphrase an old motivational quote: Hypothermia is temporary; Boston is forever. **MR**

🪧

ORIENTATION

Start // Hopkinton, Massachusetts
End // Boston's Copley Square
Distance // 26.2 miles
Getting there // Logan Airport (BOS) offers easy access to all parts of Boston; because of limited space and narrow roads around the start, taking private vehicles is strongly discouraged – the buses provided are much less stressful.
When to go // Race day is the third Monday of April.
Where to stay // Demand for hotel rooms is very high, especially those near the finish line in Copley Square. Consider an Airbnb or hotel farther away, but near a T line.
What to wear // Weather is a wild card, varying from scorching heat to freezing rain and snow.
More info // www.baa.org/races/boston-marathon
Things to know // There is a 5km race on the Saturday before Marathon Monday, giving companions of visiting marathoners a chance to do some racing themselves.

*Opposite: runners pass through
Manhattan's Times Square during the
New York City Marathon*

MORE LIKE THIS
BUCKET-LIST US MARATHONS

NEW YORK CITY MARATHON, NY

Like NYC itself, the New York City Marathon is big – the biggest in the world, in fact, with a field size north of 50,000 – and pulsing with an energy that no other marathon can replicate. Held on the first Sunday of November, the race is a 26.2-mile tour of the city's five boroughs. Runners start in Staten Island and then, in a scene that's become iconic, stream across both levels of the Verrazano-Narrows Bridge into Brooklyn. The race winds through Queens, Manhattan and, briefly, The Bronx before returning to Manhattan, where runners sail down Fifth Avenue and then slingshot around the southern edge of Central Park to the finish line, near the famed Tavern on the Green restaurant. Each borough has its own personality, but the one constant is the crowd – an estimated two million spectators turn out, and they aren't shy about expressing their enthusiasm.
**Start // Fort Wadsworth, Staten Island
End // Central Park West at 67th St
More info // www.tcsnycmarathon.org**

CHICAGO MARATHON, IL

Another tremendously popular fall race, Chicago (in early October) is one of the six World Marathon Majors – along with Boston, New York, London, Berlin and Tokyo. It's big, too, with a field size of around 45,000. The course begins and ends in Grant Park, in the city's downtown business district, and sends runners north on LaSalle St, parallel to Lake Michigan. Between miles 7 and 8 the course doubles back and runners return downtown before heading west and passing the halfway point. The remainder of the course is a series of Etch-A-Sketch turns that lead runners, gradually, south of downtown before turning north one final time, to the finish line. This race is pancake-flat and famously fast – four world records have been set here. If you're looking to PB, Chicago may be the race for you.
**Start/End // Grant Park, Columbus Drive
More info // www.chicagomarathon. com**

DISNEY MARATHON, FLA

Hey, don't laugh. Traditionalists may sneer or scoff, but the Walt Disney World Marathon is all about over-the-top fun. With a course that snakes through the Disney World resort – yes, that includes Cinderella's Castle – you'll find it hard not to smile right along with the costumed characters you'll see along the way. It's all a little trippy, though the organisers would likely prefer the word magical. The marathon is just one event, by the way, of a weekend-long whirlwind of running: there's also a 5km, 10km and half-marathon, plus a series of short kids' races. Ambitious runners can also take on the Goofy Challenge (half-marathon and full marathon) or the Dopey Challenge (5km, 10km, half-marathon and full marathon). One thing: be prepared for some godawful wakeup calls – each race starts at 5.30am, sharp. Fun!
**Start/End // Epcot Parking Lot
More info // www.rundisney.com/ disneyworld-marathon**

HAVANA'S EL MALECÓN

For a window into what makes Cuba's capital tick, hit the road along the city's seafront and be prepared for sensory overload.

As heavy drops of saltwater hit me in the face, the distinctive aroma of tobacco leaf mixed with diesel fumes drifts over from the houses opposite. A lone trumpeter sitting on the seawall, unperturbed by the crashing waves, diligently practises his arpeggios. I couldn't be running anywhere else in the world but Havana.

Buoyed by an unusual burst of early morning energy, I hasten steadily in the direction of the iconic Hotel Nacional, eyes fixed on the road ahead. In front of me, the Malecón, Havana's evocative 4.3 mile (7km)-long sea drive, curls its way round the city's northern shoreline in a protective embrace. Long a favoured meeting place for courting couples, wandering musicians, amateur fishers, daring divers, day-dreaming Florida-gazers and assorted tourists in Che Guevara T-shirts, this is the city's most expressive and typically Cuban thoroughfare. Local habaneros like to call it the world's longest sofa, a potent slice of open-air theatre, where half the city shows up at sunset to meet, greet, date and debate.

© Buckheadj7zo | Lonely Planet

"Local habaneros call it the world's longest sofa — it's a potent slice of open-air theatre, where half the city shows up to meet, greet, date and debate"

For me, it will always be Cuba's most entertaining running route, the first place I visit when returning to Havana after a lengthy break. Here, amid the crashing waves and mildewed buildings, I feel I can reconnect with the city and quickly work out what has changed since I was last in town. In less than an hour, I've got a primer on the city's mood and a visceral reintroduction to its sights, smells and sounds.

Indeed, there have been plenty of changes over the years. Back in the 1990s, during Cuba's cash-strapped 'Special Period', I used to run along the Malecón in the pitch dark during the crippling *apagones* (power outages). It was rare to see a car here in those days, let alone a tourist bus. These days, the traffic is a little thicker, but the sights are no less unique.

The starting and finishing posts for my Malecón runs are two Spanish-built forts dating from the 16th century that stand like historical bookends 4.3 miles (7km) apart. The Castillo de San Salvador de la Punta guards the jaws of Havana harbour. The Torreón de la Chorrera overlooks the mouth of the Río Almendares to the west. In between are gallant equestrian statues depicting heroes of Cuba's independence wars.

Cruising westward, I get distracted by a dazzling new sculpture outside the Hotel Deauville. Unconsciously, I veer dangerously close to the curb to get a better view, but a honking motorbike-and-sidecar quickly snaps me to attention. Running the Malecón

isn't just a test of fitness, it's a full-on obstacle course. I continue through the tightly packed residential quarter of Centro Habana towards Vedado, battling loose paving stones, slippery seaweed, gusts of ocean spray, tangled fishing twine and belching Buicks. By far the biggest obstacle is the sea itself. Even today's mild swell in the Straits of Florida is enough to send huge waves crashing over the Malecón's battered ocean defences. On one occasion, I swear I was stung by a jellyfish.

The fabulously eclectic Hotel Nacional, visible along most of the route, is probably the Malecón's most famous landmark. Running beneath its manicured gardens is a wide section of sidewalk where, in the evenings, bottles of rum are passed around, *puros* (cigars) are lit, and asthmatic Chevys glide past. This morning, a few scattered survivors of the previous night's festivities are engaged in a half-hearted after-party.

I hear a guitar being quietly strummed, and a tentative roll on the bongos. The sounds serve to revive me as I forge on towards the concrete façade of the US embassy. Marking the halfway point, the building has always been the least gregarious part of the route. Due to security concerns, loitering is strictly prohibited. There have been times when I've merely bent down to retie my shoelace and an officious Cuban policeman has blown his whistle and ushered me on.

Today, the embassy is eerily quiet as I run past looking out for any new political billboards that might have sprung up since my

THE MARABANA

The increasingly popular Havana marathon – aka Marabana – happens every November and draws more than 3000 competitors from around the globe. It's a two-lap standard 26 miles (there's also a one-lap half-marathon, plus events for 5km and 10km distances). The race makes the most of the city's iconic Malecón, running the entire length of the seductive sea-drive – twice!

From left: locals in the 'living room' of Havana; cruising the Malecón; all quiet in the afternoon; a historic lighthouse. Previous page: Havana isn't short on post-run sights. Opening page: a sunrise run on the seafront

last visit. My favourite is the cartoonish depiction of a Cuban revolutionary facing off against a bearded Uncle Sam. 'Mr Imperialist, we have absolutely no fear of you!' it cockily proclaims.

The Malecón becomes more modernist beyond the embassy, the weathered house-fronts of Centro Habana giving way to the wider avenues of Vedado. I run past a line of plush-looking private restaurants that testify to Cuba's recent economic defrosting. A bevy of leather-faced fishermen stand on the seawall by the Torreón de la Chorrera, their rods aimed towards Florida.

Once, in tougher economic times, I stopped for a short rest here. Taking off my shoes to air my toes, I fell into a pleasant lunchtime siesta. When I awoke 20 minutes later, my shoes were gone. With a mixture of embarrassment and annoyance, I tiptoed in bare feet along the frying-pan hot sidewalk to Habana Vieja in search of a shoe shop – not an easy thing to find in Fidel Castro's Cuba.

The memory of my comical robbery makes me smile as I turn around and head with fresh vigour back to my accommodation. Havana is a vibrant, complex and endlessly riveting city, but it can be maddeningly frustrating at times. Yet, stoked with a runner's high on this ridiculously seductive sea-drive, I can't help but love it. The tempestuous waves, the tangerine sunsets, the sauntering lovers, the petulant billboards and the weather-beaten buildings crying out for a face-lift. There really is nowhere else in the world I'd rather go running. **BS**

ORIENTATION

Start // Castillo de San Salvador de la Punta
End // Torreón de la Chorrera
Distance // 8.7 miles (14km)
Getting there // José Martí International Airport is Cuba's main entry point. To get to the eastern end of the Malecón (starting point for this run), get a taxi into the city centre.
When to go // November to March.
Where to stay // In a privately run *casa particular* (Cuban home-stay). Hostal Peregrino (www.hostalperegrino.com) is conveniently located close to the Malecón.
What to wear // Light, breathable running gear – it's hot and humid even in the 'winter'.
Things to know // The Malecón is a long out-and-back run. If you're still acclimatising to the heat and humidity, take it easy on the first day and turn back near the US embassy.

MORE LIKE THIS
CUBAN RUNS

SIERRA MAESTRA

The frighteningly steep road between the villages of Santo Domingo and Alto del Naranjo in Cuba's remote eastern mountains is generally considered to be the toughest climb in the country – for cars! Runners will need strong legs, lungs and resolve. Lying deep inside Cuba's Sierra Maestra, close to Fidel Castro's secret ridgetop HQ during the revolutionary war, the road climbs 2300ft (700m) in a mere 2.5 miles (4km). The road is paved but unrelentingly steep with a killer 45-degree section near the top. Few cars attempt it, leaving it to the preserve of burly Russian trucks and the odd equally burly runner. If you're up for it, avoid the heat of the day and be prepared for high levels of humidity. There's a hotel and basic facilities at Santo Domingo, but nothing at Alto del Naranjo save for magnificent cloud-forest views.

Start // Santo Domingo
End // Alto del Naranjo
Distance // 3 miles (5km)

VIÑALES

There aren't many opportunities for trail-running in Cuba, but Viñales National Park, 112 miles (180km) west of Havana, offers several options. Signposting and maps are scant in the park, but don't let that put you off. With a reasonable sense of direction and a rudimentary grasp of Spanish, you should be able to navigate this relatively flat rural circuit that starts and finishes in the bucolic village of Viñales. The route takes you through the pastoral Valle de Palmarito, famous for its caves, *mogotes* (steep-sided crags) and tobacco plantations, before coming out near Dos Hermanas, where a massive mural recalling prehistoric times has been painted on the cliffside. From here, it's a quiet jog on country roads back to Viñales village. Bank on meeting plenty of cigar-puffing *guajiros* (country folk) en route to ask for directions.

Start/End // Viñales
Distance // 3–5 miles (5–8km)
More info // www.cubanaturaleza.org

CIENFUEGOS

Graceful Cienfuegos on Cuba's south coast has always had more of an athletic sheen than other Cuban cities. It's not unusual to see people out training here, rowing their boats in the beautifully placid bay or running along the tree-lined Malecón in small groups. Cienfuegos' sea-drive is less famous but just as pretty as Havana's, connecting the main body of the city with the sinuous Punta Gorda that sticks out into the bay. For an attractive morning run, you can start amid the fabulous eclectic mansions of Punta Gorda, join the Malecón into the city centre, and head onto an elegant European-style boulevard known as 'El Prado' with a wide central walkway. From here, you can meander for several more kilometres past eye-catching statues, fine classical buildings and gossiping Cienfuegueros.

Start // Punta Gorda
End // Paseo del Prado & Via CS
Distance // 4 miles (6.5km)

From top: tobacco crops in Viñales, Cuba; the grand Palacio de Valle in Cienfuegos

Havana's El Malecón

MESA TRAIL

Easy-access wilderness on the outskirts of Boulder, Colorado holds a trail run so good it will turn burned out pavement junkies into off-road addicts.

I probably would have quit running forever if it weren't for a run I did 20 years ago. Since then, I have probably run this trail more than a thousand times, as it sits just a stone's throw away from my adopted hometown of Boulder, Colorado. Indeed it has become much more than my favourite place to log miles over the years – it's my go-to destination for athletic fitness, deep thinking and self-calm, not to mention a special place to run with my dog or with friends, manage career stress, and even mourn the passing of my father.

Like a lot of runners, I was at a point of being burned out, broken down and just plain bored of pavement, training for the same 10K runs and enduring the same kind of suffering through a big city marathon every year. Oddly, the same meditative – almost therapeutic – monotony that draws us to running often becomes the thing we despise most.

Then, by way of some unsolicited advice from a neighbour, I stumbled upon this utopian singletrack trail that helped change my life. Mesa Trail is a rolling, 6.7-mile (10.8km) dirt trail skirting beneath the iconic mountains that make up Boulder's western horizon line – most notably, Green Mountain, Bear Peak and the Flatirons. Long one of the trail-running capitals of the US, Boulder has more than 40 unique routes and 300 miles (480km) of singletrack, dirt roads and craggy mountain ridgelines. And for many reasons, the utilitarian Mesa Trail is the best of the bunch.

I didn't know it at the time, but that first run on Mesa Trail stirred something in me. It's an idyllic route, one that spoils you with both mild and challenging sections, but nothing too steep that it cannot be run at a slow pace. Most importantly, it has a flow about it, a moderately undulating profile that continually rolls up and down without sending a runner's heart rate off the charts.

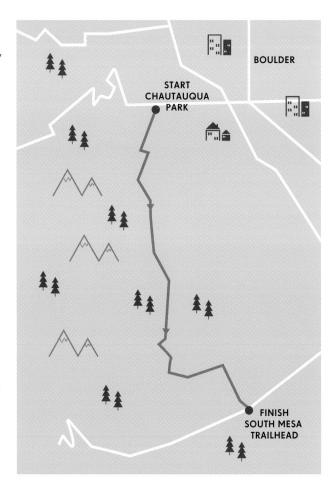

The day I finally decided to see what Mesa Trail was all about, I brought with me a bit of baggage. My angst and malaise towards running weren't the only things weighing me down – I was woefully out of shape. In fact, when I laced up my shoes and drove to the trailhead, I began to talk myself into just going for a short hike.

I started off from the stunningly expansive Chautauqua Park, immediately captivated by the impressive mountainscapes towering overhead. I was gasping for breath while adjusting to the thinner air of Boulder's 5430ft (1655m) elevation so I began by walking the robust uphill section at the beginning. But the moment the route turned to a winding dirt track that disappeared into a thick forest, I was compelled to start running. Why? It's hard to explain, It was sort of a Forrest Gump moment. And like Gump, I haven't stopped.

When I started out, I had no idea where Mesa Trail went or wound up. There were plenty of signposts and maps, and no chance of getting lost, so I just followed the route as it twisted and turned, climbed and descended over the rolling foothills. Running over the dynamic terrain of Mesa Trail was a pathway into another world. Instead of the consistent gait I was accustomed to while running on the roads, I found myself running with a bit of a staccato pattern as I dodged rocks, roots and other obstacles, negotiated steep declines and sharp ascents and used my arms to

"The dynamic terrain was a pathway into another world – I dodged rocks and used my arms to keep my balance"

keep my balance. Instead of manoeuvring around pedestrians, obeying traffic lights and keeping my eyes peeled for cars, I found myself enjoying the views, soaking in the aroma of the pine trees and marvelling at the rainbow of wildflowers along the trail. Without thinking about how far, how fast or how long I was running, I was already several miles along the trail and enjoying a mellow but enlightened vibe that must have been my first taste of trail runner's high.

I finally turned around after running about 5 miles in 45 minutes – avoiding a long descent into a valley at the south terminus of the trail – and headed back whence I came. The way back was just as exhilarating, given that a trail looks and feels unique when heading in the other direction.

That afternoon, my Mesa Trail run was much less about running and all about the experiential moments I was having as I ran: the gusts of fresh air blowing in my face, my legs and feet meeting the unique challenges of the natural terrain, watching a deer prance

FLATIRON FUEL

After a morning run on Mesa Trail, locals refuel on the porch of the 120-year-old Chautauqua Dining Hall. The restaurant is known for its Colorado bistro cuisine, featuring favourites like the Cowboy Skillet (eggs, elk chorizo, baked beans, steak, jalapeno and grilled sourdough toast) and the Denver Croissant Sandwich (eggs, ham, green peppers, onion, cheddar cheese, chimichurri aioli and sliced melon).

From left: it's not only runners who love Chautauqua Park outside Boulder, Colorado; the iconic slanted shape of the Flatirons. Previous page: enjoying the flats near the Flatirons

through the grass in the distance, and the sound of bubbling Bear Creek as I hopped over rocks to the other side.

Though I didn't immediately become a regular trail runner after that, it certainly helped me rediscover my love for running. I returned again and again, often running all the way to the termination point at the South Mesa Trailhead and back, while also connecting adjacent trails to form unique loops on the fly, and eventually running to the high mountain peaks overhead. My staccato stride movements turned into a rhythmic dance, my long runs got longer, and in many ways Mesa Trail did eventually turn me into a trail runner. (And yes, my experiences running Mesa Trail even helped me become a better road marathoner.)

Now, 20 years on, I have run that trail, or some derivation of it, more times than I can count, in spring, summer, winter and fall. It's the reason I never quit running and would never consider such a preposterous idea again. It has taught me such a lot about life, especially the notion that the journey is always the destination – not the time, distance, pace and other stats your watch feeds you. I have now ventured far and wide around the US and the world to run inspiring trails and unfathomably long races. Ultimately, my sense of being as a runner, and perhaps my sense of being me in my adult life, will forever be firmly rooted on Mesa Trail. **BM**

ORIENTATION

Start // Chautauqua Park, Boulder
End // South Mesa Trailhead, Eldorado Springs
Distance // 6.8 miles (11km) (one way)
Getting there // Denver International Airport is an hour's drive to either trailhead.
When to go // Mesa Trail is runnable year-round, but the best months are from April to October.
Where to stay // St Julien Hotel, Boulder and Chautauqua Cottages, Boulder.
What to wear // Trail running shoes with good traction and protection, appropriate running clothes for the season.
More info // www.bouldercolorado.gov
Things to know // There's wildlife aplenty on this trail throughout the year, including deer, foxes, black bears, coyotes, rattlesnakes, mountain lions and a variety of birds.

*Opposite: sunrise over the Blue Ridge
Mountains in North Carolina*

MORE LIKE THIS
FAMOUS US TRAIL RUNS

OLD CROTON AQUEDUCT TRAIL, NY

An idyllic wooded run hidden within the
urban gridlock of Westchester County, this
flat, mostly dirt, trail follows the historic
route of a 19th-century underground
aquifer built to bring fresh water to New
York City. With only a few mild rolling hills
and entirely devoid of technical features,
the 26.2-mile (42km) stretch is an ideal
place for long runs, tempo runs, recovery
runs, fartlek interval and other race-
prep workouts. Shrouded by trees most
of the way, the route occasionally offers
picturesque views of the Hudson River
and a variety of historic sites. Old Croton
Aqueduct Trail offers numerous places to
start out-and-back runs or long, one-way
jaunts combined with a return trip on the
Metro-North Railroad. Although it has
numerous road crossings, it is a surprisingly
continuous off-road running escape that's
easily accessible via a short drive or train
ride from Manhattan.
Start // Yonkers, NY
End // Croton Dam Rd, NY
Distance // 26.2 miles (42km)
**More info // www.parks.ny.gov/
parks/96/details.aspx**

WATERFALL GLEN TRAIL, DARIEN, IL

This wide crushed-gravel loop in suburban
Chicago gradually rolls through classic
Midwestern oak and maple woodlands,
diverse native prairies and lush ravines
as it encircles Argonne National
Laboratory. That's the federal laboratory
that once worked on nuclear reactors
for the Manhattan Project in the 1940s
but now primarily conducts clean energy
and environmental research. One of the
highlights of the trail is an overlook of a
beautiful tiered waterfall on Sawmill Creek,
built by the Civilian Conservation Corps in
the 1930s. The preserve contains more than
400 native plants and more than 300
species of wildlife, including deer, foxes,
coyotes, owls and a variety of non-venomous
snakes. This is a mild running loop with a
few moderate climbs that have made it a
popular place for local marathon training
groups to do hill workouts and long runs.
Start/End // Waterfall Glen parking area
Distance // 9.5 miles (15km)
**More info // www.dupageforest.org/
places-to-go/forest-preserves/
waterfall-glen**

ART LOEB TRAIL, BREVARD, NC

This rolling 30.1-mile (48km) north-south
trail has become one of the most famous
in the eastern US, especially popular
with long-distance runners. It meanders
through the densely wooded Pisgah
National Forest in western North Carolina,
traversing several high peaks along the
way, including Black Balsam Knob (6214ft;
1894m) and Tennent Mountain (6040ft;
1841m). Due to heavy logging in the 1920s
and 1930s, many of the high points are
treeless summits that reward you with
expansive, 360-degree views. Named
after a mid-20th-century naturalist from
the Carolina Mountain Club, the trail can
be conveniently parsed into four vehicle-
accessible sections that range from 4 to 12
miles (6.4–19km) or run end-to-end for an
epic ultra-distance journey.
**Start // Davidson River Campground,
Brevard, North Carolina**
**End // Daniel Boone Boy Scout Camp,
Canton, North Carolina**
Distance // 4–30.1 miles (6.4–48km)
More info // www.hikewnc.info

A TOUR OF VANCOUVER'S WORLD-CLASS SEAWALL

Hugging 400 hectares of rainforest and parkland, the stunning Stanley Park Seawall wows visitors and inspires even the most jaded local runners.

For local runners, Vancouver's Stanley Park Seawall is their treadmill – part of a routine that belies its beauty, an after-work or weekend ritual that is somehow both routine and rare at the same time. However, there's a reason it's often mobbed with tourists and all a local needs to do to be reminded how spectacular it is, is to look at the face of one of the hundreds of people who visit each day, as they stroll, cycle, sit and sightsee.

I certainly never need reminding of how spectacular this stretch of coastline is. These days, I guess you could say I'm both a local and a tourist. I lived in Vancouver for years, but now live 7500 miles (12,000km) away in London. I only get to run the seawall when I'm visiting. But to be clear, running the Seawall is the first thing I do whenever I do return to my hometown – and each time it feels like an embrace from an old friend, rekindling memories I thought I'd lost forever. I have wondered if it would mean this much to me if I did still live here and ran it every day. The answer is yes – it's that good.

During one recent visit, I couldn't wait to lace up my running shoes and make my way downtown. I was starting at Waterfront Station near Coal Harbour. Stanley Park is an island of trees linked to the West End of downtown by a narrow isthmus. But its famous 5.5-mile (9km)-long strand, with its paved lanes separating pedestrians from cyclists, has been extended a little over a mile further east, along Coal Harbour, which makes it possible to do a longer run from downtown than was previously possible. Some say the Stanley Park Seawall is the longest uninterrupted waterfront footpath in the world.

It is certainly the ultimate way to experience Vancouver, as it winds past stands of towering evergreens, skirts along sandy beaches and

even affords sublime views of downtown. It also affords great views of the North Shore Mountains and islands floating in the Strait of Georgia, leading out to the frigid North Pacific.

It was early and I felt like I had the city to myself. I jogged westward along West Cordova St before cutting north along a pedestrian mall and down some steps to West Waterfront Rd and the Winter Olympics' cauldron. A few more steps downward landed me squarely on the Seawall's pavement. Floatplanes bobbed peacefully on the docks – later in the day they would all have engines blaring, and be ferrying people to and from remote islands in the sound.

By the time I hit Coal Harbour Quay further west, I was fully in my stride. Since my last run here the trees over the footpath had grown, as had the height of the glass condominium towers and the size of the shiny white yachts. I smiled when I spotted a couple of my favourite brightly coloured houseboats, their more modest façades gleaming red and yellow in the early light, a reminder of a more modest time in the city.

At the end of Coal Harbour I turned eastward and could see yet another enduring landmark: the Vancouver Rowing Club. Its stilted wooden clubhouse, connected to the Seawall by a wooden bridge, has been a permanent fixture since 1911. Running towards the city skyline I could see Canada Place, an enormous building that cuts giant sail-shaped silhouettes across the morning sky. It's a building I've marvelled at since first seeing it at Expo 86 as a boy. This section of the Seawall weaves in such a way that one moment you are looking at the city, the next you are deep in the park's forest, then, again, looking at the city. This is one of my favourite sections, as I enjoy that juxtaposition of nature and the modern world, which is particularly stark given Vancouver's recent growth.

As I rounded the park's eastern tip and approached Brockton Point Lighthouse, I was staring straight up at the forested upper flanks of the North Shore Mountains. On rare clear winter days, you can see snow-topped summits from here.

I continued westward towards the distant but unmistakable towers of Lions Gate Bridge. The iconic span began to pop in and out of view as I meandered through the trees on the shoreline. But then it appeared in all its glory, and never disappeared again – its inorganic form sprouting from the forest

"I enjoy the juxtaposition of nature and the modern world, which is stark, given Vancouver's recent growth"

TWO-WHEEL TRAFFIC

Vancouverites' love of outdoor activities can actually cause a unique traffic jam on the Stanley Park Seawall. After a lengthy cycling ban – which started in the 1970s – a separate bike-only lane was finally added in 1984 (roller-blading was later permitted in this lane too), though it has a strict 10mph (16km) speed limit and you are only allowed to travel counter-clockwise. Runners and other pedestrians, meanwhile, can travel in either direction along the seawall.

Clockwise from top: mild maritime weather makes the seawall a year-round run; the crowds come out after work; Vancouver cityscape. Previous page: old-growth forest meets the sea

© Michael Wheatley | Getty Images

© Michael Wheatley | Getty Images

directly above me and arching out across First Narrows. As I ran, a hulking freighter silently made its way between the towers and into the inner harbour. But even a giant ship like this is dwarfed by the bridge's mass.

As I continued around Prospect Point, panoramic views of English Bay opened up before me. A dozen more tankers, scattered like toy ships, dotted its calm surface. Further out, I could just make out the faint outline of Vancouver Island (it's worth returning at sunset for this view alone).

Closer to shore, a couple of kayakers cruised in the shallows. And by the time I reached Siwash Rock, a small but famous outcrop jutting out from the water just off the Seawall, I could see the forests of lofty Point Grey that surround my alma mater, The University of British Columbia, in the distance.

Finally, I passed Third Beach, the perfect respite on a rare scorching summer day. It's a place where, as a child, I spent many hot afternoons, swimming and splashing to keep cool. From here, I could see the high-rise residential buildings of Vancouver's West End coming into view. I increased my pace as I skirted Second Beach, then crossed my imaginary finish line in the sand.

Afterwards, I sat on one of the beach's logs to catch my breath and soak in a little more of the bay view. Still not quite finished, I decided to stroll another kilometre along the Seawall to English Bay Beach to partake in yet another Seawall ritual. In fact, it's something that has become as much a part of this run as putting on my shoes: a cappuccino and the world's greatest cinnamon bun at Delany's Coffee House. **MP**

ORIENTATION

Start // Waterfront Station
End // Second Beach
Distance // 7 miles (11km)
Getting there // Public transport is extensive, with TransLink (buses, SkyTrain and SeaBus).
When to go // Mild winters make this runnable year-round. July and August are sure bets for sunshine.
Where to stay // The charming ivy-covered Sylvia Hotel (www.sylviahotel.com) sits on English Bay Beach, a few strides from the Seawall.
What to wear // Shorts and shirt in the summer. Tights, thermals and a light rain jacket in winter.
More info // www.vancouver.ca/parks-recreation-culture/stanley-park.aspx
Things to know // Extend this run another mile or so by heading inland along Lost Lagoon from Second Beach to the park section of the Seawall at Coal Harbour.

MORE LIKE THIS
SCENIC CITY WATERFRONTS

SYDNEY HARBOUR, AUSTRALIA

This 4.5 mile (7km) run takes runners past some of Sydney's most iconic sites, as well as some of its most breathtaking viewpoints. The route starts from North City Wharf – getting there on one of the city's ferries is half the fun – then continues north through Milson Park. After turning south, make the climb over the Sydney Harbour Bridge. The vistas over the harbour and the Sydney Opera House are the best in the city. This run then descends down the steps and east along Argyle St before following the water's edge around Circle Quay to the opera house, before continuing along the shore of the Royal Botanic Gardens to Mrs Macquarie's Chair. After hugging the west side of Woolloomooloo Bay, it finishes at the Art Gallery of NSW.
Start // North City Wharf
End // Art Gallery of NSW
Distance // 4.5 miles (7km)

CAPE TOWN, SOUTH AFRICA

Cape Town not only has a beautiful shoreline, but also the famed Table Mountain, looming magnificently over the city skyline. But to get the most out of the Atlantic waterfront without having to tackle the city's hills is to run the Sea Point Promenade between the Green Point Lighthouse and Bantry Bay, a return outing of around 5.5 miles (8km). The first half heads south, along the waters of Table Bay to the west, and the dramatic summit of Lion's Head straight ahead. The route passes pretty petite beaches of sand, such as Milton and Sunset, as well as long sections of rocky shore. The paved path is car-free and much of it is well-maintained parkland. You can add around three miles to the route by starting and finishing in the V&A Waterfront.
Start // Green Point Lighthouse
End // Bantry Bay
Distance // 5.5 miles (8km)

STOCKHOLM, SWEDEN

A city spread over 14 islands, Stockholm has dozens of great waterfront runs. A favourite is the loop of Södermalm, one of the city's largest islands. While it's possible to circumnavigate the shoreline for a flat 6.8-mile (11km) run, it's worth the extra effort to throw in some elevation changes along the north side. This route takes in Skinnarviksberget, a rocky hilltop outcrop that offers stunning views over the city, and Gamla stan, the old town of Stockholm. If inspired, it's also possible to add a few kilometres with a loop through this neighbouring island (the two are linked). The run through the southern part of the Södermalm is dotted with leafy parks and marinas.
Start/End // Several bridges access Södermalm and any one of them is a fine place to start
Distance // 6.8 miles (11km)

*Clockwise from top: Stockholm's
Old Town; the famous Opera House
in Sydney Harbour; Sea Point
Promenade in Cape Town*

Vancouver's Seawall

THE BARKLEY MARATHONS

In this insanely secretive and mythical ultramarathon in Tennessee, even the entry process is designed to defeat and deflate — the course itself will downright crush you.

It was night, pouring with rain and the water droplets were making it hard to read my compass. I had been crashing through the brush in the Tennessee wilderness for over 15 hours and, even though I had covered the same terrain just a few hours prior, I was now running in the opposite direction and nothing was recognisable. All I knew was that I needed to run in a southeasterly direction, down the steepest part of the hillside to the river below, where navigation would, hopefully, be easier.

I grabbed tree branches to keep me from falling over in the mud, and I strained to hear the sounds of running water. Then, when I did finally reach it, it was flowing in the wrong direction. I pulled out my map. At this point, I didn't even care about finishing the Barkley Marathons ultra. I just wanted to make it back to camp in one piece.

If you haven't heard of Barkley Marathons ultra, that's because you're not really supposed to. The entry process is a closely guarded secret and the more you research it, the more questions you have. The website tells you to submit an essay on 'Why I Should Be Allowed to Run the Barkley'. It doesn't tell you when the entry period is or even to whom you should send your essay. When I first heard about the race almost 10 years ago, I could never have imagined actually competing. However, for me, ultrarunning has always been about pushing my comfort zone. So after completing almost all of the major races on my bucket list, all roads seemed to be leading me to the Barkley. Though I knew I was physically capable – I had placed well in some seriously tough mountain ultras over the years – I had zero navigational experience.

You see, the mysterious registration process is the easy part of the Barkley. The course consists of an unmarked loop

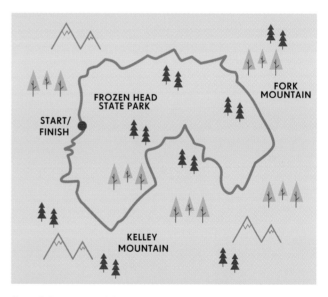

through Frozen Head State Park near Wartburg, Tennessee, which runners must complete five times in 60 hours or less – in opposite directions. Watches, GPS devices and phones are strictly forbidden. To prove that the course has been correctly followed, runners tear pages out of books hidden along the way that match their bib numbers. Runners have been known to spend hours just searching for the hidden books.

Every year around April Fool's day, 40 invitees from all over the world line up at the yellow gate, in the hope of just finishing. In the 30-plus years the race has been going, less than 20 people have finished it. In 2018, the year I ran, no one even came close

to finishing. In fact, if or when someone does finish, they just make the course harder.

The event is the demented brainchild of local distance runner Gary Cantrell, better known as 'Lazarus Lake' (or 'Laz'). Back in the 70s, Cantrell had heard of the escape of James Earl Ray – the man who assassinated Martin Luther King Jr – from Brushy Mountain State Penitentiary. After a 55-hour manhunt in the woods, Ray was found just 8 miles from his starting point, defeated by the harsh terrain. To Cantrell, this was a rather unimpressive performance. He figured he could run at least 100 miles (160km) during that same time. And so runners have been attempting to do just that ever since the inaugural Barkley (today's course even passes through a tunnel under the very penitentiary from which Ray escaped).

The day before the race, I found Cantrell ceremoniously hanging up licence plates from former competitors. The race registration fee is $1.60 and, for virgin racers like me, a licence plate from their home state or country. My hands were sweating as I handed over the plate that I'd had specially made, which was emblazoned with the words "BKLYVIRGIN".

Laz's eyes twinkled as he passed me my race bib and an emergency device, warning me that it could only be activated once; he implored me to handle it carefully. Then I realised that the device was completely fake; on my race bib it said 'help is not coming'.

I spent the next few hours marking my map and memorising each line, squiggle and dot before heading to bed. Instead of a start time, runners are given a 12-hour window in which the race could start. I slept in my race clothes.

At 8.33am, after a restless night of tossing and turning, the sound of a conch shell reverberated ominously throughout the camp. This signals one hour to start. At 9.33am, Laz lit his cigarette – the Barkley version of a start gun – and we were off.

I spent the first few hours stumbling around like a squirrel on a competitive acorn hunt, running back and forth between trees and twitching with confusion as I stared at my map. Everything looked the same and it was difficult to get my bearings. Though none of

RACE HAZING

The Barkley Marathons is probably the one race in which you do not want to be wearing the number 1 race bib. Rather than singling you out as a favourite to win, it actually marks you as the 'human sacrifice' and the runner most likely to fail first. In Laz's opinion, if he gives you the number 1 bib, you have no business being out on the course. If you do get the number 1 bib? Well, it's best to deal with it Barkley style and try to prove him wrong.

Clockwise from top: founder Gary Cantrell; first-timer licence plates; organised chaos; pulling an all-nighter. Previous page: the race's many travails

"In the 30-plus years the race has been going, less than 20 people have finished it. And when someone does, they make it harder"

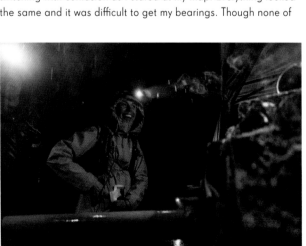

the climbs were longer than about 2500ft (760m), the gradients were beyond anything I had imagined for Tennessee. My calves were in agony.

I latched on to a couple of veterans whose course knowledge outweighed their slower speed. They methodically navigated their way through the brush, pointing out landmarks as hints for the next loop. As we discovered each new book, the titles never failed to disappoint: *Let's Pretend This Never Happened*, *61 Hours*, and *Left Behind*...

I was faring pretty well until I got to a descent called 'Leonard's Butt Slide'. Not realising the name is also advice on how to get down, I attempted to run it. After ending up facedown in a tangle of limbs and hiking poles, I realised I needed to change my strategy.

The first few hours of the Barkley are as disorienting as anything I had ever experienced. I only really got into a groove once I fully embraced the chaos. What took over was a determination to simply stay out on that course until I found all of my pages, even if it took me days.

A lot happened during the subsequent loops. Though, in the spirit of the race itself, I'll leave some to the imagination. Let's just say I did not finish and I returned to the yellow gate far more beat up than I had hoped. But I had finished two whole laps and, the truth is, I couldn't have felt more proud. I hadn't quit. Only two other women made it that far and the strongest men only finished one more loop. Once again, The Barkley had won. But that's just how it should be. **SC**

ORIENTATION

Start/End // Big Cove Campground, Frozen Head Park, TN

Distance // 100 miles (160km), 60,000ft (18,000m) of elevation

Getting there // Fly into Knoxville (50 miles; 80km away) or Nashville (150 miles; 240km away) and drive to the park.

When to go // Around April Fool's Day (the date changes).

Where to stay // In tents, vans or motor homes in the park, or a hotel in Oakridge in the days before the race.

What to wear // Sturdy gloves and pants or shin guards for surviving the briar patches.

More info // www.barkleymarathons.com. Documentary film *The Barkley Marathons – the Race that Eats its Young* shows the mental and physical challenges of the race.

Things to know // Bring laminating sheets or clear packing tape to protect your map from rain and mud. And bringing treats for Laz – favourites include Dr Pepper and Camel unfiltereds – is never a bad idea.

MORE LIKE THIS
BARKLEY-INSPIRED RACES

BIG DOG BACKYARD ULTRA, TN, USA

Another one of Lazarus Lake's concoctions, this October race challenges competitors to run a 4.166667-mile loop within an hour at whatever speed they choose – and then to repeat this as many times as they can until there is only one runner left. All eating, sleeping and bathroom breaks must be squeezed in during the moments of downtime every hour, so there is not a lot of room for error. During the day, runners follow a dirt trail in Laz's own backyard in Tennessee, while at night they run out and back on a country road near Laz's house, reportedly to avoid the many snakes in the area. In 2014, the last two runners finished together after 49 hours, stopping at just over 204 miles (328km). However, as they violated the 'Last Man Standing Rule' – dictating a single winner – Laz gave them both a DNF and declared no winners that year.
Start/End // Millersburg Rd, Bell Buckle
Distance // As far as you can go
More info // www.ultrasignup.com

THE BARKLEY FALL CLASSIC, TN, USA

Often called the 'Barkley for Beginners', this September race is a shorter and easier version of the Barkley Marathons, also held in Frozen Head State Park. Like the Barkley, runners do not know the course until the night before the race and GPS equipment is strictly prohibited. There is a 9.5 hour cutoff at 22.1 miles (35.5km), at which point runners must decide whether to run just 0.7 miles (1.1km) to end their race or continue on for another 9 miles (14.5km) to finish the full 31-mile (50km) race. Male and female runners are awarded guaranteed spots in the Barkley Marathons, should they choose to accept them after getting a taste of some of the deceptively steep ascents and descents hidden away in Frozen Head.
Start/End // Frozen Head State Park
Distance // 31 miles (50km)
More info // www.ultrasignup.com

CHARTREUSE TERMINORUM, FRANCE

The Chartreuse Terminorum is a French ultra inspired by the Barkley Marathons, that covers 186 miles (300km) in the wild foothills of the French Alps. Founder Benoît Laval is a veteran of the Barkley race, and so the course maintains the same general principle: runners navigate through dense forest trails in an attempt to find books hidden under rocks and inside trees, guided only by confusing written instructions, their compass and a map. The winner must complete five loops, but unlike the marathon-length Barkley, each loop is 37 miles (60km). To date, no one has come close to finishing within the 80-hour time limit.
Start/End // Saint-Pierre-de-Chartreuse
Distance // 5 laps of 37 miles (60km) in 80 hours
More info // www.chartreuse-terminorum.fr

*From top: Pravouta Pass in
Saint-Pierre-de-Chartreuse,
France; feeling the pain in
Tennessee's Frozen Head
State Park*

The Barkley Marathons

A RAINFOREST RUN IN COSTA RICA

A fast, flat trail in Cahuita National Park mixes pristine Caribbean beaches, tropical rainforest and wildlife encounters.

The Caribbean isn't made for running. Sunning, yes. Running, not so much. The vibe is baggy T-shirts and bare feet, not Lycra and technicolour shoes. Yet, here I am, pounding along a wonderfully forgiving sand-on-dirt trail in Cahuita National Park, the sound of the surf to my left, howler monkeys doing their thing somewhere behind me, and the jungle coming to life in the dawn.

On a family holiday to Costa Rica, this is my time – the sun pink on the horizon, the trail empty and my kids still sleeping off their jet lag back at the guesthouse. Just after the park entrance I stop and scan the trees. Yes, it's still there – a day-glow yellow coil, high up on the side of a trunk. It's an eyelash pit viper, its banana-bright skin warning of its deadly venom. The reason I know this is that yesterday we made the best decision of our trip – on our first day in the country, we had spent six hours here with a wildlife guide. In Pierre's enthusiastic company we learned how to spot sloths, tarantulas, Jesus Christ lizards and more. For iguanas,

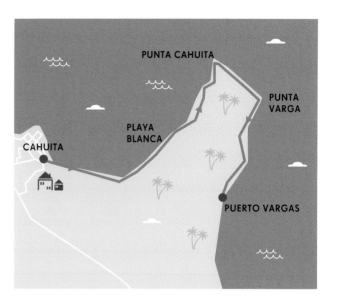

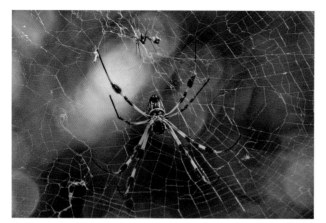

"The spider's web is the biggest I have ever seen and spans the entire width of the path – clearly not many people have made it this far recently"

we looked on sunny branches high up, where they bask in the sun undisturbed. If we crunched over freshly discarded almond shells, we were probably standing under a troop of capuchin monkeys. If we heard a strange coughing in the distance, it was a toucan and we should keep our eyes peeled for the source of the sound.

So this morning I am keen to put my new-found knowledge to the test. But first I have to put some distance between me and the park entrance, where a few other early birds are out, binoculars at the ready, walking at the snail's pace of the wildlife spotter.

I get into my stride, my breath coming easily, and realise what a great trail this is for running – I'm 25m from the crashing surf, the promise of a beach on my left, but my trail is broad and shady, made of soft, rich earth covered with a thin layer of windblown sand. As running surfaces go, it's perfect – quiet, springy and wide enough that I can look around. I open my stride.

Soon it's just me and the trail and any dawn critters I come across. At my running pace, there are lots of animals I'm not going to spot – such as anything that relies on camouflage. But there's plenty that I stand a much better chance of seeing than I did yesterday, even without the eagle eyes of my guide. I'm running on my own, up before the crowds, fast and quiet. The onshore breeze carries my scent away behind me. And the ever-present crashing of the waves masks the sound of my breathing and footfall. The element of surprise is on my side.

I come to an area where blue land crabs scuttle into their holes as I pass and I catch my first new spot – two crab-eating raccoons are out hunting. They look startled, but as I see them I stop dead and they run parallel to me into the jungle, giving me a wonderful view – fox-like faces made mischievous by bandito eye-stripes.

When I reach the Río Suárez, I look nervously at the mudbanks upstream. I've been running just 10 minutes, yet this is as far as we'd made it yesterday. Pierre had told us that caiman sometimes bask here. Of course they aren't out this early, and even if they were, I'm nowhere near them. But still, I take off my shoes and socks and tiptoe quietly across the cool creek.

From here on, it's virgin territory to me. I re-enter the jungle and as I round a corner I almost trip over a coati, the strange long-nosed cousin of the raccoon. He ignores me and carries on about his business, long tail pointing to the sky like a hushing finger as he sniffs out insects in the path. I carry on with a buzz in my belly from the feeling that somehow I'm a guest in his world.

Now the trail starts to change character as the forest to my right turns into swamp. The path moves further inland and there's a long section of boardwalk carrying me over the fragile, wet and crawling-with-god-knows-what shallows below. I realise how unfrequented this area is, just a mile or so further than most tourists come. I'm picking my way around the edge of a mangrove, planning my route over a fallen tree ahead when all

© Insights | Getty Images

SLOW YOUR ROLL

Usually, the three-toed sloth stays pretty high in the rainforest canopy, which makes it tricky to spot them. But once every three weeks or so, it has to make a trip to the ground – to poop. So if you see a sloth slowly clambering down towards ground level, looking furtive and perhaps a little desperate, give it plenty of space as you observe – it will be feeling very vulnerable.

From left: golden silk orb weaver spider; eyes peeled for the eyelash viper; three-toed sloths hang out high above. Previous page: jungle meets surf at Punta Cahuita

of a sudden... Whoa! I stop dead in my tracks, the rim of my cap pressing against the biggest spider's web I've ever seen, my arms windmilling for balance.

A huge, beautiful golden orb weaver sits at its centre, the yellow spots on her back matching the stripes on her long furry legs. She's mesmerising. Her web spans the entire width of the path, so clearly not many people have made it this far recently.

I clamber over a tree to avoid disturbing her and, after a few more minutes, I find myself at the end of this jungle peninsula. I stop and walk onto the beach. It's not sand here but coral and shells, white under the sun and scratchy underfoot. I stand and catch my breath. Like something out of a kid's cartoon, a couple of the shells start cautiously sneaking away from me. I pick one up, and am presented with the purple pincer of an annoyed hermit crab inside.

Out at sea, a line of white surf breaks over the reef. It's a sound that has been accompanying me, as regular as my breathing, for the past 10 minutes.

It's 6.40am. The sky no longer holds any of the colour of dawn. The air promises a hot day already. I look at the trail stretching round the headland in front of me, inviting me forwards. Back in Cahuita, my children still sleep.

This place was made for running.

I run on. **PP**

ORIENTATION

Start/End // Cahuita, Costa Rica
Distance // 8 miles (13km)
Getting there // Cahuita is in southeast Costa Rica, a 4.5-hour drive from the international airport at San José. It makes an ideal first stop in the country.
When to go // You can visit year-round, but March/ April and September/October are the driest months. In November and December the trail sometimes floods.
Where to stay // Playa Negra Guesthouse (playanegra. cr), where owner Pierre moonlights as a wildlife guide.
Things to know // Keep your eye out for three-toed sloth, yellow eyelash viper, coati, golden orb weaver spider, blue land crab, poison dart frog, Jesus Christ lizard, iguana, toucan, monkey and caiman.

MORE LIKE THIS
WILDLIFE RUNS

CRADLE MOUNTAIN, TASMANIA

If you're from the northern hemisphere, pretty much anywhere in Australia has incredible wildlife – the birds are more colourful, the mammals hop and the reptiles come with a public health warning. To combine this with the country's most spectacular running, head to Cradle Mountain in Tasmania. The run up the mountain itself gets all the press, but just as rewarding is a dusk run near the park entrance. As the sun goes down an array of improbably named creatures emerges from the bush – pademelon, echidna, wombat and maybe even the elusive Tasmanian Devil. Take the road to the Dove Canyon Track. Run it, then the Cradle Valley Boardwalk to Snake Hill. At sunset, return along the road, where the wildlife is easiest to spot.
Start/End // Cradle Mountain Visitor Centre
Distance // 8.5 miles (13km)
More info // www.parks.tas.gov.au

BRIGHTON SEAFRONT, ENGLAND

Some of nature's most magical sights are surprisingly ubiquitous. The starling is common throughout much of Europe, Asia and North America. While a single bird is nothing special, in some places the birds return to their roosts each winter evening and form huge murmurations – flocks of thousands that fly in hypnotic swirling clouds, painting vast ever-shifting patterns in the sky. The wide seafront of Brighton, just an hour south of London, provides the perfect backdrop for a contemplative run watching this show. From November to January, hundreds of thousands of these birds roost on the city's iconic piers, meaning a seafront run on a winter's evening is sure to lift the spirits. A 6-mile (10km) there-and-back takes you as far as Hove Lagoon. The route is well-lit at night.
Start/End // Brighton Palace Pier
Distance // 6 miles (10km)
More info // www.starlingsintheuk.co.uk

CERRO GUANACO, TIERRA DEL FUEGO

Argentina's Parque Nacional Tierra del Fuego really is the end of the world. It lies west of Ushuaia, the southernmost town on the planet. It's a rugged land where the glaciers of the Andes meet the stormy waters of Cape Horn. If you like your running wild, there's nowhere else like it. And with two protected biospheres in the park, wildlife flourishes here. Run the Senda Costera if you don't like steep and boggy, but if you're a glutton for punishment, the trail up Cerro Guanaco affords unforgettable views over the Beagle Channel. Along the way you might see the Magellanic woodpecker, austral parakeet, grey fox, condor and, of course, the guanaco (a type of llama) after which the peak is named.
Start/End // Alakush Visitor Centre, Tierra del Fuego National Park
Distance // 5.5 miles (9km)

From top: starlings swarm over the old
Brighton pier; guanaco llama in Tierra
del Fuego National Park

A Rainforest Run, Costa Rica

A PATRIOTIC PATH AROUND THE NATIONAL MALL

Washington DC's spread-out monuments can leave you drained. But for a runner, it is perhaps the most fascinating city park workout in the world.

Celebrated documentary filmmaker Ken Burns once described Washington DC's National Mall as 'America's Front Yard'. Indeed, this manicured stretch of parkland surrounded by some of America's most important monuments has been the site of everything from presidential inaugurations to fierce historic demonstrations. The memorials and monuments surrounding it celebrate both the nation's bold achievements and its tragic losses.

Some 24 million people visit the mall each year. But spanning a half mile in width and more than 2 miles end to end, it presents obvious logistical challenges to those exploring on foot. On any

given day, you'll find throngs of out-of towners sitting down to nurse sore legs and resign themselves to the disappointment of missing a few things, after grappling with the great expanses between sights. Some give up after the long slog between the US Capitol and the Washington Monument.

I decided instead to tour the mall during a well-planned run – it was a surprisingly fun and fast way to take it all in without spending most of my day walking. Suddenly, landmarks like the Washington Monument become an essential marker on an interval-filled dash from the Lincoln Memorial. Most importantly, you can see it all – and in less than 40 minutes flat if going at a decent clip. On an

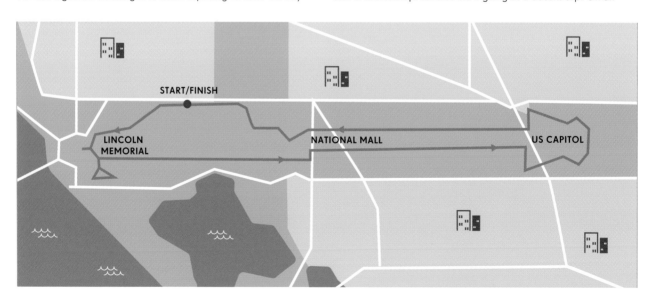

inspiring but efficient 4.5-mile (7km) loop, you can tick off every single monument and memorial, while mentally mapping out sights warranting further attention on a more in-depth visit later in the day.

It was late March, the cherry blossoms were just appearing on the trees and the morning was crisp and clear, with the promise of a warm day ahead. All was surprisingly quiet as I crossed Constitution Avenue and headed into the mall itself. In the pre-dawn light, I began the day's run along a winding path around the pond at the heart of Constitution Gardens, a 50-acre (20 hectare) expanse that forms a park within a park.

My body was still waking up as I passed graceful willow trees along the water line and a wooden bridge leading to a tiny island. The gardens are among the lesser-visited serene spots hidden in quiet corners – things you might skip touring the highlights.

At the end of the pond, I merged onto a curving lane beneath shady elm trees and ran past the entrance to the Vietnam Veterans Memorial. If it were later in the day, it would have been crowded with both tourists as well as relatives of Vietnam vets. But at 6.30am, no one was out, and I had the space to myself. I followed the black polished granite wall as it descends into the earth. Towering columns of row after row of names – some 58,200 who never returned – flashed past, no less powerful at a distance.

As I rounded the corner, the Lincoln Memorial came into view. One of the grandest monuments in the world, it anchors the

"I couldn't help but imagine Martin Luther King Jr standing atop these steps delivering his famous speech"

western end of the mall. I couldn't help but imagine the famous black-and-white images of Martin Luther King Jr standing atop these steps before a crowd of 200,000 onlookers for his 'I Have a Dream' speech. I picked up the pace and made a dash up the famous steps, enjoying the burn in my quads. At the top, I came eye-to-eye with honest Abe himself, seated on his marble throne, five times the size of the real man.

Before galloping back down the steps, I soaked in the view – it's one of the best in Washington. From here, I could see across the full length of the mall to the Capitol on the eastern edge, and I got a full view of the soaring Washington Monument shimmering on the pool in the foreground.

Back in my stride, I charged past a platoon of motionless soldiers who appeared to be on patrol. In the early morning light, these larger-than-life stainless steel figures take on a ghostly grey cast, their forms vaguely reflected in a long black granite wall to their south flank. Leaving behind the Korean War Veterans Memorial, I set my sights on the 555ft (170m)-high Washington Monument, DC's tallest building. For the next three-quarters of

THE 'SWAMP'

Despite the commonly made claim, neither the National Mall nor Washington, DC was actually built on a swamp. DC's most famous patch of green was actually laid out on low, flat land near three waterways (the Anacostia, the Potomac and Tiber Creek) and was prone to flooding during heavy rains, not only creating marshy areas, but also inspiring that politicians' cry to 'drain the swamp'.

From left: Washington DC's Vietnam Veterans Memorial; the city's famous cherry blossom bloom; the US Capitol Building. Previous page: the Washington Monument

a mile, it loomed ever larger as I headed eastwards. I raced along the reflecting pool – one of the mall's most dramatic features – as silvery clouds shimmered on the mirror-like surface.

At this point, I decided to slow down as I neared the Washington Monument, which is roughly the midpoint of the mall. Even at a clip, it's hard not to feel the majesty of this surprisingly simple structure, which was modelled on the obelisks of Ancient Egypt and is a strange homage to a man who wanted to be forever done with hero-worshipping monarchies.

I tried to not lose my footing on the downhill slope at the monument's base. From here, it was a flat mile along a wide gravel path to the US Capitol Building. This long straightaway is slow-going for non-runners – many complain that the domed building just keeps moving back as they walk forwards. Not for me. I relished this open stretch, picking things up a notch, leaning into an exhilarating high-intensity pace, determined to reach the grand house of congress in less than seven minutes.

By the time I arrived at the edge of the reflecting pool, I felt as if I was flying. There's something inexplicably satisfying about racing along the edge of a vast field ringed by the great power centres in the heart of a nation's capital. As I looped around the pool and began the return journey, it really did fee like America's collective 'front yard'. Few other places in the world can evoke so much on such a short run. **RS**

ORIENTATION

Start // 18th St NW & Constitution Ave
End // Constitution Gardens, near 18th St NW & Constitution Ave)
Distance // 5 miles (8km)
Getting there // The metro is convenient. There's also Capital Bikeshare, which has hundreds of stations.
When to go // April to October.
Where to stay // For lodging, great restaurants and nightlife, stay near Dupont Circle. Woodley Park has classy B&Bs along leafy streets, while Georgetown is home to upscale guesthouses tucked along cobblestone lanes.
More info // www.nps.gov/nama
Things to know // Crowds can be a real issue in summer if you want to get up close to any monuments you pass. In the early morning, you'll have them all to yourself.

Opposite: bookend a Russian run in
Moscow's unmistakable Red Square

MORE LIKE THIS
CAPITAL CRUISERS

OTTAWA, CANADA

Canada's capital is great for running, with more than 100 miles (160km) of pedestrian paths. Like DC, Ottawa has some grand buildings and monuments, which you can see easily on a 5-mile (8km) out-and-back run, starting near Rideau Hall, the official residence of the Governor General of Canada. From here, a tree-lined lane passes the prime minister's residence and then follows along Ottawa River. At Green Island, you can loop past monuments such as the Commonwealth Air Forces Memorial. Eventually, you'll reach the castle-like Royal Canadian Mint, with the spectacular National Gallery of Canada and the soaring towers of Notre Dame Cathedral Basilica just beyond. Nearby is the grand Parliament of Canada, the gothic revival Confederation Building and the Supreme Court of Canada building. From here, you can loop back along the waterfront, taking a leafy pedestrian-biking path on the return to the starting point.

Start // Rideau Hall
End // Supreme Court of Canada
Distance // 5 miles (8km)
More info // www.ottawatourism.ca

CANBERRA, AUSTRALIA

Like Washington, Canberra was an entirely planned city, built from scratch outside any state. Canberra is smaller and younger – dating from the early 20th century – than its American counterpart, though its compact centre also makes an ideal setting for a run. A good place to start is the leafy campus of the Australian National University. From there, it's a pleasant stretch along Sullivans Creek to the edge of Lake Burley Griffin. Turning left, a path loops along the peninsula out to the National Museum of Australia, an architectural showpiece as well as one of the country's best history museums. Continuing along the shoreline, the route leads across the Commonwealth Ave Bridge and cuts past the National Library of Australia and the picturesque Old Parliament House. Finally, cross Kings Ave Bridge and drop down into Kings Park, which offers a memorable panorama of the verdant scenery surrounding the city.

Start // Australian National University
End // Kings Park
Distance // 6 miles (10km)
More info // www.visitcanberra.com.au

MOSCOW, RUSSIA

Moscow is rich in history, culture, architecture and nationalistic monuments, making it possible to lace up your kicks and go on a remarkable self-guided sightseeing tour, while also getting in a pretty good 6-mile (10km) run. Because it's centrally located and easy to reach via public transportation, you can start from St Basil's Cathedral adjacent to Red Square and link Zaryadye Park, Gorky Park, Moscow River pathways and Alexander Gardens before returning to Red Square. Along the way, you'll weave together a tapestry of sights that links Russia's journey from the Middle Ages to the 21st century, including the Zaryadye Nature Centre, Underground Archaeology Museum, Gorky Park Museum, Cathedral of Christ the Saviour, Monument to Alexander II, the State Historical Museum, several ancient monasteries, numerous international embassies, stunning bridges, views of adjacent modern skyscrapers and, of course, the Kremlin.

Start// St Basil's Cathedral
End // Red Square
Distance // Roughly 6 miles (10km),
depending on exact route

THE DIPSEA
TRAIL RACE

At America's oldest offroad running race, California's hills are only half the challenge:
knowing who to pass and who not to let pass you is the real secret to success.

The toughest part of the Dipsea, said to be the America's oldest trail-running race, might not be the first mile, which contains nearly 700 stairs rising through the forests above Mill Valley. It is not the jiggly legged drop into Muir Woods, or the steep rise up Dynamite, so named because your churning legs might feel ready to explode. And it is not even the next big hill, called Cardiac, or the treacherous plunge towards the ocean, along the crooked depths and broken steps of Steep Ravine.

No, unexpectedly, the toughest part of the 7.5-mile (12km) Dipsea, a topographically schizophrenic romp that was first run in 1905, could be mental. It is knowing that the slowest runners are given head starts and the fastest ones begin at the back. It is like unloading a zoo's worth of animals in reverse order of mobility and releasing the cheetahs at the end.

The Dipsea is handicapped in an unusually calculated attempt to get the top runners in every age group to the finish line at the same time. A different wave is released from the starting line every minute, each one (theoretically) moving faster than the one before it. As seven-time speed record holder Alex Varner, 32, puts it: 'You're either the hunter or the hunted.'

That is why the winners over the past decade include an 8-year-old girl (barely beating a 68-year-old woman) and a 72-year-old

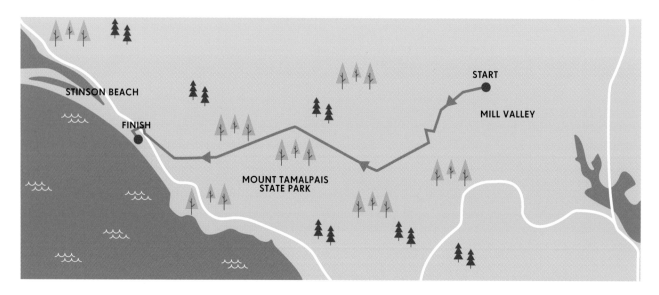

DIPSEA START
TAMALPA
1188
1933
1165
1918
1433
1366
1589
1887
1920
1580
1133

man. And that is how I started Sunday's race setting off five minutes behind the defending champion, a 47-year-old woman named Chris Lundy.

I live not far from where the race takes place, and I jog the hills a few times a week. When I had coffee with Barry Spitz, author of *Dipsea: The Greatest Race*, he asked me what other races I regularly ran. Well, none, really, I said. He silently and sceptically scanned me from head to toe and back again. 'I don't mean to be negative, but you probably won't pass anyone,' he said.

In 1904, as Spitz tells it, more than 30 years before Marin County was connected to San Francisco by a bridge across the Golden Gate, someone had the idea of racing between the Mill Valley train depot and the Dipsea Inn, on the sand of what later became Stinson Beach. There was no course, just wild terrain and a few scattered trails up and around the shoulders of 2571ft (784m) Mt Tamalpais. A man named Charles Boas apparently beat another named Alfons Coney and, deemed a success, the two-man event was renewed into an annual race beginning in 1905. It is considered the second-oldest major running race in the country, behind the Boston Marathon, which started in 1897.

The local flavour makes the Dipsea feel like a throwback in an era of gimmicky races. The starting area in Mill Valley on every second Sunday in June has the mellow air of a farmer's market. The race has no costumes, no man-made obstacles, no music. Sponsor names are not strewn about the course or the backs of T-shirts. The Dipsea is routinely approached by big-name sponsors, including one recently, offering lots of money and outfits for the army of volunteers.

I never saw Alex Varner go past. But less than a mile into the race, climbing staircases so long that the top cannot be seen from the bottom, I was aware that dozens were passing me. They were getting younger by the minute. Beyond the race's midpoint, heading downhill, the field thinned. I was alone when I ducked under a fallen tree to take a well-used shortcut called 'the swoop', a thin, tangled thread of a trail dropping fast through thorny thickets and trees. Relieved to hear no footsteps behind me, I tripped over a hidden root and fell into a bush, bruising only my ego.

More people caught me. It is the downhill dashes where the top runners make up the most time, bounding down steps and rocks and daringly passing the competition on narrow and tight corners like short-track speedskaters.

There is a lot of touching, hands on sweaty backs and shoulders, to keep in control. (The late Jack Kirk, who finished the Dipsea 67 times in a row, the last when he was 95, took to wearing a shirt that read 'Do Not Touch Me' on the back.) Only occasionally does the convivial civility turn to trail rage. One man shoved another at the finish line, sending him tumbling into the timing equipment.

I was not there yet. Darting down a meandering trail overgrown with bushes, I heard footsteps behind me. 'On your left!' a voice shouted over my shoulder. It was followed by an 'Oops! and a 'Sorry!' as the man bounced past me on the right and disappeared into the bramble.

FAMOUS FINISHERS

Actor Robin Williams ran the Dipsea a couple of times. 'Besides the hills, the stairs and the downhill, it wasn't bad,' he said after finishing a respectable 232nd in 1984. So did a young Robert S Mueller III, long before he became director of the FBI. There are no prizes other than the vaunted black T-shirts for the first 35 finishers (everyone else gets a coloured race shirt – blue or green in most years), a few trophies and a carved bear for first place.

Clockwise from top: the Dipsea's odd staggered start makes things interesting; the race ends at Stinson Beach; for many, the trail run is an annual tradition. Previous page: the start in Mill Valley, California

"Slow runners are given a head start and the fastest runners start at the back – you're either the hunter or the hunted"

© Jim Sugar | Getty Images

© Adam Derewecki | Shutterstock

Nobody gobbled up more runners than Varner, who began with a one-minute head start on the scratch runners. He ran at Davidson College and finished 26th at the 2013 Boston Marathon. He lives in Marin County, does a few trail races a year, and seems pleasantly unbothered by his inability to win the Dipsea. By the last mile, he had only one more person to catch: Lundy, a local veterinarian and an accomplished national trail runner. In 2017, she had an 11-minute head start on Varner and beat him to the finish by 20 seconds. This time, she had a 10-minute head start.

She, too, had passed hundreds by the time she topped out at Cardiac, where the Pacific Ocean comes into view. When she slid past 60-year-old Diana Fitzpatrick, a former champion, on the spiralling steps into Steep Ravine, about 6 miles (10km) in, she figured she must be in the lead.

Varner ran out of time and space again. Despite one of his fastest times ever, 48:51, and the race's overall fastest time for the eighth time, he finished in second, again, this time 15 seconds behind Lundy.

Nine of the top 11 came from different start groups. Winners of the 35 black shirts included three teenagers and seven runners in their 60s. Their median age was 53. The top scratch runner finished 30th.

I finished 580th. By my calculations, analysing the final results, I was passed by 247 people. The good news is that I passed 39. And in another two years, if I get the urge to do the Dipsea again, I will gain another minute of a head start. **JB**

ORIENTATION

Start // Mill Valley, CA
End // Stinson Beach, CA
Distance // 7.5 miles (12km)
Getting there // San Francisco airport is 28 miles (45km) south of the start in Mill Valley.
When to go // The second Sunday of June.
Where to stay // Airbnb is your best bet in Marin County, or take your pick of hotels in San Francisco, 15 miles (25km) away.
More info // www.dipsea.org
Things to know // This is a very popular race, with preference given to people who have run it the previous year. Only half of the 3,000 people who apply get a spot so read the race's detailed application carefully for the best shot at a bib. When packing, consider this area's cold, foggy mornings – even in June.

MORE LIKE THIS
FAMOUS TRAIL RACES

PIKES PEAK ASCENT, MANITOU SPRINGS, COLORADO, USA

There are more than 50 mountains in Colorado that soar above 14,000ft (4250m) elevation, but few are as awe-inspiring as Pikes Peak. That's due to how massive it appears as it towers over Colorado Springs and because it's the only '14er' in the Centennial State with a race to the summit. First contested in 1936 and held every August since 1970, the race sends competitors up Barr Trail as it winds its way to the 14,114ft (4302m) pinnacle. As daunting as it sounds, the route has a very mild slope and is runnable the entire way – even amid the increasingly thin air. While front-of-the-pack athletes reach the summit in a little over two hours, there are plenty of runners who finish in the three- to four-hour range. Once at the top, you'll understand why Katharine Lee Bates was inspired to write the song 'America the Beautiful' after reaching the summit in 1893.

Start // Manitou Springs
End // Pikes Peak summit
Distance // 13 miles (20km)
More info // www.pikespeak marathon.org

GROUSE GRIND MOUNTAIN RUN, NORTH VANCOUVER, BC, CANADA

Sometimes big things come in small packages. Such is the case with the Grouse Grind, one heck of a 1.8-mile (2.9km) race that climbs up the slopes of Grouse Mountain resort every September. Aptly known as Mother Nature's Stairmaster, the Grouse Grind trail sends runners and hikers 2800ft (850m) up a stair-step trail to the top of Grouse Mountain. (That's slightly more than the equivalent of climbing the steps to the world's tallest building, the 160-storey Burj Khalifa in Dubai). Needless to say, the men's (23:48) and women's (30:52) course records were set by world-class athletes with a penchant for suffering. For most, it takes 60 to 90 minutes to reach the top at a hiking pace. From the 3700ft (1128m) summit, runners and hikers are treated to spectacular views of Vancouver and its surrounding sea and mountains – as well as a gondola ride back down the bottom!

Start // Base of Grouse Mountain
End // Summit of Grouse Mountain
Distance: 1.8 miles (2.9km)
More info // www.grousemountain.com/ grousegrind

DALE HEAD FELL RACE, CUMBRIA, ENGLAND

Held during the Borrowdale Shepherds' Meet – a historic farmer's show that highlights many aspects of the Lake District, including cattle, dry-stone walling, beer and trail running – the Dale Head Fell Race is a classic up-and-down trail run that harks back to the origins of the sport. Starting from grassy show fields at Borrowdale's Rosthwaite Institute, competitors head out on a farm road and cross the trickling Derwent River before running over a rough and tumble farm pasture. From there, it's a sharp and rocky ascent alongside Rigghead Quarry on a path to the Dale Head summit (2215ft; 675m), where everyone tags the cairn at the top, turns around and races back down to celebrate with locally brewed beer, freshly made cheese and great merriment among the local villagers. Like all fell races in the Lake District, conditions are often windy, wet and sloppy.

Start/End // Rosthwaite Institute
Distance: 4.8 miles (7.8km)
More info // keswickac.org.uk/event/ dale-head/

*Clockwise from top: nearing the top of
the Grouse Grind above Vancouver;
Pikes Peak in Colorado; fell runners in
Borrowdale, England*

The Dipsea Trail Race

COPACABANA
AT DAWN

Rio de Janeiro's famous strand of sand rages day and night. But a sunrise sortie from Copacabana to Leme reveals a quieter slice of local life.

Nestled among soaring rainforest-covered granite mountains, Rio de Janeiro makes fine use of its gorgeous topography. Sky-high viewing platforms – like the famous one atop Corcovado, where Christ the Redeemer opens his arms over the city – provide dazzling vantage points over an island-dotted bay and glimmering beaches. But the quiet beauty of its natural setting belies the dynamism of the city's famous Copacabana shoreline. To truly feel the energy of the *cidade maravilhosa* (marvellous city), you have to come down from the lofty heights and get out onto the beaches of the vibrant *zona sul* (south district).

It's here that the scrum of tanned and toned bodies pack the sands, with vendors hollering out their wares – ice cold *mate* (sweet tea), Globos (a puffed rice snack) and, of course, *cerveja* (beer) – as they wind through an endless maze of Cariocas, as Rio residents call themselves, wearing string-bikinis and Speedos.

When I first started running in this city, this is the Rio that

COPACABANA

FINISH

LEME BEACH

START

unfolded before me as I jogged nearly every day along the beachside walkways. Just crossing the road was a challenge, amid swerving motorbikes and racing buses – not to mention the bikers, skateboarders and power walkers who clog the narrow cycle lane skirting the beach.

You see, for some reason, I had never done this run at sunrise (perhaps it was because of the late nights at the samba clubs in Lapa). So, finally, I was curious to see one of the world's most famous beachscapes, without the crowds, at a cooler and drier time of day. One early Sunday morning, with the sun just a hazy suggestion beyond the horizon, I laced up my shoes and stepped out onto Avenida Atlântica.

Named after the great ocean at its doorstep, the avenue is normally packed with cars. But on Sundays, the seaside lane of the boulevard is closed to traffic, and for the first time I had the wide stretch of pavement to myself. Fringing the road are the undulating waves of black and white cobblestones, a striking pattern designed by Roberto Burle Marx, one of Brazil's top landscape architects.

Beyond is the wide expanse of Copacabana Beach, which is also normally packed with locals navigating the popular walkway along the length of Copacabana. But that morning only a few early birds were out, including a few barefoot runners tracing the water line along the sands.

Warming up, I jogged slowly over to the Colônia dos Pescadores (fishermen's colony). I stopped to stretch while checking out the brightly painted fishing boats being hauled in. Closer to the road, vendors wore long aprons as they set up piles of the daily catch. Tracing the line of high-rises, I could just make out the end point of my 5-mile out-and-back route, which would take me from the southern tip of Copacabana to Pedra do Leme, the soaring rockface where beach and neighbourhood came to an abrupt end.

Enjoying cool morning temperatures and a light breeze, I set off near Posto 6. This is the southernmost post and lifeguard station in Copacabana and a popular gathering spot for standup paddleboarders. Fighting back the urge to kick things up a notch, I settled into a steady rhythm.

To my left, the high-rises lining the oceanfront were reflecting the first rays of daylight, while behind them rose the undulating forested peaks. A few minutes in, I caught glimpses of the Cantagalo favela, just inland. This informal community is home to some 5,000 residents who live in makeshift homes built of brick and cinderblock, teetering on the edge of the steep hillside. It's one of an estimated 1,000 favelas in Rio, which house more than 1 million people. A little further up the boulevard is the art deco facade of the Copacabana Palace, now a Belmond hotel. That these two worlds can coexist in such close proximity alludes to the great chasm between rich and poor that divides Brazilian society.

A few blocks beyond the Palace, I zipped past Avenida Princesa Isabel, which forms the imaginary boundary between the Copacabana and Leme neighbourhoods. From my waterfront perspective, however, there was no division, just the one long stretch

FAMOUS NAME

The name Copacabana originates from a small Bolivian village on Lake Titicaca. According to legend, a statue of the Virgin Mary of Copacabana (Bolivia's patron saint) was brought to Rio in the 17th century by Spanish merchants and consecrated inside a small chapel on the southern reaches of present-day Copacabana. Over time the name of this chapel was adopted as the name of the village, and then later the name of the entire neighbourhood that grew around it.

Clockwise from top: Copacabana's boardwalk meets the sand; the iconic Christ the Redeemer statue watches over Rio; beat the heat in the morning. Previous page: Copacabana is South America's most famous strand

"Normally, a scrum of tanned and toned bodies pack the sands, as runners, power walkers and skateboarders clog the walkway"

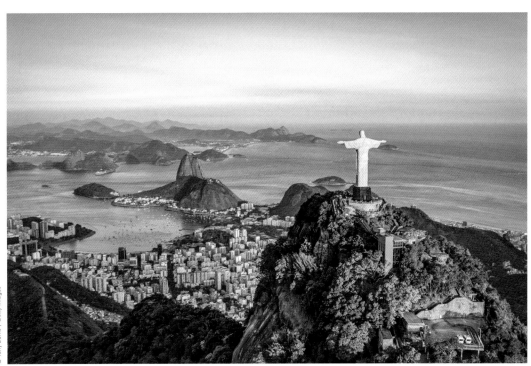

of near-empty beach. Meanwhile, just ahead was Pedra do Leme, the hulk of granite with patches of forest spreading atop its rockface. I cranked things up and ran hard for the next half mile. My pulse was racing by the time I reached a seawall that hugs the mountain.

I slowed down and jogged up a ramp that carried me above the crashing waves. From here, the view across the coastline was mesmerising – one long strand of elemental beauty: golden sand, green mountains and a cityscape kissed by the gold hues of the rising sun. This was my turnaround and, as I began the run back, the neighbourhoods were slowly coming to life. Vendors were setting up for the day, unstacking chairs and tables, and unloading fresh coconuts into coolers. As I ran past, a shirtless young man pedalling a three-wheeled cargo bike pulled up with a delivery of ice – Cariocas like their drinks 'estupidamente gelada' (stupidly cold).

Towards the end of my dawn run, more and more runners had been lured out by the temptation of a perfect, sun-drenched morning. Also zooming past me now were cyclists, speed walkers and longboard skaters.

For me, however, the Equatorial sun was now too high in the sky to continue. Instead, I parked myself at a beachside kiosk and ordered the coconut water I'd been daydreaming about since I passed it earlier. The attendant hacked off the end of a nut with a machete, stuck in a straw, and handed it to me. I sipped away, perched over one of South America's most magnificent city landscapes.

Having now seen an enchantingly peaceful side of Rio, I enjoyed watching it come to life and resemble something I was much more familiar with, as Cariocas flocked to the shoreline to celebrate yet another glorious day's sun and surf in Rio. **RS**

ORIENTATION

Start // Colônia dos Pescadores (corner of Rua Francisco Otaviano and Avenida Atlântica)
End // Pedra do Leme (Praça Almirante Júlio Noronha off Avenida Atlântica)
Distance // 2.6 miles (4km) one way
Getting there // From Rio's Galeão International Airport, it's a 45-minute taxi ride to Copacabana.
When to go // Year-round.
Where to stay // Rio Design Hotel (www.riodesignhotel.com) is a block from the beach, while the Marta Rio Guesthouse (www.rioguesthouse.com) has a spacious penthouse overlooking it.
What to wear // Lightweight gear; bring a rain layer if there's any cloud cover.
Things to know // You can run it there-and-back, or run it one way and take the metro. The nearest station is Cardeal Arcoverde, a little over a mile west of Pedra do Leme. Taxis are easy to hail along Avenida Atlântica.

MORE LIKE THIS
BUSTLING BEACHSIDES

MIAMI BEACH, FL, USA

Swaying palms and gorgeous white sand makes a fine backdrop to a run in Miami Beach. Pretty shoreline aside, Miami Beach is also famed for its colourful art deco architecture and lively, open-air eateries near the waterfront. A memorable 4-mile (6.4km) run begins at Indian Beach Park, near the entrance of the Miami Beach Boardwalk. This old-fashioned wooden walkway passes through verdant greenery and provides picturesque views over a surprisingly pristine stretch of coastline. Around 1.6 miles in, near 23rd St, the path becomes paved as it continues into the heart of South Beach. There's great people watching and plenty of architectural ogling as the run skirts along world-famous Ocean Drive, past buzzing restaurants and bars set in gorgeous pastel-hued art deco buildings. The run ends at peaceful South Pointe Beach, about 0.7 miles past the frenetic epicentre of South Beach.

Start // Indian Beach Park
End // South Pointe Beach
Distance // 4 miles (6.4km) one way

PROMENADE DES ANGLAIS, NICE, FRANCE

Along the southern coast of France, the city of Nice has long enchanted visitors with its beach-lined coast, belle-époque architecture and sunny Mediterranean climate. A run along the 4-mile (6.4km) Promenade des Anglais is a memorable way to take it all in, with a wide pedestrian-only lane. Aside from the Mediterranean views and refreshing sea breezes, the run passes some striking buildings, including the Hotel Negresco, a palatial neoclassical design built in 1912. Other highlights include rows of blue chairs facing the azure sea. Curiously, *la chaise bleue*, in existence since the 1940s, has become a symbol of this city on the French Riviera, and near the eastern end of the promenade 'La Chaise', a sculpture by local artist Sabine Géraudie, even pays homage to them. Though there's no bad time to run along the promenade, early evenings are particularly impressive, when the sun is setting.

Start // Cadran Solaire
End // Port Nice Carras
Distance // 4 miles (6.4km) one way

WAIKIKI BEACH, HONOLULU, HI, USA

One of the world's most spectacular urban shorelines, Waikiki Beach dazzles the senses with its views of powdery white sands, aquamarine waters and pounding waves – it's a favourite among surfers, especially in the winter months. Off in the distance, the Diamond Head volcano looms majestically. The run begins at Queen Kapiʻolani Regional Park near the Waikiki Aquarium, then follows the palm-lined seaside path, with beach-front high-rises in the distance. As the park ends, the route continues along Kalakaua Ave. This bustling commercial strip skirts the beach, giving fine views of this sandy playground. The run follows this road before turning left down Beach Walk, then right onto Kalia Rd. This leads into Fort DeRussy Beach Park, where the Fort DeRussy Boardwalk leads to the gorgeous Duke Kahanamoku Lagoon. It's worth taking a loop around the placid waters before making the return trip.

Start // Queen Kapiʻolani Regional Park
End // Duke Kahanamoku Lagoon
Distance // 3.1 miles (5km) one way

*Clockwise from top: the promenade
in Nice, France; sweating in Miami's
South Beach; Hawaii's famous Waikiki
Beach on the island of Oahu*

THE CHICAGO SHORELINE

After decades in development, the Windy City's Lakefront Trail is an impressive network of city parks and adventure playgrounds.

Chicago's 18-mile (29km) Lakefront Trail passes plenty of the city's trophy sights: splashy beaches along Lake Michigan, world-famous museums, downtown's mighty skyscrapers, and one very big Ferris wheel. But more importantly, the opening of this continuous path that spans Chicago's entire sprawl provides a tour of local life in all of its disparate glory, from struggling forgotten communities to mansion-lined streets, from oppressive urbanity to breathtaking wilderness.

On balmy days it seems the entire city makes a dash for the waterfront and it doesn't matter how fit – or not so fit – you are. The Lakefront Trail has a way of showing you that this city of 2.7 million people somehow remains small-town and neighbourly. Heartland values reign supreme here, strangers wave to strangers along the way. Fast runners politely pass slower runners.

It begins – or ends, depending on which direction you're travelling – outside the South Shore Cultural Center, a former country club where the Obamas held their wedding reception. The flat, paved trail hugs Lake Michigan, one of the world's largest freshwater expanses. It's an inland 'sea' vast enough to sink 1500 ships over the years. Its frothy waves ripple over the horizon with no end in sight. For locals who feel hemmed in by the asphalt jungle, the lake is powerfully restorative.

You can run the Lakefront Trail in either direction, but starting in the less travelled south means more legroom for the early miles. That's my way. I take a bus from downtown, passing through a jumble of working-class neighbourhoods, past low-slung apartment buildings and the occasional vacant lot.

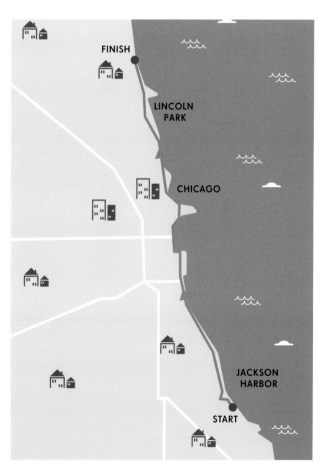

"Running the entire Lakefront Trail has a way of showing you that this city of 2.7 million remains small-town — heartland values reign supreme here"

I exit the bus and walk a few minutes to a sign on an obscure street corner that marks the start. At first the trail is just an unremarkable sidewalk skirting a public golf course. But after just a half mile, I round a bend and the turquoise lake appears, stretching out to meet the sky, while the trail unfurls elegantly along its shores.

In the first few miles, the path takes me past Jackson Harbor, where sailboats wobble in the water and old men cast for bass off the docks. Here, locals from the surrounding neighbourhoods gather outside, tailgating-style, blasting hip-hop and tending to grills that sizzle with sausages.

But not much further along is another strand of sand popular with students from the University of Chicago, whose ivory towers loom a few blocks west. Also nearby is the Museum of Science and Industry, the largest science museum in the western hemisphere – visitors often wander down to the shoreline after a visit.

For the next few miles, the path travels between the lake to the east and cars whizzing by on busy Lake Shore Drive to the west. But there is still plenty to distract me from the sounds of the city. When the water is low you can actually see a shipwreck offshore from 49th St; the *Silver Spray* ran aground on a rocky outcrop called Morgan Shoal in 1914. Today, its iron boiler pokes out of the lake. At 41st St Beach, muscled dudes do pulls-ups and crunches at the outdoor fitness station.

Suddenly, I'm in the middle of nowhere.

Gone is the hum of traffic and the exhaust fumes. The sound of birdsong and the sweet smell of grasses tells me I've entered the Burnham Centennial Prairie. Tall buildings fall away and busy roadways disappear. They are replaced by butterflies and swaying coneflowers that buffer the trail. It's as if I've passed through a portal and onto a trail run in the grasslands of Nebraska.

Once on the other side of this wild section, I enter yet another one of Chicago's iconic urban cores. Bronzeville is the historic heart of the city's African-American cultural scene, the neighbourhood where Louis Armstrong and Gwendolyn Brooks once lived. The neighbourhood's pride is 31st Street Beach. Often crowded with happy, tight-knit families, it also has some of the city's best public recreation facilities for a population that loves outdoor living.

Next up is a burst of famous Chicago landmarks: Soldier Field, Shedd Aquarium and Buckingham Fountain, which marks the trail's halfway point. It's also a section where the trail sort of disappears. The Chicago River actually blocks the way forward and getting past it is messy. It's a section that is still in-the-works, with a pedestrian bridge slated for completion in late 2019.

Meanwhile, deep-dish pizzas, margaritas and an insanely tall Ferris wheel wink from Navy Pier. This is commercial Chicago on steroids. Love it or hate it – most locals feel both – it sets

ALFRESCO ART

Chicago is an international centre for public art, and there are several great sculptures along the Lakefront Trail. Among the notable pieces are Tom Friedman's *Looking Up*, a fairy-tale-like giant made of aluminium foil and pans (near 48th St) and John Henry's *Chevron*, a 52ft (16m)-tall windmill-esque piece (near Diversey Pkwy). The artwork changes every few years.

From left: Navy Pier on the shores of central Chicago; runners flock for pre- and post-work workouts. Previous page: some sections of the Lakefront Trail cut through city, others escape it

the tone for the next few miles through the posh, consumerist neighbourhoods of Streeterville and an area known as the Gold Coast. The path here fringes Ohio St Beach, a favourite open water swimming training ground for triathletes. In fact, it stays close to the shore all the way until reaching Oak St Beach.

Flashy high-rise buildings keep things interesting until North Avenue Beach, Chicago's most expansive shore. It's chock-full of water-sport vendors and volleyball courts, giving it a southern California vibe.

Towards the end, the trail enters leafy Lincoln Park. Urban planners have praised this 'green lung' as one of America's great public spaces for its zoo, theatre and gardens. But really, Chicago's entire Lakefront Trail is now the city's most impressive public space. Chicago's forefathers mandated that the shoreline remain forever open and free of development. It's thanks to their vision I can run through this city end to end.

Finally, the trail swings north through more parkland, then into the communities of Uptown and Edgewater. Young toughs shoot hoops on basketball courts, Latino teams collide on soccer fields and elderly Vietnamese couples rest on trail-side benches. This far north, the lakefront is once again more a window into daily life than a show for visitors. At Osterman Beach, the end of the line, I decide to grab a Coke at the snack bar and blend right back in with the rest of my fellow Chicagoans. **KZ**

ORIENTATION

Start // 7100 S South Shore Dr
End // W Ardmore Ave, just east of N Sheridan Rd
Distance // 18 miles (29km)
Getting there // From downtown, take bus 6 (Jackson Park Express) to the South Shore Dr/71st St stop. Walk east a few blocks on 71st St to the Lakefront Trail Mile 0/18 sign.
When to go // Spring; weekdays are least crowded.
Where to stay // The Loop and Near North neighbourhoods.
More info // www.chicagoparkdistrict.com/park-facilities/lakefront-trail. Check @activetransLFT on Twitter for updates on trail conditions.
Things to know // It's easy to get on/off anywhere along the trail and run a shorter distance. Abundant restrooms and water fountains are available at the beaches and parks.

*Opposite: New York City's
Brooklyn Bridge*

MORE LIKE THIS
US URBAN PROMENADES

BROOKLYN BRIDGE, NEW YORK CITY

Yes, it's mobbed most of the time, but it's worth the crowds. Start amid the skyscrapers of lower Manhattan, make your way up the slow rise towards the bridge's towering crisscrossed cables, pass through the granite towers and eventually drop into Brooklyn's groovy waterfront district known as DUMBO (an acronym for 'down under the Manhattan and Brooklyn Bridges'). Once over the span, Brooklyn Bridge Park rolls out a waterfront path that makes it easy to add more miles, with stellar views across the East River, toward the high-rises of Wall Street, One World Trade Center and even the Statue of Liberty, further out into the harbour.

Start // City Hall, Lower Manhattan
End // Pier 6, Brooklyn Bridge Park
Distance // 2.5 miles (4km)
More info // www.nycgo.com

EMBARCADERO, SAN FRANCISCO

San Francisco's Embarcadero is a promenade that wraps around the city's eastern edge, following the Bay north. A run here lets you breathe the salt air and soak up maritime views, including a close-up of the hulking Bay Bridge. The route also passes by the Giants' gorgeous baseball stadium and hipster foodie hangout the Ferry Building, as well as the more touristy Fisherman's Wharf. The entire area draws a crowd, both local and from out of town, but don't be put off: the path is wide and flat, with views clear to Berkeley and Oakland in the distance the entire time. Pier 39 makes a fine stop for clam chowder, a microbrew, or a bucket of mini doughnuts as your post-run reward.

Start // AT&T Park baseball stadium
End // Pier 45
Distance // 3 miles (5km)

WEST RIVER PARKWAY, MINNEAPOLIS

The Mississippi River churns right through downtown Minneapolis, and the West River Parkway hugs its storied shore. The trail starts at the foot of the hip Warehouse District and zips by vintage bridges, spooky old flour mill ruins and the famed Guthrie Theater, with its cobalt-blue Endless Bridge that seems to dangle in midair. Onwards, it passes the University of Minnesota campus and swooping silver Frank Gehry-designed Weisman Art Museum. Minnehaha Park is an oasis of trees, verdant knolls of grass and bluffs above Old Man River and a poetry-inspiring waterfall. The trail is part of the Grand Rounds, a 51-mile (82km) network that loops around the city, connecting several other scenic routes for longer runs.

Start // Plymouth Ave, opposite Boom Island
End // Ford Parkway at Minnehaha Park
Distance // 8.9 miles (14.5km)
More info // www.minneapolisparks.org

THE BADWATER 135

Due to its face-melting heat and altitude extremes, just reading about this iconic ultramarathon across the California desert will be harder than your morning run.

At mile 127 of the Badwater 135 ultramarathon, the pain I felt in my legs was no ordinary pain. It was an illuminating pain that, strangely, has lured me back to this race year after year. I'd say it's what lures a lot of us here. It's a pain that asks you who you are and who you want to be. No race on the planet cleanses mind and body quite like this one.

This was my sixth time running Badwater and yet I've never felt quite prepared for it. For some reason, knowing what's coming doesn't help. I'm always stunned when the car door opens at the start, exposing my prickly cool, climate-controlled skin to a veritable furnace blast. Fittingly, Badwater starts in Death Valley, California,

the massive desert region named by a group of pioneers who, in 1850, found themselves hopelessly lost here, with death being the almost certain outcome.

Badwater is designed to bring runners from the lowest point in the lower 48 to the highest point. Starting at Badwater Basin, racers plod along narrow desert highways all the way to Lone Pine on the east side of California's Sierra Nevada mountain range, before turning westward up to the top of Whitney Portal Rd at 8360ft (2548m), the base of the tallest peak in the lower 48 (the original course finished on the 14,505ft (442om) summit of Mt Whitney until the park service shut it down due to safety concerns).

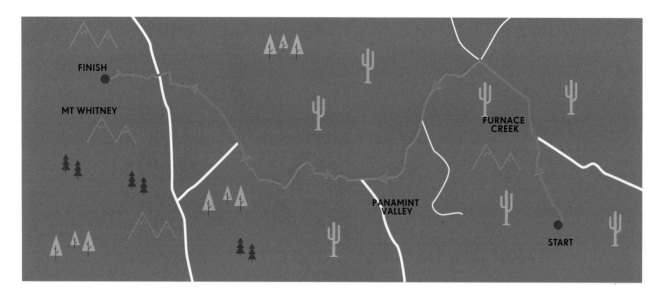

Even in the sport of ultrarunning, where the word 'extreme' is somewhat overused, the Badwater 135 stands out as a truly sadistic test of endurance. Considered by many to be the toughest footrace on the planet, its origin is firmly rooted in the age-old, ill-advised question: 'I wonder if I can do this?'. Al Arnold, a fitness guru from Walnut Creek, CA, was the one asking and set off for an answer in the early 70s. Then, after two failed attempts, he successfully covered the distance in 1977, thus dooming hundreds of future adventure seekers to take on this same challenge. Despite running dozens of ultras through the years – even winning more than a few – I still consider the Badwater 135 to be the ultimate challenge.

As I arrived at the starting line of the 2013 Badwater 135 my anxiety grew, and a familiar question arose: 'Do I really want to do this again?' It was mid July, the hottest time of the year, because to race at some other time of the year would defeat the purpose. I guess you could say that purpose was to have such an intense clarifying experience that it would scrape out my insides and replace them with some deeper understanding of what I'm made of.

Every racer is required to bring their own support crew, as there are no aid stations along the course. Without a crew, racers might not survive the race, much less finish it. My crew were all rookies that year, but I was fairly confident they wouldn't let me die. Lined

> *"The pain in my legs was no ordinary pain – it was an illuminating pain that has brought me back, year after year"*

up at the start with my fellow adventurers, I glanced up to my right and saw the words 'sea level' scrawled on a rock face, 282ft (86m) above me. When the 10am start time arrived, we shuffled away from the line like a bale of turtles. I let the faster runners go ahead, reminding myself that Mt Whitney is a long 135 miles (217km) away and I should try to enjoy this early, relatively pain-free section. It wouldn't last for long. Not much later, my watch cruelly reminded me it was already 128°F (53°C). And that's the good news. The bad news is that the 200°F (93°C) surface temperature caused what I can only describe as a sort of open-space claustrophobia.

I moved through Furnace Creek and then past furrowed dunes on my way to Stovepipe Wells. It had taken 42 miles of slow gradual climbing just to reach sea level and this small town. Some racers were stripping down and jumping into a motel pool, but it felt more like a hot tub to me so I just kept moving. I slogged my way through the 17-mile climb up to Towne Pass, 5000ft (1500m) above the desert floor. Then I scurried down the 10-mile descent to the Panamint Valley.

DOUBLE THE FUN

Distance is only half the challenge at Badwater, as the course crosses two mountain ranges, for a cumulative elevation gain of more than 19,000ft (5790m). Nonetheless, there are a handful of men and women who have done what are known as the Death Valley 300 (a round trip), a Badwater Triple (three crossings) and even a Badwater Quad (two round trips).

From left: runners near the finish at Mt Whitney; heat and dehydration are ever-present dangers. Previous page: temperatures in Badwater Basin can hit 130°F (54°C)

The setting sun meant mercifully cooler temperatures and the lavender sky was a beautiful reward for my hard work so far. As dusk turned to full dark, I was startled by a rattlesnake in the road. At mile 72, I passed the Panamint Springs Resort, then Father Crowley's Turnout, finally reaching mile 90 and the turnoff to Darwin, a small inhabited ghost town with a sign reading 'NO television, NO WIFI, NO cell signal, NO stores; visitors welcome.'

The pleasant 97°F (36°C) nighttime temperature beckoned me to turn off my headlamp and take in the mind-blowing celestial show. A few hours later, dawn began to breach the horizon as I passed through the small mining town of Keeler at mile 108. Up ahead was Mt Whitney and the stunning Sierra bathed in a dawn Alpenglow.

I was fully energised as I finally reached Lone Pine at mile 122. The final, and arguably hardest, section of the race is this 13-mile (21km), 5000ft (1500m) climb up the foothills. As I made my way up, the temperature cooled and the wind picked up. Every S-curve through the towering pines brought a new view of the impossibly vast desert below. Then, the final turn revealed a small crowd near the finish line at 8300ft (2530m), causing me to unleash a hobbling sprint. It had taken me 26 hours and 15 minutes to get here. As I looked back one final time, I said to myself, 'Goodbye Death Valley – never again'. As I write this, I am currently signed up to run it again in 2019. **CE**

ORIENTATION

Start // Badwater Basin
End// Top of Whitney Portal Rd, above Lone Pine, California
Distance // 135 miles (217km)
Getting there // Fly to Las Vegas, then drive 140 miles (225km) to Furnace Creek.
When to go // Third week in July.
Where to stay //The Furnace Creek Ranch (www.oasisatdeathvalley.com) is a good luxe option near the start. The Dow Villa Motel (www.dowvillamotel.com) has simple rooms near the finish in Lone Pine.
More information // www.badwater.com
Things to know // Everyone focuses on the heat, but it's the dry air you have to worry about – start hydrating at least a week before your arrival.

Opposite: Climbing past cypress trees
on the Spartathlon ultra

MORE LIKE THIS
GRUELLING ULTRAMARATHONS

SPARTATHLON, GREECE

Steeped in history, this event transports runners back in time. While racers face extreme heat and tight cutoff times, they can marvel at a course that traces the full route of Pheidippides himself, who in 490 BC was dispatched from Athens to Sparta, before the battle of Marathon, in order to seek help for the Greeks as they waged war on the Persians. Starting at the base of the Acropolis, the course winds along ancient provincial roads, passes through olive groves and past vast vineyards. Then it's up the 3900ft (1200m) Parthenon Mountain, where legend claims that Pheidippides encountered the god Panna. The citizens of Sparta turn out to enthusiastically welcome the runners as heroes, as they kneel at the feet of the statue of King Leonidas. All finishers are crowned with an olive wreath and are offered a bowl of water from Evrotas, just as the first Olympians were honoured in ancient times.

Start // Acropolis, Athens
End // Sparta
Distance // 153 miles (246km)
More info // www.spartathlon.gr/en/

ARROWHEAD 135, MINNESOTA, USA

The Arrowhead 135 takes place in the coldest part of winter in the coldest city in the lower 48 states, International Falls, Minnesota. The multipurpose Arrowhead State Trail is a mix of wide, flat trails and rugged, rolling hills with ice-cold lakes and streams. Expect to see moose and wolf tracks, as well as deer, lynx, foxes and snowshoe hare. The southern section of the trail has vast areas of exposed rock and enormous boulders, detritus left behind from glacial erosion that ground down ancient mountain ranges. There are scenic vistas overlooking the lakes and old iron-ore mines, as well as massive stands of old-growth hardwoods. Pay attention and you might also spot osprey, snowy owl and bald eagle nests along the way. The race ends near Lake Vermillion, but with a finishing rate below 50%, many racers find a warm place to bail out along the way.

Start // International Falls, MN
End // Lake Vermillion, MN
Distance // 135 miles (217km)
More info // www.arrowheadultra.com

BRAZIL 135, MINAS GERAIS

The Brazil 135 is held in the Serra da Mantiqueira mountains. This lush mountain range separates Rio de Janeiro from Minas Gerais state and is one of the few remaining areas with extensive Atlantic Coastal Rainforest. Even though the Brazil 135 is widely considered the most difficult foot race in Brazil, it is totally worth the effort. The race is run on the most challenging segment of the Caminho da Fé (Path of Faith) a well-known pilgrimage path. Racers run past pretty little towns with friendly hostels and amazing food. The path also meanders through many national and state parks. Though the 60-hour cutoff seems generous, runners will need to keep moving to finish in time... especially if it rains.

Start // São João da Boa Vista
Finish // Paraisópolis
Distance // 135 miles (217km)
More info // www.brazil135.com.br

BAY TO BREAKERS

San Francisco's most famous running race is not about split times and speed records. It's more like a fast-paced protest march through the streets, freak-flags flying high.

Making my way up Howard St in the first miles of the Bay to Breakers race across San Francisco, I couldn't help but feel people were staring at me. I was an oddity that day – one of the few runners dressed up as, well, an actual runner.

On this cool Sunday morning in late May, I was surrounded by a woman wearing a panda costume; two men wearing black leotards, multicoloured tutus and fluorescent yellow feather boas; and two more dressed up as the Blues Brothers. Nearby, a group of runners were dressed entirely in green, wearing cardboard signs decrying oil drilling and deforestation and global warming. To my right were

'centipede' teams of identically outfitted runners, tethered together with a small cord. And then, of course, there were the naked people. Naked men, naked women, bandying about, wearing nothing but running shoes and lightweight backpacks.

When signing up for this event, I'm not sure I fully understood what the Bay to Breakers run was all about, or what it meant to so many people. Yes, it always attracts an odd collection of humanity, but perhaps even stranger was the notion that we were all there – 50,000 of us – to run 7 miles (11km) across San Francisco, from the bay shore at its eastern edge to the Pacific ocean in the west.

For me, the Bay to Breakers was actually supposed to be a simple tune-up for an upcoming marathon. But it became pretty clear even before the race start that I was an outsider looking in. As my race wave approached the startline, a group of runners wearing inflatable rubber ducky pool toys did some sort of choreographed warm-up dance. An Elvis impersonator belted out a few bars of 'Love Me Tender'. In my wicking T-shirt, nylon running shorts and a beat-up pair of Nike Pegasus, I actually felt a bit foolish, perhaps even some shame, that I had seemingly missed the entire point of what I now know is the most peculiar race in running, as well as one of the most significant events in San Francisco.

In fact, I cruised through the entire financial district, shortly after the start, contemplating what kind of costume I would wear if I came back to run it again in the future. Maybe a superhero? A bunny rabbit with big floppy ears? Maybe I'd just wear a brightly colored pair of Speedos. It's the sort of event that makes you second guess things like personal time goals, which somehow feel a little inconsequential.

Bay to Breakers has long been one of the world's most iconic running races, both because it's one of the oldest – it originated in 1912 – and because it so distinctively oozes the passionate energy of the city that spawned it. It was started as a way of lifting the city's spirits after the devastating 1906 earthquake. But decades later it transformed into the massive public party it is today. It's more than just a race. Much like San Francisco itself, it stands for self-expression, personal fitness, political activism and counterculture liberation.

'Yes, it is a big party, but it's certainly much more than just that. It's a San Francisco institution,' says one runner who has run on a fast centipede team almost every year for more than a decade. 'It's an excuse to dress up for fun, but also for whatever social cause you believe in.'

A few miles in, the two women beside me wearing pink sports bras, pink Spandex shorts, pink running shoes and bright pink wigs seemed perfectly normal. The course zig-zagged from Howard to 9th St to Hayes Valley, where I began the trudge up the notoriously steep Hayes St Hill – an ascent that climbs as sharply as 11% for 2000ft (600m). When I finally reached the summit, people were out in force, partying on porches, dancing to a street-side band playing – what else – Grateful Dead covers.

When the first wave of the American running boom swept the US in the early 1970s, Bay to Breakers grew from hundreds of participants to thousands. Shortly after, it ballooned into the world's largest running event. It has actually shrunk a bit since then – thanks to rising entry fees and buzz-kill citizens fed up with the debauchery – yet still attracts thousands of unregistered 'bandit' runners, as well as more than 100,000 enthusiastic spectators.

The Panhandle near Golden Gate Park and the Haight Ashbury neighbourhood marks the halfway point. Here, I was passed by the first of many centipede teams. No other race in the world allows runners to compete while linked together as a team. Nowadays,

RECORD SETTER

Held every year since 1912, Bay to Breakers has been run for more consecutive years over a given course and length than any other footrace in the world. During WWII, participation sometimes slipped below 50 registrants, but the race carried on without interruption. Meanwhile, it also became the world's largest running event; the 1986 race set a world record thanks to 110,000 runners.

Clockwise from top: essential race kit; the Golden Gate Bridge; 50,000-strong. Previous page: runner-revellers hit Alamo Square

"I cruised through the financial district contemplating what sort of costume I might wear next time. A superhero? A bunny rabbit? Or maybe I'd just wear a pair of Speedos."

winning centipede teams run faster than a 5:30-mile pace, a true sight to behold as runners stride in unison just five feet apart for the entire length of the course.

Running through Golden Gate Park, I passed the domed greenhouse of the Conservatory of Flowers and the manicured gardens fronting the Japanese Tea Garden. This is also the high point of the course and running downhill along John F Kennedy Dr, the final miles went by in something of a blur. I realised I had abandoned my target long ago, in favour of people watching, so it felt good to finally pick up some speed. After a slight zig-zag to Martin Luther King Jr Dr, I ran past the famous Dutch-style Murphy Windmill in the southwest corner of the park.

Turning onto the Great Hwy, I got my first glance of the ocean, its powerful waves breaking to my right the entire final hundred yards to the finish line. When it was over, I immediately felt an uncanny sense of remorse. Not because I didn't run as fast as I'd initially hoped, but because I had been paying attention to my time at all. I immediately headed to the beach to watch others cross the finish line, and inhale whatever second-hand freakiness I could before the crazies started heading home.

I've run races all over the world and the truly great ones are a reflection of their physical and cultural landscape. In much the same way your experience of the New York marathon is defined by the fact that you get to run through all five boroughs, Bay to Breakers bares the soul of San Francisco. It's definitely not about running fast, or even about running at all. It's about expression. **BM**

ORIENTATION

Start // Near Howard and Stuart streets
End // Great Hwy, Ocean Beach
Distance // 7.46 miles (12km)
Getting there // San Francisco International Airport is about 35 miles (56km) south of the starting line.
When to go // The third Sunday in May.
Where to stay // Hotel Griffon (www.hotelgriffon.com) or Hyatt Regency San Francisco (www.hyatt.com) are good options near the startline.
What to wear // If you want to truly enjoy your experience to the fullest – and really fit in – wear a costume or run for a cause. That said, don't forget a good pair of running shoes – 7.5 miles is a long way to go wearing fake duck feet.
More info // www.baytobreakers.com
Things to know // This is one race where you should not forget your smartphone to take pictures.

Opposite, from top: the cheese takes the lead on Cooper's Hill, Gloucester; Las Vegas welcomes all, even marathon runners

MORE LIKE THIS
FAMOUS FUN RUNS

COOPER'S HILL CHEESE-ROLLING AND WAKE, BROCKWORTH, ENGLAND

Cheese-wheel racing down Cooper's Hill has been happening every spring on the last Monday of May in Brockworth, a small village in the county of Gloucestershire in southwest England, since at least the mid-1400s. The event has persevered through wars, food-rationing, bubonic plague and numerous injuries. The premise is simple: hearty competitors chase a locally made cheese wheel down a dastardly steep grassy hill. The first one to the bottom to retrieve it is declared the winner. The cheese wheels have traditionally weighed about 9lbs (4kg) and reportedly travel as fast as 70mph (112kph) down the hill. However, the cheese has been replaced in recent years by a slightly slower-moving foam replica to reduce the chance of spectator injuries – or deaths.
Start // Top of Cooper's Hill in Gloucester, England
End // Bottom of Cooper's Hill
More info // radseason.com/event/ coopers-hill-cheese-rolling-gloucester- united-kingdom/

ROCK 'N' ROLL LAS VEGAS HALF MARATHON, NEVADA, USA

One of the biggest spectacles in running, this early November race sends runners up and down the Las Vegas Strip on one of the two nights of the year it's closed to car traffic. Beginning with a headliner music act and a pyrotechnic starting line, runners dash through the heart of Sin City, passing the famous 'Welcome to Las Vegas' sign, renowned casinos such as Mandalay Bay, Luxor, Excalibur, MGM Grand, Caesar's Palace and The Bellagio, plus numerous wedding chapels, pawn shops and the amazing light show of The Fremont Street Experience. There are also full marathon, 10km and 5km events, but the half marathon distance is the sweet spot as far as seeing it all, with enough left in the tank to experience Vegas afterwards.
Start // MGM Grand Hotel Casino
End // The Mirage Hotel Casino
Distance // 13 miles (21km)
More info // www.runrocknroll.com

AUSTRALIAN DUNNY DERBY, WINTON, QUEENSLAND, AUSTRALIA

Dubbed 'The Constipation Stakes,' this is a down and dirty outhouse race. Toilet humour aside, it's a mad dash of homemade latrines on wheels. Each five-person team includes one 'jockey' squatting on 'the throne' and four runners acting as human horses, two pulling from the front and two pushing from behind. The 200m race starts off Le Mans-style, with the jockey sprinting to his seat and then each team manoeuvring their outhouse through a series of obstacles to the finish line in front of a local pub. Cue heroic drinking.
Start/End // Eric Lenton Memorial Recreation Grounds
Distance //200m (650ft)
More info // www.outbackfestival.com. au/event/dunny-derby/

A WINTER WARM-UP IN QUÉBEC CITY

Sometimes the only way to have your favourite city run all to yourself is to do it when the mercury drops below zero and most people are still in bed.

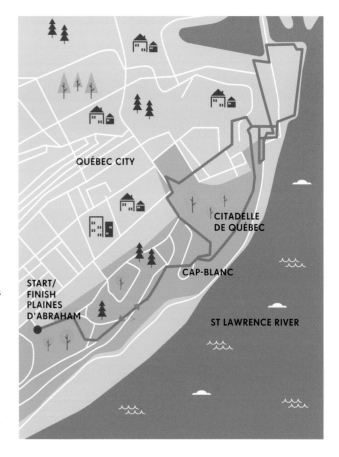

Winter mornings have never been a runner's best friend – unless you happen to live in Québec City. I do live in Québec City for part of the year, and have found that the season is such a part of our culture and landscape, it's actually a time when that internal early morning struggle – the negotiation with oneself for a few more minutes in bed – disappears. In winter, I get up with the alarm, excited to discover how snowy it might be outside, curious about how cold it might be. On go the layers and the four-season running gear – the thermals, the tuque, the YakTrax – and off I go.

Outside, it's always minus a few and my breath steams up in great clouds around me. I never grow tired of what lies ahead: centuries of history and gorgeous natural surroundings along my favourite city run on the planet. It's a run I do a few times a week when I'm here, and it's actually best in the coldest months. However, even in winter, Québec City gets packed with people, which is why early morning is my favourite. A quiet dawn workout is the perfect way to start the day.

Québec sits high on a cape known as Cap Diamant, between the St Lawrence and St Charles Rivers. The old city was built on the site of an Iroquois village, chosen by French explorer and city founder Samuel de Champlain in 1608.

Because of its geography, the oldest part of the city is a two-tier affair. The upper city sits high on a promontory with its meandering, history-drenched thoroughfares, imposing ramparts, and the impressive Château Frontenac hotel. The lower part of

town is full of impossibly narrow cobbled streets and quaint shops, in what's known as the Quartier Petit Champlain, a neighbourhood leading to the Old Port area.

I always begin this run near the snowy expanse of the city's largest city-centre park, the Plaines d'Abraham. When it's really cold, say, 5°F (-15°C), I head here first for a warm-up along the flat, green, manicured gardens and tree-fringed lawns. In winter, it's a huge, snowy playground with cross-country ski tracks, a skating rink and snow-running tracks.

Once at the south end of the plains, I pick up some of the off-road trails that lead through the heart of the park. Ice-crusted snow sparkles in the streetlights, early morning skiers glide by and a handful of runners leave trails of frozen exhales in the still air.

By the time I reach the Old City though, I'm often the only runner around. There's still fresh white snow on the pavement and no sound other than the rhythmic crunch underfoot. I run over ground where in 1759 the French and British fought the bloody Battle of Québec for control of the city.

Ahead is the nearly 200-year-old Citadelle, one of the best-preserved forts in North America. I jog through one of the city gates, Porte St Louis, opposite Québec's ornate icicle-adorned parliament, before passing more architectural wonders such as the château-esque Hôtel de Ville de Québec (the city hall) and the Notre-Dame de Quebec Basilica, first built on this site in 1647. This early, I have these places all to myself and it's wonderful to be able to take them all in, in solitude.

Once at the riverside, I head down the Escalier Casse-Cou (Breakneck Stairs), a steep stone stairway where I hold tight to the railings as I clamber down, being careful not to slip on hidden ice. I then enter the narrow, cobbled streets that run between the squat, stone buildings of Quartier Petit Champlain, the oldest commercial district on the continent. These tiny shops have been selling their wares here for 400 years; today the quartier is a tourist magnet, selling everything from tacky souvenirs to fine art. I often revel in the fact that the cobbles have a fine covering of crunchy snow, which makes them slightly grippier in winter than they are during the summer.

Beyond the cobblestone is the Boulevard Champlain at the St Lawrence riverside. The river is wide here – more than a kilometre across – and steam rises in the early light. Chunks of ice jostle in the turbulent water, catching the low sun as they tumble and bob past the city.

From here, I hit the paved walking tracks that lead me north to the Old Port, before looping south again, back to the Quartier Petit Champlain. This time I'm heading uphill, as I cruise up slender Rue Petit Champlain, which is usually packed with shoppers, many of whom ride the nearby funicular that parallels the street. But not this early. Long before the shops will open, their lit windows paint the untouched snow with a warm, yellow glow.

Eventually, I arrive at the iconic view of the city: the Château Frontenac hotel, towering above me as I duck under the Porte

WINTER WORSHIP

Québec City loves its cold winters so much that the town and its residents celebrate the season with a 10-day-long winter carnival festival in February each year. The city comes alive with every kind of winter sport imaginable, including sleigh and toboggan rides, as well as snow and ice carvings, music, steaming hot food and parades. The centrepiece is a vast ice palace, made with thousands of blocks of clear ice, brought to life with cinematic lighting.

Clockwise from top: Québec City is transformed under a blanket of snow; grippy tread keeps runners on their feet; hit the road before Old Town wakes up. Previous page: stairs get slippery under ice in winter

"The cobbles have a fine covering of crunchy snow, which makes them grippier than they are in summer"

Prescott city gate. Built as a hotel in 1893, the château is vast and imaginatively spectacular. Its fairytale turrets, sharp-pointed spires and steep copper roof, sprinkled here and there with snow, make it seem like a magical winter castle. It's florid now in the rising sun. To get even closer, I climb a stone stairway and emerge onto the boardwalk of Terrasse Dufferin, which is a delight underfoot: springy, wooden, flat.

My run ends with an exhilarating climb up 300 stairs to gain the ground I have lost. It's actually several sets of steps, mercifully interspersed with flat sections. I'm careful to tread gingerly and keep an eye on my feet as I ascend the icy steps – doing this run in reverse would require a precarious plunge down the slippery descent.

Finally, I pop out at the top, next to the Citadelle and onto the Plaines of Abraham once again. The city is now awake and my tracks have long been trampled by commuters. There are people now walking – and skiing – to work. There are others out doing their morning runs. But the winter sun still is low in the sky, just enough to warm my face.

With the temperature rising, it's a slushy run back across the park. The tuque comes off and I bask in the last of the cold, clear air for a few final moments.

Of course, this is a run that's brilliant when the snow melts, too. Autumn is particularly beautiful, with the crunch of leaves underfoot. But, for me, this is an early morning winter run, a time when I have it all to myself. **GM**

ORIENTATION

Start/End // Plaines d'Abraham
Distance // About 5.5 miles (9km)
Getting there // Fly into Québec City's Jean Lesage international airport or arrive by train. It's a 3.5-hour train trip from Montreal.
When to go // To experience winter running in Québec City, visit between December and March when there's usually snow on the ground.
Where to stay // The funky C3 art hotel (www.lec3hotel. com) is just opposite the Plaines d'Abraham, making it the perfect starting place for Québec City running.
More info // www.toursvoirquebec.com/en/
Things to know // For cold winter running, bring long running trousers and thermal layers for your top half, including a light windstopper running jacket. Bring a warm hat or headband, windbreaker gloves, waterproof socks, all-weather runners and snow grips for your shoes.

*Opposite: Montréal's Angel of
Mt Royal*

MORE LIKE THIS
WINTER RUNS IN CANADA

MT ROYAL PARK, MONTRÉAL

Just east of Montréal's downtown lies the 280-hectare Mt Royal Park, designed by Frederick Law Olmsted, who also designed New York's Central Park and named the extinct volcano at its centre. Mt Royal Park has a hundred kilometres of tracks and trails to explore, and winter transforms them. There is skating on Beaver Lake, cross-country ski tracks, downhill skiing and, of course, running tracks. A jog on the packed-snow trails, after a fall of fresh snow with the bare trees dusted in white – and the quad-burning climb to the 764ft (233m) Mt Royal summit – is an essential Montréal experience.
Start/End // Le Serpentin Trail off West Pine Ave
Distance // 3–6 miles (5–10kms)
More info // www.lemontroyal.qc.ca/en

ST JOHN'S, NEWFOUNDLAND

The 240ft (73m)-high Signal Hill – known for being the site of the first transatlantic radio transmission – is a brutal climb with a breathtaking reward. Start in downtown St John's, where a maze of narrow laneways snake between colourfully painted wooden houses above the harbour. Follow the waterfront northwest to the northernmost head of the Narrows. Here, you climb a series of walkways and staircases to the top. Though St John's gets more than 10ft (3m) of snow a year, the Signal Hill trail is often clear underfoot because of the city's cycle of snow and thaw. Wind, however, can make this a tricky outing, so visit when things are calm. It's 5–6 miles out and back from the city centre, depending on where you start.
Start/End // St John's downtown
Distance // 5–6 miles (8–10kms)

MT TREMBLANT, QUÉBEC

As soon the snow begins to melt on the slopes of Québec's best-known ski resort, local trail runners bust out the running shoes. The classic route is a 10.5-mile (17km) circuit, known as the Johannsen-Sommets-Grand Brule circuit, that starts and ends in Mt Tremblant Village. This hilly, technical trail takes you through gorgeous, deep green forest, across grassy ski trails, over rushing mountain streams and past gushing waterfalls. You climb over 1950ft (600m) in total and take in killer views over the ski village and surrounds from the summit of Mt Tremblant and Pic Johannssen.
Start/End // Mt Tremblant Village
Distance // 10.5 miles (17km)

THE BIG SUR MARATHON

California's ruggedly stunning Highway 1 is a race venue that's perfect for deep thinking and self reflection – if you can forget about the quad pain, that is.

It was mile 22 when I hit the wall. I remember it pretty clearly. My calves pulled up into a sinewy ball, muscles went into spasm and I felt like I could no longer breathe. I had survived the brutal two-mile ascent to Hurricane Point, and sailed across Bixby Bridge, spurred on by vast ocean views and the sound of crashing waves. Yet, here I was, with one last steep climb and just 4 miles to go, and finishing no longer seemed possible. Making matters worse, in that moment, it felt as though if I didn't finish I'd probably end up in a life of ruins.

You see, the reason I was running the Big Sur Marathon along California's central coast in the first place was because life wasn't going quite as planned. I was in what you might call a rut. Heck, some might even say my life was a shambles. I was overweight, single and inspired by nothing. My assets in life amounted to the computer I used for a job I didn't love and some debt. I was a beat-down 30-something writer and emergent alcoholic. Worst of all, I was starting to feel numb to it all.

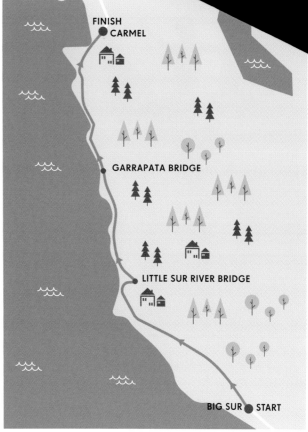

Perhaps more out of survival instinct than intention, I turned to the one thing in my life that had always remained a constant companion: running. My friend Brian had always had this beautiful poster of the Big Sur Marathon hung on his office wall. One day, I asked him if I could have it. The very next day I showed up to my own office with the poster in hand, and promptly hung it right beside that damn computer. And it stayed there for three full months as I trained for the 26.2-mile race that allows VIP access to one of the most beautiful stretches of highway on earth, completely devoid of cars between the villages of Big Sur and Carmel, a stretch that is normally swarmed with road-trippers.

The Big Sur International Marathon hosts roughly 4,500 runners, mostly from other states and countries. No one comes here to set any records or qualify for anything. Runners come to simply soak in the ocean views, rolling hills and rugged coastal wilderness. The race's motto is 'running on the ragged edge of the western world.' Ragged is another way of saying it's really hilly. It has 2182ft (665m) of elevation gain and 2528ft (770m) of loss – it's not the race to try for that personal record.

It's a run where you tune into the sounds of huge waves crashing against tall rock cliffs of tungsten and orange, where you can stare out across coastal mountains that ripple with verdant green ferns and redwoods so tall they seem to touch the sky.

© Courtesy of Big Sur Marathon Foundation | Ian Higuera

© Courtesy of Big Sur Marathon Foundation | Heather McWhirter

© Courtesy of Big Sur Marathon Foundation | Chris Cleary

Even my training regimen began to lift me out of my malaise. I was able to prep for all those hills with a few of my old familiar routes around my house, in the funky college enclave of Berkeley a few hour's drive north from the race's start. I also made regular training trips up around the gorgeous stone buildings and quads of the University of California campus, as well along the paved trails of Inspiration Point in Tilden Park. Eventually, my body began to feel tighter, stronger. More importantly, my mind was clearer. Despite the fact that I had never run a marathon, and that my longest training run had only topped out at 18 miles, I even felt ready.

On race day, I mingled among the other runners, including a handful of elites up front, a few diehards that use the Big Sur Marathon as a way of training for another upcoming race, and then, of course, a bunch of middle-of-the-packers, like me. Shivering with excitement and slightly chilly from California's icy coastal mist, we huddled together, talking about race strategies. My stated goal was simple: to finish. However, secretly, I wanted to do it under 4 hours 10 minutes so I could beat my friend Brian's time.

The race began slightly inland, but when California's glorious coastline finally revealed itself, the runners let out a collective gasp. The pace even picked up, and there were a few whoops and cheers.

At the midway point is Bixby Bridge, perhaps one of the most famous landmarks along the way. Race organisers had tuxedoed musicians playing on grand pianos here to energise us for the

back nine. The curving bridge provides what are perhaps the best panoramic views of the coast along the course.

Right about the time the views start to get monotonous in their beauty, there is more live music and some costumed race fans cheering us on from the sidelines. But there are also a few runners lying splayed out in front of the first-aid tents. That's exactly when I began to think about my own precarious state.

I stopped momentarily to take a deep breath, stretch my calves and scarf down a banana. Then I began moving again. Not fast, just forwards. One step after another. I looked up at the clouds in the sky, then down to the crashing waves. I looked back at vaulting mountains behind us. That's when the proverbial lightbulb appeared. I actually began gaining speed. Working through it. Finding what I guess you could call 'the now'.

My mile 22 catharsis came and went in the blink of an eye. As I moved through the final miles I realised that, while I was here with 4,500 other people, I was actually running this race alone. Likewise, my dissatisfaction with the world around me – my job, my computer – was about me. And if I could only focus on the me in every moment of every day, just as I was here in every step of this race, I knew I'd be OK. Some might call this runner's high.

Whatever it is, it freed my mind to take in the powerful beauty of the coast all the way to the finish. More importantly. it allowed me to finish that race in a Brian-beating 4 hours and 2 minutes. **GB**

Clockwise from left: runners high; the coastal road is rarely closed to cars; clifftop views keeps things exciting; some hills help, most hurt. Previous page: Bixby Bridge marks halfway

© Courtesy of Big Sur Marathon Foundation | Jason Bump

"No one comes here to set any records or qualify for anything. Runners come to soak in the ocean views and rugged coastal wilderness"

RACE WITH A VIEW

Big Sur Marathon founder Bill Burleigh was a Superior Court judge who commuted between Big Sur and Monterey every day. On his way home, Burleigh always passed a sign that indicated Big Sur was 26 miles away. Then lightning struck. The recreational runner who had never finished a marathon himself decided to test the waters. The first run took place in 1986.

ORIENTATION

Start // Big Sur, California
End // Carmel, California
Distance // 26.2 miles (42km)
Getting there // Monterey has an airport, but flights are cheaper to San Jose or San Francisco (100 miles and 130 miles; 160 and 210km north, respectively). There are shuttles to the start, from Carmel and Monterey.
When to go // Last Sunday of April.
Where to stay // Big Sur has some of the most beautiful campgrounds in the world, as well as some of the most honeymoon-worthy – and expensive – hotels in the world. More modest B&Bs can be found in Carmel or Monterey.
More info // www.bigsurmarathon.org
Things to know // Leave a few days to explore the coastal redwoods, killer restaurants and Monterey Aquarium.

MORE LIKE THIS
RUGGED US COASTAL RUNS

OUTER BANKS MARATHON, NORTH CAROLINA

The Outer Banks is a string of barrier islands off North Carolina offering spectacular coastal views and amazing sand dunes. The Outer Banks Marathon starts in Kitty Hawk – where the Wright Brothers flew their way into the history books with the first powered flights – then cuts through the Nags Head Woods Ecological Preserve on a hard-packed dirt road, before heading out for several miles below the East Coast's largest sand dunes. The final miles take you rocketing past the arching Washington Baum Bridge and Roanoke Island.

Start // Kitty Hawk
End // Manteo
Distance // 26.2 miles (42km)
More info // www.outerbanks.com

MT DESERT ISLAND MARATHON, MAINE

With over 1500ft (450m) of ascents, this hilly marathon passes through six gorgeously preserved New England villages, surrounding Maine's Acadia National Park. Runners will see the East Coast's only fjord, Somes Sound, and quintessentially New England scenes of golden trees, misty coasts and centuries-old maritime villages. It all starts in downtown Bar Harbor, heads over the ridges of the Champlain and Dorr Mountains, past the rugged cliffs and headlands of the island's southeast tip. It all ends with a fast mile-long descent to the charming village of Southwest Harbor, and a cup of piping-hot clam chowder.

Start // Bar Harbor
End // Southwest Harbor
Distance // 26.2 miles (42km)
More info // www.runmdi.org

CAPE LOOKOUT, OREGON

This rugged 4.7-mile (7.5km) out-and-back takes you through mossy fern forests and cedar groves, to a lookout over the Pacific Ocean. Fallen logs and slippery roots add some fun technicality and gentle switchbacks ease the climbing. Expect rain and mud – it is the Pacific Northwest, after all – and embrace it as you continue on for spectacular views of the cape, 400ft (122m) drops down to the sea, wildflowers, and the final vista, which feels like the edge of the world. The trail is easily accessed from Tillamook, Oregon, where you'll find world-famous cheese factories and access to excellent hiking, kayaking and other adventuring along this less crowded portion of Oregon's coast.

Start/End // Cape Lookout Trailhead
Distance // 4.7 miles (7.5km)
More info // www.oregonstateparks.org

AN ILLUMINATING ASCENT IN LA PAZ

For those feeling beat down by Bolivia's two-mile-high capital, a run through its diverse and complex socioeconomic strata leads to gratitude.

A couple of decades ago, while living and working in La Paz, Bolivia, I found myself cursing the place as I trudged my way through the thin air, up to the city's 13,300ft (4050m)-high plains. Like a rag-doll robot, I pulled my way to the top of the canyon rim, a foot at a time: two steps, deep breath; two steps more, deep breath. Life in Bolivia's sky-vaulting capital had been extremely frustrating. Perhaps the din, decay and traffic jams that define all big cities in the developing world were revealing new dimensions in the hypoxic air.

But as I neared the edge of the canyon, stepping closer with each stride to where it levels off on what is known as the *altiplano* (high plains), I suddenly gained some much-needed perspective. The altiplano extends all the way to the Chilean border and I felt as though I was literally, and figuratively, on top of the world. I could see the arch of the earth. I could feel the pull of the tides from Lake Titicaca and the ancient kings. I could see the city in a new light. For some reason, I suddenly thought about how my Asics running shoes cost more than what many of these people make in a month.

I had been living in La Paz for nearly a year at this point, working as a cub reporter for the *Bolivian Times*. During the first 10 months, the city's hidden alleyways, the remarkable views of the Cordillera Real mountain range and the turbo-charged nightlife were enchanting. Then I got mugged. And I was also pickpocketed at least a half dozen times. I was realising my stomach hadn't felt normal for most of the time I'd been here. I was also somehow broke in a place where dinner and a Coke costs a dollar. La Paz had become my adversary, a foe determined to break me.

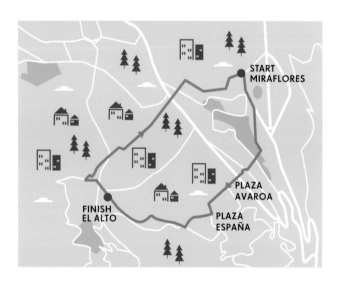

One day, feeling especially fragile, I decided to lace up and sweat it out. I hadn't been running for months, nor did I have a planned route. But I did have a very specific plan. I knew that from my house, I could run through some of both the richest and poorest neighbourhoods in town. Without my wallet or anything worth stealing on me, I could even blast through poor shanty towns that gringos seldom visited. I felt the need to see it all, to go from low to high in search of some much-needed perspective.

My own neighbourhood of Miraflores has tight alleyways that immediately lead to impossibly steep streets. In some cases, I was ascending little more than mud and brick stairways. I reminisced about my first scent of tear gas during the state of siege that I had

covered for the newspaper; it was around that same time that I was strangled with a wire by a gang of kids and left for dead. I thought about the many all-night parties fuelled by wine, beer and coca leaves.

Once I passed the national stadium, I turned downhill for a high-speed descent to the central part of town. I crossed from one side of La Paz's vertiginous valley to the other, over the towering span of Puente de las Americas. La Paz is built in a violently steep canyon formed by the Choqueyapu River. No matter where you run here, you'll either be going up or down. I was heading up.

As I reached the eastern side of the canyon, I entered the Sopocachi neighbourhood, where the rich, young intellectuals live and play, and where I spent most of my evenings. It had been one of my favourite parts of town. Although, as I ran, I was struggling against the altitude, kicking harder against the uneven pavement and cobblestones, perhaps just a little more aware of gross inequalities. The streets were packed with people who could afford to go to university, buy hamburgers at Mongo's – where we often danced on the tables until 4am – and go to the hospital when they were sick. I was one of those people.

As I ascended away from Sopocachi, the houses gradually got worse. The streets turned from cobblestone to dirt. People's homes

"La Paz is built in a violently steep canyon. No matter where you run, you are either heading up or down"

weren't built out of brick any more, they were made from mud and adobe.

Further up is where the vast majority of La Paz's indigenous population live, where the descendants of Aymara kings and Inca conquerors still sacrifice llamas to honour Pachamama (Mother Earth). They are very poor but extremely proud, and highly insular, having been cheated by land-grabbing foreigners for more than a century.

This was not my first time on the altiplano. Perhaps it was my first time with eyes wide open though. As a journalist, I had interviewed indigenous leaders from these neighbourhoods made of cardboard, mud and tin. I had met with rural farmers who lived on less than $2 a day, and proud artists who created fantastic images of revolution and strife using bold hues of red and orange. Like so many others, I had always forgotten about their struggles too quickly after returning to the lowlands.

Though there is always an element of danger in visiting this

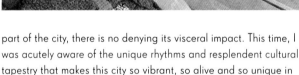

From left: many homes in La Paz cling to hillsides; Bolivia's indigenous culture runs deep in the capital. Previous page: Nevado Illimani Mountain looms over the city

part of the city, there is no denying its visceral impact. This time, I was acutely aware of the unique rhythms and resplendent cultural tapestry that makes this city so vibrant, so alive and so unique in its imperfections.

From here, I was able to look across the broad valley, but also back towards my own home in Miraflores. My view extended in all directions, beyond the horseshoe canyon rim. I could see the vast expanse of the poorest neighbourhood in La Paz, El Alto, which is home to about one million people, all living in dreary apartment blocks and mud sheds. However, it's also a place in which I could tell hope is on the rise and change is afoot.

Indeed, the citizens of La Paz were months away from electing Bolivia's first indigenous president, Evo Morales. I once had the pleasure of interviewing him for the paper. The country was also making important strides toward more equality and economic development (there's even now a gondola that takes you from downtown to where I stood that day in El Alto).

As I looked out over the valley, contemplating my descent and catching my breath, frustration was slowly disappearing, giving way to a sort of appreciation. I was falling in love with it all over again. More importantly, an entirely new feeling was taking over: gratitude. **GB**

🪧 ORIENTATION

Start // Miraflores
End // El Alto
Distance // 6 miles (9.5km)
(about 2000ft; 600m elevation gain)
Getting there // From El Alto International Airport at 13,300ft (4050m), take a taxi downtown.
When to go // Winter – May to October – offers beautiful crisp clear days, but very cold temps up high.
Where to stay // Many of the best hotels are in the Sopocachi neighbourhood and the area around the Mercado de Hechiceria (Witches Market).
More info // www.lapazlife.com/running-in-la-paz/
Things to know // Give yourself a few days to acclimatise before running above 12,000ft (3658m). Get your blood flowing on some easy hikes down valley in the Zona Sur.

MORE LIKE THIS
SOUTH AMERICAN RUNS

ISLA DEL SOL MARATHON, LAKE TITICACA, BOLIVIA

At 12,500ft (3800m), Lake Titicaca is the highest navigable lake in the world. Along its azure shores are small Andean villages, and within the lake itself are a few islands worth exploring. One of the best runs on the lake follows the marathon route around the Isla del Sol (Island of the Sun) on a 26.2-mile course across rough paths, some ancient pavement and small villages, where *campesinos* still live a simple life. The run starts on the lake's edge in the village of Yumani. From there, it's up over a rough trail to the Chinkana ruins, which were built by the Tiwanaku civilisation and predate even the Inca. As you cruise across the northern reaches of the island, it's back to the water's edge in the village of Challapampa.

Start // Yumani
Finish // Challapampa (and back)
Distance // 26.2 miles (42km)

VILCABAMBA, ECUADOR

Located in a green valley in the low-elevation corners of southern Ecuador, the beautiful little Andean village of Vilcabamba is surrounded by mist-shrouded mountains on all sides. The best part about running here is you'll generally be coming from Ecuador's main attractions that sit well above 10,000ft, to an oxygen-rich 5000ft. A favourite run out of town is a challenging 9-mile (15km) round trip to the El Palto waterfall. Along the route, you'll pass through farmlands and cross small rivers, while taking in amazing views to the valley down below. The towering waterfall is well worth the extra push to the top. From there, it's all downhill. Vilcabamba is known for its warm air, long-living residents, spas, and new-age treatment centres. After this run, you probably deserve that hour-long massage you were thinking about.

Start // Vilcabamba
Finish // El Palto Waterfall
Distance // 9 miles (15km)

VALPARAISO, CHILE

Valparaiso is a city of poets and street art. But this port city also offers some of the most challenging hill running you could ever ask for. One popular quad-burner starts in the central Plaza Sotomayor. From there, you head up your first hill to the Palacio Baburizza, a fantastic art museum with fine views over the bay. It's a little difficult navigating the hilly streets from here to your next stop – your best bet is to go down to the flats and head over to the base of the next hill, where you'll make your way up again – but it spits you out at the incredible murals of the open-air Museo a Cielo Abierto, where you'll find some of the town's best street art. It's worth the additional trudge up the steeps to La Sebastiana Museum, the hilltop house of Chile's famous poet Pablo Neruda.

Start // Plaza Sotomayor
Finish // La Sebastiana Museum
Distance // 3 miles (5km)

Clockwise from top: Lake
Titicaca's Isla del Sol
in Bolivia; the hills of
Valparaiso, Chile; some
of which are so steep they
require a funicular

PORTLAND'S EPIC PARK RUN

Forest Park is one of America's greatest urban wildernesses, a vast untamed oasis in Oregon where the trail running is so good you'll forget you're in a city.

Portland, Oregon has two tourist destinations that truly and reliably live up to the hype. One is Powell's City of Books, the independent bookstore that occupies a full city block on West Burnside. The other is Forest Park. (Sorry, Voodoo Doughnut.) Interestingly, they have a lot in common. Both are huge, exerting a gravitational pull that attracts visitors from near and far, and both are supremely satisfying places to lose yourself for an hour or two. Both are cathedrals – Powell's, to books; Forest Park, to nature.

But Forest Park is truly special in what it has to offer an especially picky outdoorsy and fit population. The bar is set quite high for greenspace in a city that is a short drive from both the ocean and the mountains. Sitting just across the Willamette River from downtown, it occupies a huge expanse just above the entire western shore. During my four years here, I've seen everyone on Forest Park's trails, from elite runners (Portland is home to quite

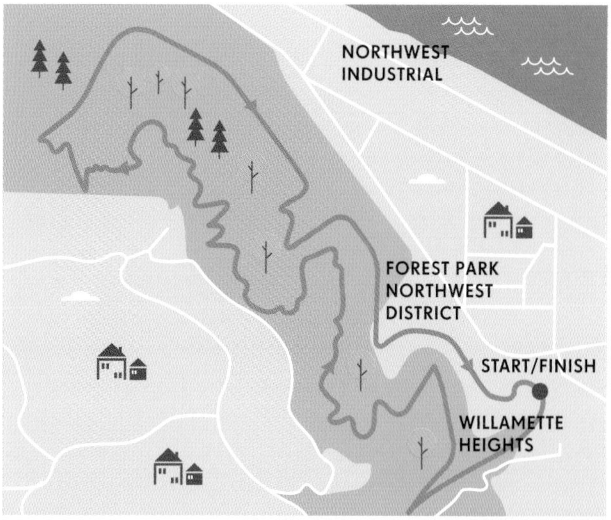

© Sankar Raman | Getty Images

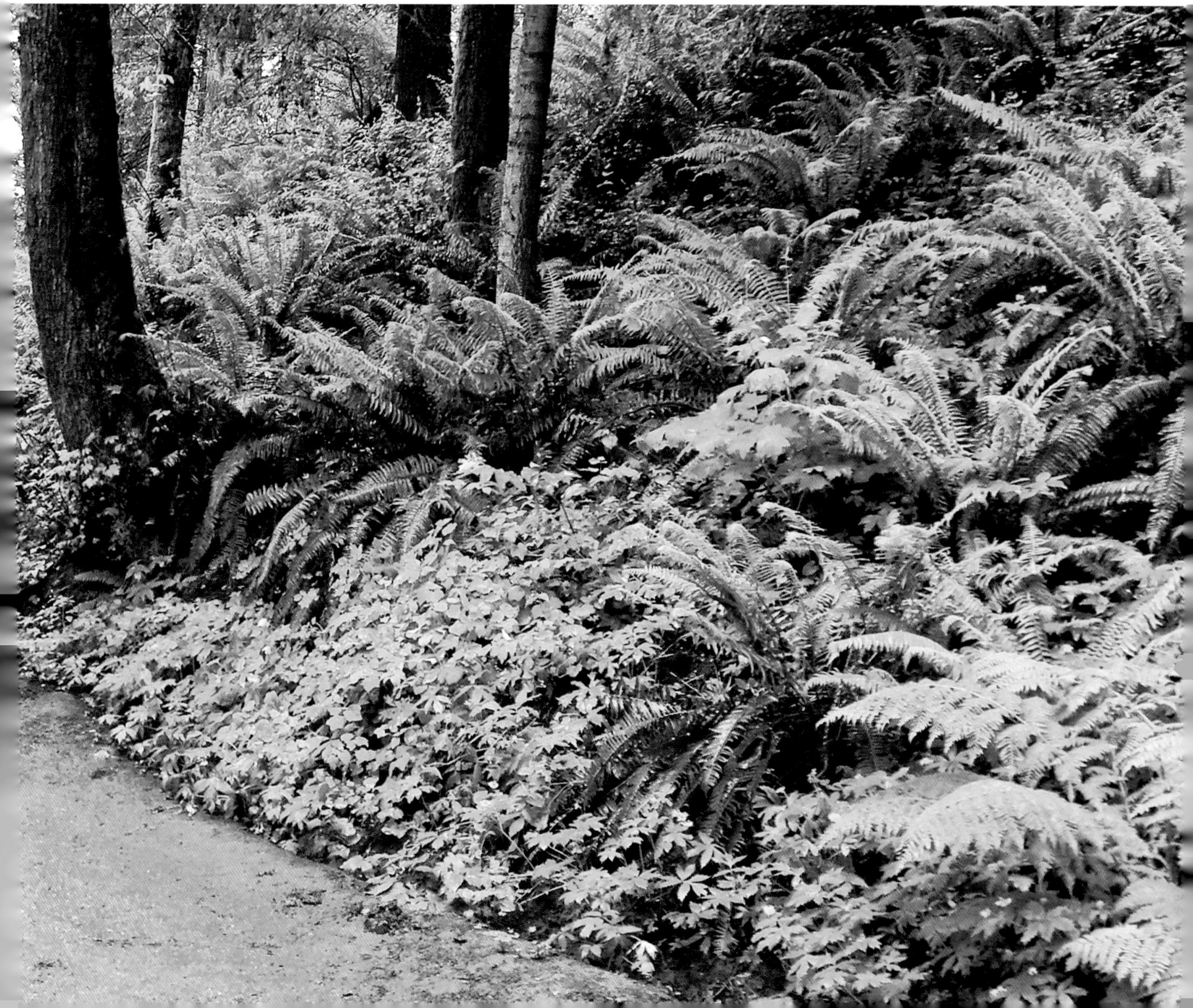

a few) to families with dozing newborns. It's also a magnet for anyone craving a bit of tranquillity and perspective within city limits. It's true, Portland is not exactly a high-stress city, but even we sometimes need a local escape, and that's exactly what I've come to rely on it for.

On a recent summer Sunday, I was in need of both tranquillity and perspective. Between the usual work-life tension and a string of unusually awful news cycles, it had been a brutal week. I decided to tackle something a little more challenging than normal, a 12-mile (19km) combo of two of my favourite runs. But I was also in need of a bit of solitude, so I planned on spending some time on the less-travelled Wildwood Trail. I call my route the Chestnut Loop.

As I dipped onto I-84 from our neighbourhood in the northeast, the lush green of Forest Park's southern tip peeked over the horizon. I knew I'd be there in 10 minutes, give or take, and already I felt better. Stretching more than 7 miles (11km) along Northwest Portland's western edge, Forest Park is immense. It's one of the largest urban forests in the country – 5200 or so densely wooded acres, thick with Douglas fir, western hemlock, western red cedar and big leaf maple. Under this canopy is a network of trails, fire lanes and paved sections – nearly 80 miles' (128km) worth, including the 30.2-mile (48.6km) Wildwood Trail (narrow, tortuous, and technical) and the 11.2-mile (18km) Leif Erikson Drive (wider and smoother).

My Chestnut Loop begins and ends at Lower Macleay Park, at the southern end of Forest Park. The fact that it's just a short hop away from excellent bagels and coffee means parking spots can be scarce up here, but that day I lucked out. I locked the car and was on my way.

The Lower Macleay trail starts out paved but within moments I was on dirt, following Balch Creek into the woods. Less than a mile in, Lower Macleay meets the Wildwood Trail at a structure called the Stone House, also known as the Witch's Castle. The Stone House, or what's left of it, dates to 1929 and once served as a rest station with bathrooms and running water. Damaged badly in a 1962 storm, the building was stripped and abandoned. Today it's a graffiti-covered oddity and a common backdrop for selfies. Had I continued straight on Wildwood, I'd eventually end up at Pittock Mansion and the Oregon Zoo. I took a hard right – deeper into Forest Park.

Wildwood is a fun topographical scribble. Immediately I was climbing and clambering – rocks and roots are near-constant obstacles. I settled in and tried to find some sort of rhythm. The next 5 miles were nearly all uphill, some of it gentle, some not. Much of it is the sort of terrain you fast hike rather than run. And I was OK with this, because I don't come to Forest Park to run fast. I come to Forest Park – with apologies to Thoreau – to run deliberately.

On Wildwood – and in Forest Park in general – it's easy to 'run deliberately', to focus not on things like pace but on things like, well, anything else. Apart from birdsong, the occasional plane humming high above and, of course, my own footfalls, Forest

SECRET SQUATTERS

In 2004, it was discovered that a man and his 12-year-old daughter had been living in Forest Park, secretly, for four years. They had dug their camp into a hillside and built a small vegetable garden nearby. The father, a Vietnam vet, had been homeschooling his daughter using old encyclopedias. The story even inspired a book, and later a film called *Leave No Trace*, which starred Ben Foster as the father and premiered at the Sundance Film Festival in 2018.

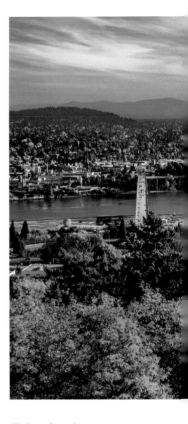

Clockwise from above: autumn envelops the Portland skyline; another ascent in Forest Park; there are many obstacles down in the woods. Previous page: the park offers a mixture of paths and lesser-trodden trails

"After nearly eight miles of climbing and juking over technical terrain, I was grateful for the break"

Park was a deep-green sea of calm. I exchanged nods with other runners but, for me, this is always a solo run.

At around 6 miles (9.5km), where Wildwood intersects with Firelane 1 in a large clearing, I slowed to catch my breath. Once ready for more, I plunged downward, dropping an exhilarating 270ft (82m) over the next half-mile. In fact, it's literally all downhill from here. But the terrain remains tricky, so it's impossible to zone out. Instead I focused on the trail 5, 10, 20ft ahead, anticipating minor turns and obstacles and adjusting my form, almost unconsciously, step-by-step. Paradoxically, I find, this sort of hyperfocus frees up other parts of my brain to sort themselves out – like a hard drive defragging itself in the background. Herein lies the magic of all great trail runs.

Once I reached Chestnut Trail, I was on narrow singletrack, hemmed in by weeds, as it snaked lazily downhill before dumping me on the much wider Leif Erikson. After nearly 8 miles of climbing and juking over technical terrain, I was grateful for the break. I shook out my arms and opened up my stride for the final few miles.

Closer to the end, distraction was easy to come by: walkers and other runners appeared more frequently – this is the part where you tend to see families with small children, and other casual strollers – and cyclists come and go. It's also where I began to catch occasional glimpses, through the trees to my left, of the Willamette River and Northwest Portland's industrial district down below. It is a gradual re-introduction to civilisation, but by now, I was ready for it. **MR**

ORIENTATION

Start/End // Lower Macleay Park Trailhead, off NW Upshur St

Distance // 12.1 miles (19.5km)

Getting there // The Lower Macleay trailhead is about 30-minutes from Portland International Airport (PDX). Head west on Northwest Upshur St, which dead-ends at the trailhead. There is a Nike 'Biketown' bike-share hub about half a mile from the Lower Macleay Trailhead.

When to go // Late spring to fall is generally the safest bet, as winter's heavier rain can trash dirt trails.

Where to stay // All downtown hotels are a short ride from Lower Macleay Park, via bike, public transit or car.

More info // www.forestparkconservancy.org/forest-park

Things to know // Beyond the trailheads, drinking water is nonexistent. Tuck a map of the trail system into a pocket. Don't expect to rely on GPS; mobile reception in Forest Park is very spotty.

MORE LIKE THIS
WILD US CITY PARK CIRCUITS

CENTRAL PARK, NEW YORK CITY

This 843-acre (341 hectare) sanctuary, established in 1857, sits smack in the middle of Manhattan, running approximately half a mile wide and two and a half miles long. Everyone from runners, triathletes and cyclists to harried residents and tourists flock here day and night to escape Manhattan's hustle and bustle. Runners will find a surprisingly complex web of paths and trails, but the most popular routes take advantage of the Park Drives. The 'full loop' (just over 6 miles; 9.6km) takes you on a tour of the park that includes the Harlem Hills and Lasker Rink in the north, the Metropolitan Museum of Art on the east side, and the Sheep Meadow and Strawberry Fields on the west side. Bonus: you can breathe easy. After years of pressure from activists, the park officially went car-free in the summer of 2018.

Start/End // Engineers' Gate, 2 East 90th St

Distance // 6.1 miles (10km)

More info // www.centralparknyc.org

GRIFFITH PARK, LOS ANGELES

Billed as one of the largest municipal parks in North America, Griffith Park covers more than 4200 acres (1700 hectares) in north LA and offers sweeping views of the city. (You can see the famous Hollywood sign from several spots.) There's a lot going on in this sprawling park – facilities for golf, tennis and soccer; a rail museum; a world-class observatory; the Los Angeles Zoo – but an impressive amount of the acreage remains untouched and wild. Runners will find more than 70 miles (112km) of off-road trails, fire roads and bridle paths. For an 8.6-mile (13.8km) tour of the park's eastern and northern portions, start at the Los Feliz Blvd/Riverside Dr entrance and take Crystal Springs Dr north to Griffith Park Dr; following that to Zoo Dr and Crystal Springs Dr back to your starting point.

Start/End // Los Feliz Blvd at Riverside Dr, near the William Mulholland Memorial

Distance: 8.6 miles (14km)

More info // www.laparks.org/griffithpark

WISSAHICKON VALLEY PARK, PHILADELPHIA

Inside this 1800-acre (728 hectare) gorge lie 57 miles (92km) of trails, including Forbidden Drive (aka Wissahickon Valley Park Trail), a gravel road that follows Wissahickon Creek for 5 miles. The park's upper trails are narrower, steeper and more rugged. Heavily wooded, the park includes several landmarks, including the historic Valley Green Inn roadhouse and Philadelphia's last remaining covered bridge. For a quick 4.25-mile (7km) loop, park at the Kitchens Lane lot and take the Orange Trail (near the Monastery Stables) along the creek's eastern edge. Follow the Orange Trail north past Fingerspan Bridge and Devil's Pool, then cross at Valley Green Rd to return south on Forbidden Dr to the Kitchens Lane Bridge, and back to the car park.

Start/End // Monastery Stables, 1000 Kitchens Lane

Distance // 4.25 miles (7km)

More info // www.fow.org

From top: Griffith Park Observatory in Los Angeles; New York's Central Park is the city's treadmill

THE GRAND CANYON'S
RIM TO RIM CHALLENGE

*If you've ever had aspirations to hit off-road ultra distances, few sights will
inspire and ignite that extra gear quite like this one in Arizona.*

Standing on the edge of the Grand Canyon for the first time, I literally became weak at the knees. It was the night before I was going to attempt to tackle my bucket-list goal of running across the entire chasm and back with two friends – and yet my legs felt like noodles before I had taken a single stride.

This run is essentially an offroad ultramarathon with elevation gains and losses unlike any other in the world. Sure, some do this as an out and back – with a car waiting on the other side – but we were all in for the full 42-mile (67.5km) adventure.

After flying to Phoenix and picking up our rental car, we drove three and a half hours northwards with purpose, hoping to get our first glimpse of the 'Big Ditch' before the sun went down. We made it with 20 minutes to spare and scurried to an overlook at Mather Point. I actually felt my throat tighten and a lump start to form, as my legs started to ache. I couldn't even see the halfway point on the North Rim, but the view I did have was overwhelming enough.

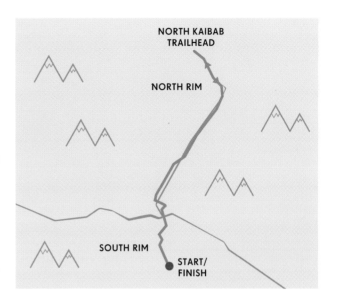

Running across the Grand Canyon is known in running vernacular as Rim to Rim to Rim (or simply R2R2R) and it's one of the toughest trail runs in the world. I had previously run one 31 mile (50km) trail race, but it was mostly flat. I trained for months to prepare for nearly 21,000ft (6400m) of vertical gain and loss, including one workout that entailed running up and down a 2500ft (76om) mountain on a 6-mile (9.5km) loop – four times in a single day. And this still did nothing to prepare me for the debilitating heat. Temperatures can soar to 120°F (49°C) in summer.

Anyone who has seen the Grand Canyon in person will agree that no photograph comes close to doing it justice. At 277 miles (446km) long, 20 miles (32km) wide and more than a mile deep, it's one of the most awe-inspiring views I have ever absorbed. Fortunately, when we started from the top of the South Kaibab Trail at 5.15am the next morning, it was pitch dark and all we could see was the 50ft of light cast by our headlamps. That made this seem like an ordinary trail run with friends. What lay ahead, though, was actually a 4700ft (1430m) descent over 7 miles (11km) towards the Colorado River.

Running downhill on the smooth dirt was rather effortless, and it helped loosen up our legs in the surprisingly chilly weather. As soon as the sun began to rise, our focus shifted to the colourful sedimentary landscape that lit up as daylight broke. We were among blazing red and orange buttes, walls and obscure rock formations created by ancient rivers and seas.

Just an hour in and we had already reached the bottom. We passed through a tunnel, roughly hewn through a massive granite outcropping, then rambled over a 440ft wooden plank suspension bridge to reach the Phantom Ranch lodge, the only public accommodation at the bottom of the Grand Canyon. We pulled snacks from our backpacks and topped off our hydration packs at the first of five water pumps.

Once back on the North Kaibab Trail, my giddiness had burned off a bit as we jogged up mildly ascending gravel along Bright Angel Creek. We had now begun the daunting task of ascending 5700ft (1740m) over 14 miles (22km) to reach the halfway point at the North Rim. We passed the miles by soaking in the astounding red rock canyon scenery and spending long periods of time in solitary contemplation. We encountered a smattering of colourful wildflowers, massive yucca plants and cartoon-like agave stalks that towered 20ft into the air. By mid-morning, temperatures had reached almost 80°F (26°C), but constant cloud cover cast a merciful shadow.

We finally reached our turnaround point at about noon. It was so chilly and damp here we even put on a wind shell, knitted hat and gloves for the descent. I hesitated for a moment, thinking that one-way rim-to-rim run would have been sufficient to quell my adventurous quest. But all it took was a few strides back down North Kaibab Trail to know I'd be able to complete the journey.

ARE YOU R2R2R READY?

It takes most well-trained trail runners between 9 and 14 hours to complete the Rim to Rim to Rim run (R2R2R), across the Grand Canyon and back. But for perspective, Jim Walmsley, a professional runner from Arizona, did it in a record-shattering 5:55:20 in October 2016. The women's record of 7:52:20 was set by Colorado's Cat Bradley in early 2018.

From left: Kaibab National Forest near the South Rim; mule deer patrol the surrounding wilderness. Previous page: looking out over the Grand Canyon from the North Rim

That confidence carried me down the 14-mile segment back to Phantom Ranch with a bit of a spring in my step, even though by now temperatures had climbed back to about 90°F (32°C) and my legs were experiencing a new level of fatigue. We refilled our hydration packs and ate the last of our snacks. We had already covered about 35 miles (56km), but the vertical mile-high ascent over the final 7 miles of trail would prove to be the biggest challenge of the day.

As I pulled myself up South Kaibab, the first few miles jogging up the trail started out OK. But soon I was dragging and was reduced to a slow walking pace behind my faster friends. Every stair step on the trail seemed taller than the previous one and I began to wonder what would succumb first, my body or my mind.

Then, just as I was ready to sit down and give up, I suddenly remembered I had stashed a PayDay peanut caramel bar deep in a hidden pocket of my pack. I scarfed it down in three bites, took my last two gulps of water and within a few minutes I had renewed vitality and a fresh outlook. I suddenly felt like running.

Over the final mile or so, I ran with a consistent gait up the zig-zagging trail back towards the top of the South Rim, catching my flagging buddies along the way. Jogging side by side, we crested the final section of the South Kaibab Trail at 6.30pm. We high-fived and hugged. Of course, the day ended just as it had begun, as I stood on the edge of the Grand Canyon weak at the knees. **BM**

ORIENTATION

Start/End // South Rim, Grand Canyon
Distance // About 42 miles (68km)
Getting there // Sky Harbor International Airport in Phoenix is 3 ½ hours from Grand Canyon Village; McCarran International in Las Vegas is 4½ hours away.
When to go // From March to April and mid-September to early November, all of the water spigots are turned on.
Where to stay // The Grand Hotel at The Grand Canyon, Tusayan, Ariz. or Grand Canyon Lodge, North Rim, Arizona.
More info // www.nps.gov/grca
Things to know // Carry at least $20 in cash just in case you need to buy additional food at the Phantom Ranch Canteen, at the bottom of the canyon.

MORE LIKE THIS
US NATIONAL PARK EPICS

ACADIA NATIONAL PARK, MAINE

In 2017, trail runners Chris Bennet and Andrew Lombardi linked almost every high peak in this park on Mt Desert Island, including 1530ft (466m) Cadillac Mountain, and created the unofficial Acadia Mountain Marathon, a 26.2-mile trek with more than 7000ft (2100m) of vertical gain (not to be mistaken for the much mellower, and flatter, Mt Desert Island Marathon). That's a massive undertaking for most trail runners, but there are plenty of other trails ranging from 3 to 10 miles to explore. Just make sure you bring a rain shell as the Maine coast ranks second in annual precipitation to the Pacific Northwest.

Start// Lower Haddock Pond
End // Newport Cove
Distance // 26.2 miles (42km)
More info // www.acadiamountain
marathon.com

CUYAHOGA VALLEY NATIONAL PARK, OHIO

Boasting 125 miles (201km) of trails, this massive trail runner's playground in northeastern Ohio is a stone's throw from several cities and towns in the midwest. While numerous trails can be connected to run across the park, the Ohio & Erie Towpath Trail is an elegant 19.8-mile (31.8km) south-to-north route that was formerly used by mules from 1827 to 1912, as they pulled boats along the canal from Akron to Cleveland. Because it's an entirely flat route, it's as ideal for marathon training as it is a destination trail run.

Start // Botzum Trailhead, Bath Rd End
// Lock 39 Trailhead, Rockside Rd
Distance // 19.8 miles (32km)
More info // www.nps.gov/cuva

ZION NATIONAL PARK, UTAH

The most similar long-distance point-to-point run to running across the Grand Canyon can be found at nearby Zion National Park in southern Utah. While the arduous 48-mile (78km) northwest-to-southeast Zion Traverse is not for the weak of lungs, legs or heart, it's possible to run awesome out-and-back sections of that longer route, which includes the arduous run-hike up to Angel's Landing. Zion National Park boasts more than 130 miles (209km) of trails, and most of them offer distance glimpses or up-close viewing of the red rock geological features for which the park is known.

Start // Lee Pass, Kolob Canyons Rd
End // East Rim Trailhead, Highway 9
Distance // 48.7 miles (78km)
More info // www.nps.gov/zion

From top: Acadia National Park;
striding through the Observation Point
Trail in Zion National Park

THE JINSHANLING
GREAT WALL MARATHON

Running is booming in China and that's great news for anyone who has ever dreamed of setting a personal record on Asia's incredible man-made wonder.

As I hit the six-mile mark of the Great Wall Marathon and pass through one of the Wall's highest beacon towers, it hits me – the stark contrast between the ancient civilisations that conceived, built and maintained this monument back in the 7th century BC, and the exciting running boom that has emerged in present-day China. As I take in stunning views of the rolling stone against the Jinshan Mountains and the neon-clad figures plodding along the walkway, I marvel at these two worlds colliding in such a spectacular way.

Held every April, the Jinshanling Great Wall Marathon follows restored sections of the Wall about 80 miles (130km) northeast of Běijīng. It's set within a modern park, built to give local and international tourists access to the Wall. Though only small portions of the race actually run on top of it, the parts of the course that detour off the Wall add welcome diversity to the terrain and incredible views of the structure itself. You don't need to be running atop the Wall to understand its power, history and significance.

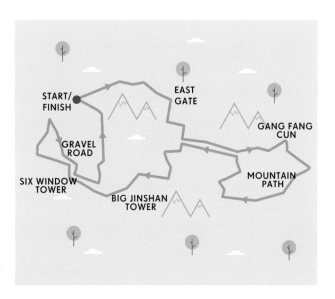

I'd been personally captivated by the Great Wall of China ever since 7th-grade history class. My middle-school self was intrigued by the notion that this 5500 mile- (8850km) long structure could have been built so many centuries ago, without any modern machinery. I was fascinated to learn that rice flour was one of the main components in the mortar that held some of the stone blocks in place, and how it protected ancient Chinese states against raiding nomadic tribes.

As I walked to the starting line, runners mingled nervously while trying to stay warm in the cool morning air. Still recovering from a 14-hour flight from Washington DC to Běijīng a day earlier, I was feeling a little sluggish, physically and mentally. I was comforted to hear the chit-chat of English-speaking runners among the 1500 or so participants, including many Brit and Aussie expats who had come from Hong Kong. Though most of the runners were Chinese citizens hailing from the densely populated areas near Běijīng – largely novice runners who were eager to express a public display of fitness and fun – this race has a distinctively international flair.

As the start time drew near, that local energy really came to life. A Běijīng running group posed for a shot under the starting line banner, two young Chinese women dressed in identical pink and orange running outfits embraced in a pre-run hug. A middle-aged local man wearing a New York Yankees cap shot me a thumbs up. Then, loud synthesizer-infused pop music began pumping out of loudspeakers and three race ambassadors appeared on a small stage to lead us in a vigorous flash-mob warm-up session. The scene was a cross between an early '90s fitness video and what you might witness on the dance floor of a Běijīng nightclub.

Within a few minutes, we were in the starting corral and ready to run. 'Wu!... Si!... San!... Er!... Yi!' A pre-recorded starting-gun blast set us on our way. The race began with a downhill on one of the park's newly paved roads. As the field of runners stretched out over the first two miles, the course veered uphill and headed towards a large brick entry gate, adorned at the top with an intricately designed blue, green and bronze pagoda. Gasping runners trudged single file upwards through the foothills, before topping out at one of the Wall's many brick beacon towers. In ancient times, the towers housed guards who would pass military messages along the Wall and create smoke-signals if intruders were approaching. In the race, the towers were unique obstacles with shadowy labyrinth-like stairwells, or dangerously steep steps.

In general, it's not easy running atop the Wall itself. In fact, it's more akin to running on rugged mountain trails at times. Not only are there very steep sections of steps, which many runners approach hand-over-hand, flat sections have a jagged surface of uneven stone blocks. You want to soak up the views, but need to look precisely where you're going. No two sections of the Wall – and no two strides – are the same. At about the 5-mile mark, I stubbed my foot and suddenly found myself twisting and flailing in an out-of-control panic that I was sure would end in a face plant. Somehow, I managed to control the fall.

STILL STANDING

The oldest portions of the Great Wall were built in the 7th century BC, but it was rebuilt, maintained and enhanced over various dynasties. Through the years the many sections extended more than 13,000 miles (21,000km) across China. Today, only about 5500 miles (8850km) remain intact. Most of the existing Great Wall was built during the Ming Dynasty between 1368 and 1389, and then it was significantly repaired from 1567–1575. The best preserved section runs from Hushan to Gansù province.

Clockwise from top: rugged mountains mean lots of ups and downs; cobblestones are precarious underfoot; there are few spectators at the Jinshanling race. Previous page: a perfectly restored section of the Wall in the Jinshanling Mountains

© Andrius Aleksandravicius | Getty Images

© Jean-Luc PETIT | Getty Images

Eventually, we exited down off the Wall via a stairway and ended up on a trail that meandered through the trees and brush of a creek drainage. The trail led down to an ancient village, where a few locals were preparing their small dusty field for spring crops. A young Chinese boy wearing khaki trousers and a blue sweater stood silently alongside the course, waving a multicoloured hand puppet at runners as they passed. Unlike big city marathons around the world, the only real spectators at this race seemed to be the friends and families of the runners.

Aid stations offered a unique take on support as well. Halfway through the race, I remember reaching for water, bananas and cherry tomatoes, before ascending once again along a steep dirt trail back towards the Wall. This time, the route ran directly alongside its shaded south flanks for about half a mile, affording a sense of just how impenetrable this thing is. Finally, we reached another Wall entrance and climbed up yet another thigh-busting staircase to the top, and the grind began once again.

About two-thirds of the way into the race, the course left the Wall for good, as it ventured back to the roads and trails of the park. This was a good thing because my legs were trashed. I trudged through the final five miles to the finish.

I completed the Jinshanling Great Wall Marathon in a little over five hours. I certainly didn't set any personal records. But looking back up at one of the Wall's impressive beacon towers, high on the beautiful natural hillside, I couldn't help but think about what an incredible report I could now give my 7th-grade class. **BM**

ORIENTATION

Start/End // Jinshanling Great Wall Park
Distance // 26.2 miles (also 10K and 13.1 mile; 21km races)
Getting there // Běijīng International Airport is about 85 miles (135km) from the race start.
When to go // April
Where to stay // JinShan Hotel is nearer the start; Plaza Hotel Běijīng is more central.
More info // www.rungreatwall.com
Things to know // The Jinshanling Great Wall Marathon attracts runners from around the world. The race organisation itself offers several travel packages for tourists interested in visiting historic sites beyond the Wall while they are in China.

MORE LIKE THIS
MAN-MADE WONDER RUNS

INCA TRAIL TO MACHU PICCHU MARATHON, PERU

More of an experiential run than a competitive race, this well-established event sends runners along the original pilgrimage trail that leads from the city of Cusco into the religious capital of the Inca Empire – the legendary 'lost city of the Incas' known as Machu Picchu. For even the most seasoned trail runners, it requires a strenuous effort over rigorous mountain terrain at altitudes ranging from 8000–13,779ft (2400–4200m) above sea level. The 26.2-mile course includes 10,400ft (3170m) of vertical gain and 11,000ft (3350m) descending. The agony of the struggle will be worth the ecstasy of reaching Machu Picchu, as well as seeing additional archaeological sites along the way. (The Inca Trail Classic 30K is a slightly truncated 18-mile run that begins outside of Cusco. Both events are part of a multi-day running tour that includes a special permit necessary to access the Inca Trail.)
Start // Cusco, Peru
End // Machu Picchu
Distance // 26.2 miles (42km)
More info // www.andesadventures.com

PETRA DESERT MARATHON, JORDAN

The Petra Desert Marathon is a historically inspiring 26.2-mile race set in the desert region of southern Jordan among spectacular ruins that featured in the third Indiana Jones film. Starting near the entrance to Petra – a city carved out of pink sandstone in 9000BC – the race takes runners on a culturally significant route past ancient tombs, temples, mountainside carvings and caves, before venturing into the arid, lunar-like landscapes of the Jordanian desert. The first half of the course rolls over sand and asphalt sections and the second half climbs abruptly over paved roads and gravel pathways to the high point of about 4600ft (1400m) near the 22-mile mark. The reward for that dramatic ascent is a 4-mile downhill section to the finish line.
Start // Petra
End // Wadi Musa
Distance // 26.2 miles (42km)
More info // www.petra-desert-marathon.com

THE TAU'A BANANA RACE, EASTER ISLAND

This tiny, remote island in the South Pacific, famous for its ancient stoic stone faces, celebrates its indigenous culture with a unique race every February during its Tapati Festival. The highlight of the two-week event is the Tau'a Rapa Nui Pa'ari triathlon, which entails paddling a reed boat 1300ft (400m), running barefoot about 3280ft (1000m) – but while carrying two 22lb (10kg) bunches of bananas – and then swimming 400m, all inside the flooded crater of an ancient volcano. Tourists are encouraged to participate, although they might not want to wear the traditional loin-cloth attire that the locals do. There are plenty of other trail-running opportunities on the island as well, including a 7-mile (11km) round trip up and down the grassy slopes of the 1663ft (507m) Maunga Terevaka and a 12-mile (19km) run from Hanga Roa to a white beach where the earliest human footprints were discovered.
Start/End // Hanga Roa, Easter Island
Distance // 0.6 miles (1km)
More info // www.easterislandspirit.com/tapati-festival

*Clockwise from top: follow the Inca
Trail to Machu Picchu; desert trails
beneath the ruins of Petra, Jordan*

HONG KONG'S VICTORIA PEAK

For a vertical tour of this towering metropolis – and views far beyond to a surprisingly verdant countryside – run up one of Hong Kong Island's highest summits at sunset.

There are many supposed ways to conquer jetlag: wearing sunglasses indoors, popping melatonin pills, even shining a bright light on the back of your knees (look it up!). But the best way? Easy. Run up a big hill. Instead of a first afternoon spent struggling with culture shock and the challenge of staying awake, you get sunshine and a hefty dose of endorphins.

Having read this theory somewhere or other, I find myself needing to test it on arrival in Hong Kong. The image I've seen on a thousand screen-savers is a city of science fiction – huge towers dancing with lights and lasers, made even taller by the reflections in the harbour. Yet everyone I've spoken to talks of an outdoorsy city of green space, mountains and islands, perfect for running. Those in the know tell me I can in fact see these two sides of the city during one beautiful sunset run up the highest point on the island, Victoria Peak.

So just before 5pm, my danger-time for dozing off, I groggily get off the metro at Hong Kong Park. I'd meant to start running right from the station, but this being my first few minutes in the city

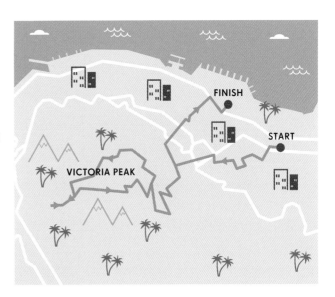

© Mike Pickles / Alamy Stock Photo

centre, I can't help but walk and gawk. Towering over me on three sides are huge skyscrapers. On the fourth, the skyscrapers recede up a peak, with glimpses of green above them. The park is crowded, a bewildering mix of tai chi gardens, turtle ponds and play parks. I feel dwarfed and suddenly very alien in this Asian mega-city.

But I know that's the jetlag talking, so I face uphill and break into a reluctant shuffling jog. At first, I have to say, it feels awful. It's instantly steep, and busy enough that I can't get a decent rhythm going. This tropical city is muggier than I'm used to, and I'm not 100% certain which of the myriad paths I should be taking. A part of me wishes I was in bed.

But then my pace begins to match the gradient, not fight it. My breathing becomes more regular as my heart and legs learn what's required. I climb through the Hong Kong Botanical & Zoological Gardens, joining the Old Peak Rd.

This traffic-free path snakes up at a ridiculous angle. Walkers are puffing up it, some of them even walking backwards to give their calves a rest. I just manage to keep my feet lifting and falling, taking tiny steps that seem to be getting me nowhere, except that I'm passing the walkers at a steady rate. Some smile encouragement, others shake their heads as though I deserve whatever it is I have coming.

The sounds of the city disappear under the hurricane of my breathing. Tropical trees shade the road. The muggy air sweats the

flight out of me. Every pump of my legs moves another little bit of fluid away from my long-haul cankles, shrinking them back down to size. Head down, I lose myself in the physical process of moving upwards. I work, enjoying the burn.

Before I know it, I've reached the top of the climb. Over to my left are the homes and condos perched along what many consider the most expensive street in the world. Above me is Peak Tower, a ridiculous anvil-shaped mall with a glass front showing seven storeys of escalators that connect people to the city below. I sense the view behind me, but am reluctant to stop here to enjoy it.

After all, this is where the fun begins. I turn right down Lugard Rd onto the famous circuit of the Peak. The crowds thin immediately. Not long after, the road does too, turning into a flattish paved path built into the steep hillside, with a black iron handrail against the drop.

And there, through a break in the trees, I see the view. Below me, the world's most vertical city is laid out around its harbour – the Pearl of the Orient shining in the South China Sea. The towers along Victoria Harbour mirror the mountains behind them. Green peaks are everywhere. The coast is a pin-cushion of skyscrapers so close together that they form their own topography when seen from up here. And cutting through it all, the South China Sea is bright under the evening sun. If I'd had any breath left after the climb, this panorama would have taken the last of it.

OFF-ROAD

Hong Kong is known for being one of the most densely populated places on earth (only Monaco, Singapore and Macau beat it). But in fact only 25% of the land has been developed. Much of the remaining 75% is protected countryside, with networks of trails that make it one of Asia's most run-friendly cities. For more info on the trail network visit www.hiking.gov.hk

From left: Hong Kong from atop Victoria Peak; Lugard Rd provides a front-row seat for sunset over the city. Previous page: the trail offers stunning views at every turn

But once I tear myself away from the views, I start to appreciate the quality of the running. The ground under my feet is urban smooth, but the terrain I'm passing through feels like trail running. It seems obvious, but my jetlag-addled brain hadn't expected it – this is a circular route around the top of the Peak, so the view is ever-changing. As I run, every corner means a bit more island scenery in front of me, a little less harbour behind me. I discover the outdoorsy Hong Kong I'd been told about – a seascape of green islands, myriad ships and distant towns. I circle back to Lugard Rd just as the sun is setting.

Returning to my favourite viewpoint, I stop. Over the next hour, Hong Kong will transform. In daylight, the city is seen in counterpoint to the magnificence of its natural setting. But the darkness concentrates the view on the human scene below, on the mind-boggling density of this urban centre and the life within it. Traffic forms ribbons of light. On the bigger skyscrapers, huge projected creatures stroll past, fish swim and clouds drift. The *Blade Runner* city blazes into life, made all the more surreal by the peacefulness of my viewpoint.

I stand leaning on the rail, sweat slowly drying. It's 7pm, and I feel wide awake. The jetlag, the culture shock, both have gone. I'm going to stay up here for an hour watching the lights. I'll sleep well tonight. And tomorrow I'll wake up fresh and excited to spend my first full day exploring the city below. **PP**

ORIENTATION

Start // Admiralty Station, Hong Kong Island
End // Central Station
Distance // 8.5 miles (13.5km)
Getting there // Admiralty MTR station is easily accessible from both Hong Kong Island and the mainland. More scenic and much slower is the tram.
When to go // HK is mild all year round.
Where to stay // Mini Hotel Central is a budget-friendly option near the start of this run. If you can afford it, stay at the Twenty One Whitfield, a needle-thin skyscraper with amazing views from floor 29 upwards.
More info // www.greatruns.com/hong-kong-peak-circle
Things to know // If you want to stay for sunset, carry a good light for the descent – the trail gets very dark.

MORE LIKE THIS
URBAN HILL RUNS

DUNEDIN, NEW ZEALAND

According to the Guinness Book of World Records, the world's steepest street is Baldwin St, in the New Zealand town of Dunedin. It's just 1150ft (350m) in length but steepens as you climb, reaching a punishing 35% gradient. Not surprisingly for the South Island, the area surrounding this street makes for a runner's paradise, with a well-developed network of trails up hills, along the coast and out over the Otago Peninsula, famed for its albatross population. From Dunedin Botanic Garden, a short schlep along North Rd then Norwood St allows a quick diversion up Baldwin St and down Arnold St – just to say you've done it – on your way to Bethunes Gully. From here, it's a trail through pine and native forest to the top of Mt Cargill, where there are views over the peninsula.
Start/End // Dunedin Botanic Garden
Distance // 10.5 miles (17km)
More info // www.dunedin.govt.nz/
facilities/walking-tracks

LISBON, PORTUGAL

Lisbon's Alfama and Bairro Alto neighbourhoods are notoriously steep, narrow labyrinths of cobbled limestone streets, palm-shaded squares and sudden views. Late at night or early in the morning, they reward the exploratory runner with a heart-thumping tour of ancient Lisbon. It's difficult to pick out (or follow) one route in this warren. Much better is to string together a series of waypoints and see where you end up. The castle is a must, as are the Sé Cathedral and Miradouro de Santa Luzia in Alfama, whereas taking in the Miradouro de Santa Catarina and Miradouro de São Pedro de Alcântara guarantees a good tour of Bairro Alto. Expect to get lost, climb plenty of stairs and have fun along the way.
Start/End // Rossio Plaza metro stop
Distance // 4–6 miles (6–10km)

TBILISI, GEORGIA

Now that the Caucasus is served by cheap flights from Europe, the charms of these almost-Asian countries on the edge of Europe is being discovered. Georgia's capital, Tbilisi, sits at the heart of a mountainous country, so it is no wonder there are some calf-busting runs right from the city centre. For the best of Tbilisi, take the 61 bus out to Vake Park and climb nearly 1970ft (600m) up past Turtle Lake to a 3280ft (1000m) peak. From there enjoy a long run down through Mtatsminda Park with its big views, along the Sololaki Ridge passing the statue of Mother Georgia to Narikala Fortress, brooding over the Old Town since the 4th century. From there, follow Kote Abkhazi then the old city walls to Freedom Sq.
Start // Vake Park
End // Freedom Sq
Distance // 8.6 miles (14km)

From top: some say Baldwin St
in Dunedin is the steepest in the world;
houses cling to the flanks of Tbilisi,
Georgia

Hong Kong's Victoria Peak

AN ADVENTURE RUN IN INDIA

The biggest hazard of running the boulder fields and ruins near Hampi is getting distracted by spectacular ancient Hindu temples or world-class rock-climbing routes.

In Hampi, India, the timeworn remains of the ancient Hindu kingdom of Vijayanagar are almost continuous with the surreal landscape of granite boulders that surrounds them. One seems to grow organically from the other, like a meeting point between the natural and supernatural world in a Guillermo del Toro movie. Sprawling over the plains of central Karnataka, 217 miles (350km) north of Bengaluru, the ruins are a beacon for a growing contingent of climbers and boulderers, lured here by kilometre after kilometre of aeon-sculpted outcrops, and the siren song of climbing world-class granite in the tropical sunshine. But even for those who aren't used to hauling around a rack of hexes and cams, there is an adventure waiting for anyone who just loves to run.

With a decent pair of approach shoes, it's easy to transform the hills around Hampi into an all-terrain assault course – a run here, a scramble there, a free-climb over there – all the while surrounded by the ruins of a vanished civilisation. This is no leisurely jog around the park, however. While only a few sections of the ancient city have gates and entry fees, the dirt trails that snake through the ruins are tailor-made for turning ankles, and the rounded granite rocks are cheese-graters, waiting to nick skin from hands and knees as you scramble between the boulders.

One day, while the rest of my guesthouse was snoring, I roused the receptionist sleeping by the door and slipped out into the first light. At this time of day, Hampi Bazaar is a town of monkeys

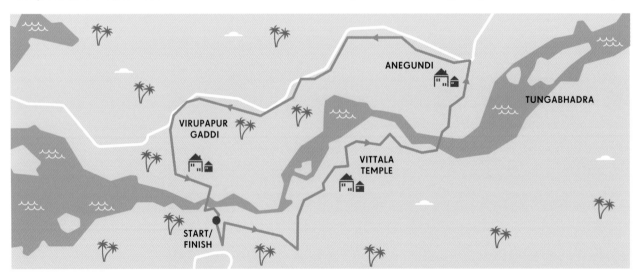

ANEGUNDI

TUNGABHADRA

VIRUPAPUR
GADDI

VITTALA
TEMPLE

START/
FINISH

rather than people. Troupes of rhesus macaques patrolled the walls, growing greater in number as I left the inhabited part of the village and jogged up the granite slope of Hemakuta Hill, past the skeletal remains of a string of Vijayanagar-era structures. On a previous trip, I traipsed up this same hill with half the travellers in town to watch the sunset settle over the still-operating Virupaksha Temple. But today my objective was the cluster of granite boulders on the hilltop, looking, in the half-light, more like fungi or succulents than physical hunks of rock.

Taking care to avoid the crude dwellings crammed between some of the crags, I found a split between two house-sized boulders that looked wide enough to chimney. I wedged myself inside and, even with a generous second skin of climbing tape, my knuckles were bloodied by the time I reached the top. From this vantage point, I planned my route between the ruins and crags. I then dropped back to ground level and ran along the broad stone arcade that once housed one of ancient Vijayanagar's bustling bazaars.

My first stop was across the ridge to the east of Hampi Bazaar, where a garden of eroded buttresses hemmed in the timeworn Achyutaraya Temple – normally crowded, but at this hour a silent congregation of *gopurams* (towers) and pillars. I stopped to work a succession of interesting-looking bouldering problems on either side of Sule Bazaar, the broad boulevard that served as the red-light district for ancient Vijayanagar.

"In the half light, the cluster of boulders on the hilltop looked more like fungi or succulents than physical hunks of rock"

Upon closer inspection, it became obvious that many of these boulders were in fact temples in the making. Natural lines gave way to orderly rows of man-made holes, left by ancient masons.

I could have happily spent the day working my way across these fascinating ruins and seeing what other forgotten relics I could uncover. But this was supposed to be a run, after all, so I dutifully tucked my chalk-bag into my waistband and got down to business, abandoning the main track for a maze of drovers' paths behind the Vittala Temple.

Once you leave the trodden path, Hampi is more obstacle course than running route. I made my way through the coarse scrub like a video game character, leaping from boulder to boulder, dodging thorn bushes and generally getting maximum value from the rocky terrain. At the end of the ridge, I found a group of farmers loading fodder into wood-framed coracles for the journey downstream. A swift negotiation earned me passage across to the white-washed village of Anegundi on the northern shore.

Here, the meditative pace was replaced by a more conventional Indian experience – the beep of motorcycle horns, hollering market

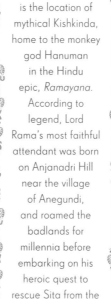

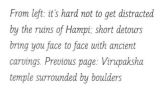

THE LEGEND

According to Hindu scholars, Hampi is the location of mythical Kishkinda, home to the monkey god Hanuman in the Hindu epic, *Ramayana*. According to legend, Lord Rama's most faithful attendant was born on Anjanadri Hill near the village of Anegundi, and roamed the badlands for millennia before embarking on his heroic quest to rescue Sita from the demon king Ravana.

From left: it's hard not to get distracted by the ruins of Hampi; short detours bring you face to face with ancient carvings. Previous page: Virupaksha temple surrounded by boulders

traders and giggling children running alongside the deranged foreigner – but this was merely an interlude. Peace returned as I ran back out into the countryside, avoiding the tarmac as much as possible for dirt tracks skirting the edges of fields.

More boulders rose like islands of ochre in a green sea of cultivated fields, but I had my sights set on a loftier prize: the Anjana Matha Temple crowning Anjanadri Hill, birthplace, according to legend, of the monkey god Hanuman in the time of the *Ramayana*.

After running up 570 stairs in the rising tropical heat, I was a sweat-soaked mess. I took a restorative rest stop to soak up the cooling breezes and admire the views. The run back to Hampi Bazaar was a stroll: a level, if circuitous route through farmland to reach the riverside village of Virupapur Gaddi, facing Hampi Bazaar across the Tungabhadra. One more riverboat ride deposited me on the ghats below the Virupaksha Temple, where a cohort of sari-clad women were hard at work beating the living daylights out of the village's laundry on carved stones that once supported temples and palaces.

As I watched, I felt a pleasing sense of closure. Every sweat-soaked stitch that I was wearing would be joining the mounds of laundry on the ghats within the hour, while I relaxed under a mango tree in a travellers' cafe to contentedly pass the hottest hours of the day. **JBS**

ORIENTATION

Start/End // Virupaksha Temple, Hampi Bazaar
Distance // 8.5 miles (14km)
Getting there // Bengaluru is served by regular flights from all over the world, and trains run on to Hosapete, a short bus ride from Hampi Bazaar.
When to go // October to April.
Where to stay // Hampi Bazaar and Anegundi have plenty of guesthouses, but the government has clamped down on accommodation within the historic area in the past, so check ahead before you visit.
More info // www.tourismofindia.com
Things to know // Approach shoes are preferable to traditional running shoes for their sticky soles, and running gloves are handy for scrambling over sharp boulders. Also, be sure to bring some Indian currency for boat fares.

Opposite: hot-air balloons over Myanmar's Bagan Pagoda, which is ringed by flat, fast running terrain

MORE LIKE THIS
RUNS THROUGH RUINS

MUGHAL, FATEHPUR SIKRI, INDIA

Most of India's magnificent Mughal monuments are active places of worship, so not ideal for runners in body-hugging Lycra. But Fatehpur Sikri has enough quiet corners that you can run without upsetting local mores, as long as you choose a modesty-preserving outfit: think loose-fitting joggers and a tee. The ruins of Akbar's ill-fated capital sprawl out into the surrounding farmland, and only the Jama Masjid is frequented by worshippers, so meander between the palaces then head for the caravanserai, the vast travellers' inn where Mughal traders set up camp, then jog out into the green fields of rural India.
Start // Fatehpur Sikri railway station
End // Sikri Hissa Iv village
Distance // 3–9 miles (5–15km)

KOH KER, CAMBODIA

Angkor Wat gets all the headlines in Cambodia, but another gloriously ruined temple city spills from the rainforest a few hours further north, with all of the jungle vines and Khmer carvings, but just a fraction of the visitors. Ideal territory, then, for runners who crave exotic flora, ancient relics and just the buzz of insects for company. Stay overnight at one of the lodges near the ruins and you may have this surreal landscape of tiered temples, collapsing carvings and empty *baray* (reservoirs) entirely to yourself. There is one caveat though: not all of Koh Ker has been de-mined, and wise runners stick to the main trails linking the excavated temples.
Start // Koh Ker village
End // Prasat Pram, Koh Ker
Distance // 2–9 miles (3–15km)
More info // www.kohker-bengmealea.com

BAGAN, MYANMAR

The plain of temples at Bagan, one of the wonders of Asia, is ideal running country – flat, dry and criss-crossed by cart tracks and farmers' paths – with a perfect end point on the banks of the Ayeyarwady while watching the blood-red sun sink slowly behind the misty hills. Time your run for the cool hours of late afternoon, when the light turns to molten gold and the red-brick pagodas become a forest of silhouettes. The temples sprawl over 10 sq miles (26 sq km), meaning you can run for as long as your legs (and the light) last. Make a short circuit from the gleaming Shwezigon Paya to the gates of old Bagan, or run for miles past outlying stupas in the patchwork of fields between New Bagan and Nyaung U.
Start // Shwezigon Paya, Nyaung U
End // Old Bagan boat jetty
Distance // 3–12miles (5–20km)

KYOTO'S KAMO RIVERFRONT

An accidental run in the temple capital of Japan uncovers a hidden treasure and reveals an often-ignored slice of real life.

One humid early summer evening in Kyoto, Japan, I accidentally set out on a short run from the city's main station. I had put my family on the bullet train back to Tokyo, and was tired and hungry. After trying to figure out which public transportation made the most sense to get back to the suburb where I was staying, I gave up and just started running. I knew where I was and, vaguely, where I was headed – I just wasn't quite sure how I'd get there. It turned out to be one of the most memorable runs I've ever done.

I now call this my '*Ichi-go ichi-e*' run. During my stay in Japan, I learned of this local concept that translates, roughly, to mean: 'In this moment, and never again'; some describe it as 'a once in a lifetime moment'. Sure, I was familiar with the idea, but I'd never thought of this in terms of running. Looking back, I now see that Japan's third biggest city – a mere provincial hamlet compared to Tokyo – is a place where '*Ichi-go ichi-e*' moments seem to lurk round every corner. The city's serenity belies the potential for incredible serendipitous moments.

Kyoto is surrounded by mountains and is full of green space. At around 1.5 million inhabitants, it's certainly not tiny, but is utterly dwarfed by Tokyo's 8.3-million-strong population. Kyoto is also one of the few metropolises in Japan where traditional houses known as *machiya* survived World War II. The moment you step off the train, after the two and a half hour journey from Tokyo, things slow down and the city seems to be blanketed in a gentle golden light at all times.

At the edge of the city, instead of sprawl, there is woodland and water, and mountains on three sides. This was indeed the Japan I had imagined and was hoping for – wooden bridges, red-gated

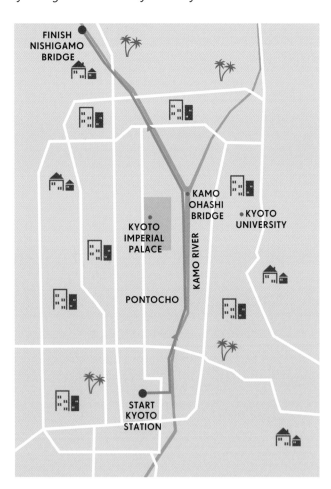

Shinto temples, of Hokusai and Hiroshige prints. Walking around for the first time, it seemed every other building was a temple. If that sounds like an exaggeration, it's worth noting there are more than 1600 of them here.

I had already done a little running in Kyoto during this trip, but these runs were planned routes in the verdant north of the city, on the grounds of the Imperial Palace. I'd also run the Philosopher's Walk, a pedestrian path that winds for about a mile and a half along a stream from Ginkaku-ji (Kyoto's Silver Pavilion temple) to Nanzen-ji, a 13th-century Zen Buddhist temple, which is a must for any runner. The curved, stepped roofs, raked gravel and glowing screens painted with herons make it feel as though you are running in a Hiroshige woodcut scene.

But I had ignored the Kamo River, which begins in the mountains in the north and runs all the way to the Shimogamo-jinja shrine in the south. City rivers are often busy places, teeming in foot traffic. Dawdling tourists – naturally, I didn't consider myself one at this point – make it hard to move at any kind of speed and river routes tend to be more exhaust fumes than views. On this day, however, it seemed to be the most sensible way to get from point A to Point B, and so off I went.

Moving away from the busy station to the river path, I entered an incredibly calming space almost immediately. There were wide green banks, abundant with flowers. Reeds sprung out of the water, while egrets fished in the river itself. Cherry blossom season

> "This was the Japan I had imagined: the wooden bridges and red-gated Shinto temples of Hiroshige woodcut prints"

was in its final throes, each puff of wind threatening to carry away the last of the flowers.

I passed bridges, but the river is wide and so shallow – less than a metre in most places – that you can actually walk across it, hopping along turtle-shaped stepping stones placed for just such a purpose. The river gently gurgled in the background as it flowed over the flat stones. Locals fish, walk and, like me, run here. Children were splashing in the water. The Kamo passes by Gion, Kyoto's famous geisha district, though most of it is hidden from view. But at the Pontocho area, restaurants back right onto the water with terraces full of tables.

Especially with a destination in mind, I often speed my running up a little, just to get it done. But that evening I found myself running as slowly as I possibly could, just to drink it all in.

A couple of miles in, near Kyoto University, I stumbled onto what appeared to be an impromptu outdoor concert. First it was just one young man playing a violin beautifully – I assumed he was a busker – but a few hundred metres further, a flautist was running up and down some scales. Another couple of hundred metres and I passed a pianist with a battery-powered keyboard. Then some

MOUNTAIN MONKS

In the mountains above Kyoto live the monks of Mt Hiei, who sometimes embark on a quest to run 1000 marathons in 1000 days in order to achieve enlightenment. Less than 50 have ever achieved this remarkable feat of endurance, and those who have done become revered as living saints. Fortunately, the casual runner can just explore the beautiful trails without committing to either epic feats of ultra running or prospective sainthood.

Clockwise from top: riverside dining on the Kamo; runners are rare here; spring brings the cherry blossom. Previous page: traditional dwellings line the Kamo Riverfront

© Todd Brown | Getty Images

© Yagi Studio | Getty Images

singers, solo and in pairs. A little further and I spotted another violinist. I only later learned this is a popular spot for university music students to practise.

Nearing the end, I came across a final scene so perfect that I actually stopped running for a moment: a couple in traditional Japanese dress walked slowly arm in arm, their backs to me. She in a light pink summer kimono and traditional *zori* sandals, with perfectly dressed hair, holding a woven bag neatly behind her. He in a dark kimono with a contrasting golden *obi* belt. It is actually common in Kyoto for Japanese tourists to rent the clothes for the day in order to go sightseeing in them, as a sort of nostalgic and romantic nod to a bygone era. And while it sounds strangely contrived – maybe even a little cheesy – it fits the scene perfectly here along the Kamo, where you are sort of transported to the past.

If, like me, you run daily, you inevitably end up repeating the same tired routes again and again. Your gaze turns inwards, trying to ignore the traffic or the hill you've come to loathe. Running somewhere new, however, brings you back to the moment and perhaps even delivers a few 'Ichi-go ichi-e' moments.

I could have kept running along the Kamo that day, and not even noticed the time passing. It reminded me that some of the best runs are those that are also adventures or explorations. But it also reminded me that 'Ichi-go ichi-e' moments exist in our everyday runs. We just don't look up long enough to notice them. **KC**

ORIENTATION

Start // Kyoto Station, west of downtown
End // Nishigamo Bridge
Distance // 6 miles (10km)
Getting there // Kyoto has bullet-train connections to Tokyo.

When to go // The river is a popular area for locals for most of the year. But cherry blossom – *sakura* – season is from the end of March to the middle of April.
Where to stay // Gion is the most picturesque area but the downtown and Kyoto Station areas offer the most hotel options and are also near the river.
More info // www.greatruns.com/kyoto-kamo-river-paths
Things to know // The paths along the Kamo River are also great for cycling or circuit training as there are benches and exercise areas en route.

Opposite: the Tokyo Marathon, one of the biggest in the world, is also one of the six World Marathon Majors

MORE LIKE THIS
MUST-DO RUNS IN JAPAN

TOKYO MARATHON

Marathon running is a national obsession in Japan and elite runners here are national icons. Even running the Tokyo marathon as an amateur you'll get to hear the cheering cries of '*Gambare*! *Gambare*! and, once you've finished, get to see volunteers form a line either side of you to clap for your accomplishment. The course takes in the widest flat roads of the city and finishes outside the Imperial Palace. If you get a chance to enter the Friendship Run – a shakeout 5k the day before the marathon – snap it up. It's a rollicking experience with runners from all over the world in national dress or with their faces painted in the colours of their flag.

Start // Tokyo Metropolitan
Government Building
End // Imperial Palace
Distance // 26.2 miles (42km)
More info // www.marathon.tokyo/en

HAKONE TRAILS, HAKONE

Just an hour and a half by train from Tokyo's Haneda Airport are the stunning trails of the Kanto region. From many parts of these trails you will, on a clear day, have wonderful views of Mt Fuji, as well as clear lakes and lush green forests. Road running is very much the dominant form in Japan, with trail running relatively new, but the Kanto region hosts many clubs and races, often run by local shops. If you're lucky enough to be in Japan in the new year, you'll be unable to miss the Hakone Ekiden, a relay race between Tokyo and Hakone that is televised live to millions of excited Japanese. There are several small peaks and ridgelines to keep you busy. Head for a stiff ascent of Mt Kintoki, where you'll find a couple of tea houses, or hit the 13-mile (21km) path around Lake Ashi.

Start/End // Hakone Station
Distance // 5–20 miles (3–12km)
More info // www.hakone.or.jp

MT HIEI, KYOTO

The scenery in the hills surrounding Kyoto is spectacular and changes dramatically by season, from the bright azaleas of spring to the autumnal maple leaves. There are various trails and routes, but whichever you take the terrain is rocky and uneven. The elevation isn't huge, just 2782ft (848m) compared with Mt Fuji's 12,388ft (3776m), but it's definitely a good workout, and the landscape visibly changes as you ascend towards the summit and Unesco World Heritage-listed Enryaku-ji temple. There are stunning views on the way up, too – you can even see all the way to Osaka on a clear day. The ultra-adventurous might tackle the entire 43-mile (69km) Kyoto Isshu trail. But for a day trip, take the train to Shugakuin Station. One popular trail starts about 1.5 miles from the station and climbs Mt Hiei to the Enryaku-Ji temple. (You can ride a cable car down if you want to avoid the descent.)

Start/End // Shugakuin Station
Duration // 7 miles (11km) round trip

THE ANGKOR WAT
HALF MARATHON

This race among Southeast Asia's greatest ancient temples is hot, sticky, magical and very disorganised – a lot like Cambodia itself.

Waking in the stifling pre-dawn heat on race day, our throats already aching for water, my husband and I laced up our running shoes and stumbled into the busy streets of Siem Reap. Climbing into our waiting tuk-tuk, my stomach turned as I forced down a banana. Normally, I'm a little nervous on race day. But as our driver expertly navigated the congested streets, I felt oddly comfortable as the familiar rush of warm air washed over my face.

It was still dark as we rode towards the Angkor Archaeological Park, which houses some of the most spectacular ruins in the world, a collection of temples that were built over hundreds of years, the earliest dating back to the 9th century. Angkor was once the largest city in the world, estimated to have held more than one million people at its peak.

Left mostly untouched during the decades of the brutal Khmer Rouge regime and the years that followed, Angkor has since erupted with tourism, and the once sleepy city of Siem Reap is

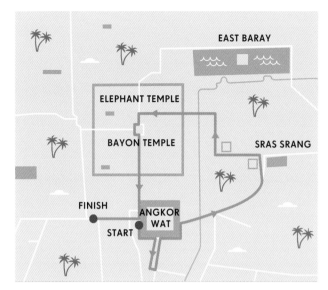

EAST BARAY

ELEPHANT TEMPLE

BAYON TEMPLE

SRAS SRANG

FINISH

ANGKOR WAT

START

© Mark Read | Lonely Planet

© EyesWideOpen | Getty Images

"The temples still stood tall and proud, even while the strangler figs of the surrounding jungle threatened to overtake them"

a bustling regional hub. Every morning, hundreds of people gather at the largest temple for sunrise; more than two million people visit the ruins annually.

On the day that my husband Joe and I visited Angkor for the very first time, however, the streets were noticeably empty of tourists. Instead, they were packed with cars and tuk-tuks carrying runners from all over the world to the start of the 22nd Angkor Wat International Half Marathon.

But well before we reached the entrance to the temples, our tuk-tuk ground to a discouraging halt. Our smiling driver turned and assured us that we were only a few minutes away and not to worry. But Joe and I had spent enough time in the developing world to know better. We were just one of dozens of vehicles inching their way towards the single car-sized opening of the gate. Let's just say there is a surprisingly relaxed approach to details like this throughout the race.

We decided instead to simply start our race early, and run the rest of the way as a warm-up. That's when I caught my first glimpse of the temples themselves, somehow still standing tall and proud, even while the strangler figs of the surrounding jungle threatened to overtake them.

Void of sound and light in the dense tree canopy, they are solitary remnants of a world long lost. 'I can't believe we're running a race here,' Joe said softly beside me. It was hard not to stop and stare, but the clock was counting down to start time.

By the time we arrived at the start, we were already sweating like crazy. The sun had not yet risen, but we could already tell that this was going to be one of the hottest races we had ever attempted. Minutes turned to hours and still no start. We anxiously watched the sun climb higher into the sky, knowing how quickly the temperature would climb with it.

Two full hours later came the blast of the starting gun. I've always loved the first few moments of a race: the over-zealous pack trying to beat each other for a few extra seconds; the heat of so many bodies compressed tightly together; the thrill of not knowing how this race, on this day, will end.

As the route took us past the first few temples, we craned our necks to take in the immensity and the intricacy, as impossibly large stone blocks balanced atop one another, each with story-telling carvings. On a thoroughfare normally clogged with tourists, tuk-tuks and tour buses, we were seeing these sites with only a handful of other runners at a time, which meant there was a peacefulness to the temples that, after touring them amid the crowds days later, I realised was something most people would never get to experience. Somewhere in those first miles, I understood that the breathless feeling in my chest was not just from the exertion, but from being immersed in the stunning architecture and history. Runners paused for selfies – this was not a competitive bunch.

ACTION!

The Angkor temple of Ta Prohm became a celebrity in the early 2000s as a stand-in for the temples in the Angelina Jolie film *Tomb Raider*. It ended up being a boon for the preservation of temples as the crew was charged a previously unheard of $10,000 for each day they filmed on site, all of which was funnelled directly back into the park.

From left: vendors sell race fuel in Siem Reap; runners get the temples to themselves in the morning; tuk-tuks deliver runners to the start. Previous page: Angkor Wat at sunset

About an hour into the race, the streets opened up to the public again. While some of the serenity was lost, the roadsides were now lined with local spectators, some merely watching from beneath the shade of a tree, others laughing wildly (more at us than with us). Local children ran out onto the course for high fives.

Towards the end, the streets were lined with foreigners like us, cheering in various indiscernible languages. I needed it – I was struggling at this point, finding it challenging to do more than put one foot in front of the other. Typically, I'm a pretty strong finisher. However, the stifling heat and humidity had me at my limit.

Then came that familiar second gear. I sped past runners who were staggering towards the end, past more towering temples, and then burst across the line. And that was it – no walk-off, no crowd of volunteers handing out apples or water, just a quick handover of medals and we were back in the ever-present traffic of Cambodia. Unlike at most races throughout the world, the crowd at the finish had no intention of dispersing quickly.

In spite of the course's mostly flat roadways, the tuk-tuks, traffic, tourists and the heat made it feel a lot longer than 13 miles (21km). Nonetheless, Joe and I found ourselves there at the end, aimlessly wandering through the crowd, making new friends from around the world, and with no desire to be anywhere other than right where we were. Apart from, perhaps, getting back into the ruins and exploring some more. **AR**

ORIENTATION

Start/End // Bayon Temple, Angkor Archaeological Park
Distance // 13.1 miles (21km)
When to go // The first weekend of December.
Getting there // The park is roughly 3 to 4 miles via highway from Siem Reap. Tuk-tuks and taxis are readily available. However, it is best to organise a ride to the start through your guest house or hotel the night before.
Where to stay // Several hotels – including the Courtyard Marriott and Angkor Palace Resort – offer packages for the race.
More info // www.cambodia-events.org/angkor-half-marathon
Things to know // The heat and humidity are the biggest challenges in this race. Water is available, but bringing additional supplies is highly recommended.

Opposite: Thailand's Ko Phi Phi island has many dirt trails that lead to otherwise inaccessible beaches

MORE LIKE THIS
SERENE SOUTHEAST ASIA

KO PHI PHI, THAILAND

Running is not the first thing that comes to mind when you're visiting the Thai islands, known for their raging parties and perfect beaches. Runners, however, take advantage of the beautiful and well-maintained trail on Ko Phi Phi that leads you away from the busy tourist area to quiet viewpoints and more secluded beaches. Start with a roughly one-mile climb up a set of concrete stairs – or the more gradual, longer paved road – to reach three viewpoints overlooking the island. The stairs are a fun quad burner but the road, winding through local villages and with limited signage, is a quieter, more peaceful option. Trails eventually lead to four beaches on the other side of the island: Ao Toh ko, Paknam, Rantee and Lo Bakao.
Start/End // Tonsai Village
Distance // 3–6 miles (5–10km)

HALONG BAY HERITAGE MARATHON, VIETNAM

The quintessential journey through Vietnam's Halong Bay is aboard a slow-cruising junk boat. But these days, more and more people are coming for the Halong Bay Heritage Marathon, a run that brings you face to face with the stunning rainforest-capped limestone cliffs that rise from the emerald waters. The route shows off the best of the bay's scenery. Runners begin with breathtaking views from Bai Chay bridge, the longest single-span bridge in Southeast Asia, and continue through mountains, small fishing villages and along coastal tracks. Unlike many other races held in the region, the average temperature for this November run hovers around 65°F (18°C).
Start/End // Fair and Exhibition Quang Ninh Province
Distance // 26.2 miles (42km)
More info // www.halongmarathon.com

VANG VIENG TRAIL, LAOS

Vang Vieng has long been a hotspot for the Southeast Asia backpackers' trail but has shifted in recent years from a party scene to one thriving on adventure tourism. The unspoilt natural beauty that surrounds this Laotian town makes it the perfect jumping-off point for climbing, kayaking and, now, trail running in the nearby karst hill landscape. The Vang Vieng Ultramarathon is an absolute monster of a route. Winding up and over the nearby mountains, the longest of the five races peaks at about 3700ft (1125m) on the highest point with over 16,000ft (4875m) of total elevation gain. The race comes in 85km and 52km ultramarathon options and the much more manageable 30km, 18km and 8km routes.
Start/End // Vang Vieng
Distance // 5–52 miles (8–85km)
More info // www.race-central.com

THE MARATHON OF AFGHANISTAN

For many, running represents freedom. For a few brave activists – and even braver local runners – it also represents a long stride towards equality.

Three hours into our race, we were barely halfway. It was taking me almost twice as long as my best road marathon time. But I didn't care. I was running in one of the most beautiful places on earth and witnessing history at the same time. I was running in the inaugural Marathon of Afghanistan, alongside Zainab, the lone female competitor, in a country where not only is sport tightly controlled by traditional tribal politics but women are often absolutely forbidden to participate in events like this.

It was a crisp autumn morning in Bamyan Province and we were both having difficulty breathing in the high-altitude air. Zainab knew all eyes were on her, some curious, some showing support, many in strong opposition. It was 2015 and, in Afghanistan, seeing a woman walking outside on her own was still a rare occurrence. The significance hit me like a ton of bricks as we ran past a group of women fully clad in the ubiquitous blue burkhas. It felt as though I was getting ready to run further than I ever had before.

Afghanistan is not quite ready to become the world's next big marathon destination. Civilian casualties are still frustratingly high and many parts of the country are still a war zone. However, there does exist a more peaceful and enchanting corner of the country in the central highlands. A 30-minute plane flight from Kabul, Bamyan Province is considered one of the safest in all of Afghanistan, virtually untouched by the surrounding conflict. Bamyan city, which means 'The Place of Shining Light', is steeped in history. Remnants of its famous Buddha statues, which were carved into the sides of cliffs facing the city – and partially destroyed by the Taliban in 2001 – can be seen from any part of town. As the home of Afghanistan's first ski club and the site of an annual ski competition, Bamyan's populace are somewhat accustomed to sports in the area.

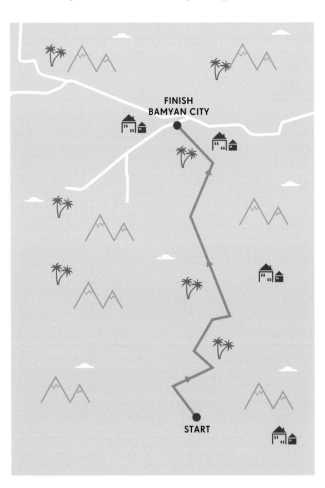

FINISH
BAMYAN CITY

START

A few years ago, adventure tour company owner James Willcox approached British race director James Bingham to ask if he would help set up the historic event. Their experience was deep and they were committed to creating an event in which everyone was welcome – but neither of them had any idea how people would react to Zainab's participation.

That was one of the reasons I was running. As president and founder of Free to Run, a charity that uses sport and outdoor adventure to create female leaders in areas of conflict – and having run in dozens of big adventure races around the world – I was heavily invested in the development of running in Afghanistan. It was clear to me that if women and girls were not able to participate, it could set back the fragile progress that was being made on gender equality.

The morning of the race, dressed in loose trousers, long shirts and head buffs instead of hijabs, we headed out by jeep to the startline, 26.2 miles away from the city centre. There, Zainab and I both hopped up and down in the cold to stay warm. Our hearts were racing with nerves. It was a day that had the potential to be great, even groundbreaking, but there was also the possibility of violence and tragedy.

A 10km race was scheduled to set off before the marathon. This was open to just about anyone, though males and females start a few minutes apart to provide some physical separation. Or at

"Zainab and I finished dead last but the accomplishment was far greater than a mere 26.2 miles"

least that was the idea. Within seconds of the male start, the women and girls could barely hold back, and it wasn't long before they, too, sprinted off the line to try to catch up. Ten-year-old girls in sandals and ballet flats shoved and jostled as they fought their way towards the front of the pack. It was pure joy and excitement at the chance to run outside.

For the main event, Zainab and I lined up behind a group of Afghan men. There were a few other foreign females in the race, but Zainab was stuck in the spotlight. As we set off, the cold mountain air was sweeping down off the surrounding Hindu Kush.

As we shuffled along the paved highway, orange-tinged sand stretching out on either side, we spent the first 10 to 15 miles largely on our own, running at our own pace and in peace. The occasional car would swerve away from us and honk as it passed. Race checkpoints were stocked with homemade cake, fruit, local raisins, nuts, water and juice. Although by the time we reached them, they were pretty depleted.

As we slowly made our way back to Bamyan city, the landscape started to change. Low-lying buildings made of mud and grass

AFGHAN ADVENTURE

Band-e-Amir National Park, just a 90-minute drive from Bamyan city, offers a rare opportunity to swim in this landlocked country (however, women are still only allowed a quick dip behind a barrier). The park also offers paddle boats shaped as swans. Alternatively, Free to Run has kayaks and stand-up paddleboards, available in exchange for a donation.

Clockwise from far left: navigating the Central Highlands; the marathon passes striking architecture; Bamyan province offers unforgettable sights. Previous page: the race is organised by Untamed Borders and Free to Run

sprung up out of the countryside, which was becoming interspersed with green patches of carefully tended farmland. Road traffic increased as we shared the lanes with everything from cars to trucks to donkey-driven carts.

As we reached the outskirts of the city, the exhaust from the traffic began to fill our noses and line our mouths, so we pulled our head buffs up from our necks to cover the lower half of our faces. Bystanders in front of small shops stared. Instead of ignoring their gaze, we waved back, smiling as we continued to clock the miles. Children giggled and older bearded men blinked in confusion. Some of the younger men and women waved back – I couldn't help but wonder what was going through their minds as we ran past.

Finally, covered in dust, dried sweat and salt, Zainab and I made it over the finish line – dead last. It took us six and a half hours. But we both knew that the distance covered and the accomplishment was far more than a mere 26.2 miles.

I have run the Marathon of Afghanistan every year since. James Bingham believes the event has grown into an important symbol of hope, diversity and national unity. More importantly, the number of Afghan women who compete in the 10km and marathon-distance races increases every year. It's not just a show of bravery, it's a sign that there is more acceptance from the citizens themselves. Friends and family often tell me I'm crazy to go running in Afghanistan. After running alongside Zainab that day, it feels crazy not to. **SC**

ORIENTATION

Start/End // Bamyan Province, Central Highlands (actual route withheld for security reasons)
Distance // 6–26.2 miles (10–42km)
Getting there // For security, it is recommended you enter the country as part of Untamed Borders' tour package.
When to go // Autumn (exact dates are kept out of the public domain due to security concerns).
Where to stay // The Gholghola Hotel in Bamyan is a large, modern hotel with wi-fi and a restaurant. A less expensive but more colourful option is the Silk Road Hotel.
More info // www.untamedborders.com; www.freetorun.org
Things to know // The security situation in Afghanistan is volatile. Follow political developments closely and register with your embassy. For women, hats and/or head buffs will help to not draw too much attention during the race.

Opposite: Iran's Dasht-e Lut desert is one of the hottest, driest places to run in the world

MORE LIKE THIS
MIDDLE-EAST MARATHONS

IRANIAN SILK ROAD ULTRAMARATHON

The Iranian Silk Road Ultramarathon is a six-stage, 7-day race across the Dasht-e Lut desert in the Kerman province of Iran. Though women and men running together is still not accepted in Tehran, out in the desert the rules are more relaxed. The Dasht-e Lut desert is one of the driest and hottest places on earth, with temperatures regularly surpassing 120°F (50°C). Runners willing to brave these extreme conditions are rewarded with stunning landscapes, ranging from Mars-like lava formations to salt flats and sand dunes.

Start/End // Dasht-e Lut desert, Kerman
Distance // 155 miles (250km), self-supported stage race
More info // www. worldrunningacademy.com/ wraextremeraces/isru

ERBIL MARATHON, KURDISTAN, IRAQ

The Erbil Marathon in Iraqi Kurdistan provides an opportunity for runners to experience modern Iraq, away from the violence across the rest of the country. The race is arranged by a non-profit body called the Erbil Marathon Organization for Sport and Peace, which uses the race to promote peace and non-violence, with men and women running together. The race consists of four loops around the 200ft (60m) ring road, finishing in Sami Abdulrahman Park, with runners passing city sights such as the citadel and Jalil Khayat Mosque. Though the race was cancelled in 2014 due to security concerns and reduced to just the 5km and 10km races in 2017 for similar reasons, its popularity has not waned, with several thousand runners from across Iraq, Europe and other parts of the world coming to participate each year.

Start/End // Sami Abdulrahman Park
Distance // 3-mile (5km) family and fun run; 6 miles (10km); 26.2 miles (42km)
More info // www. erbilmarathon.org

PALESTINE MARATHON

The Palestine Marathon takes places in Bethlehem every year in the spring, starting and ending at the Church of the Nativity. The marathon course consists of two 13-mile (21km) loops through refugee camps and along Israel's 26ft- (8m) high separation wall, bringing a sobering view of what it is like to live in Palestine under such restrictions. The race was started by the non-profit social group called the Right to Movement as a way of using running to 'tell a different story' of the conflict, and the organisation of the race has since passed over to the Palestine Olympic Committee. It may not be the most picturesque marathon, but it is certainly one of the most rewarding.

Start/End // Manger Square, Bethlehem
Distance // 26.2 miles (42km). Half-marathon, 10K and 5K family options are also available.
More info // www.palestinemarathon. org

A CLIMB INTO THE
FOOTHILLS OF NEPAL

The forested ridge south of Pokhara's Phewa Tal lake is a
scenic circuit with grandstand views of Nepal's Himalaya.

J ust as I always do when I'm in Asia, I began my run through the streets of Pokhara, Nepal at dawn, before the muggy heat set in. I set off from my guesthouse as the first light of morning was spilling onto the streets. It would be another hour or so before the sun would boil off the grey mist that hung over the town's serene Phewa Tal lake.

Downtown Pokhara was almost empty, apart from a gaggle of taxi drivers greeting the morning with steaming cups of *chi-ya* – a milky Nepali tea – at a roadside stall. As I trotted along in near solitude, I caught glimpses of the ancient Newari-style Varahi Mandir temple's tiered roof and colourful doonga boats tied up on the lakeshore.

It's one of the eternal challenges of travel: how to fit a relaxing run into the frenetic surroundings of the developing world. On dozens of trips, I've packed shorts and running shoes, only to be beaten into submission by the traffic, temperature and pollution. Nepal, however, is a little different. Sure, there's death-defying

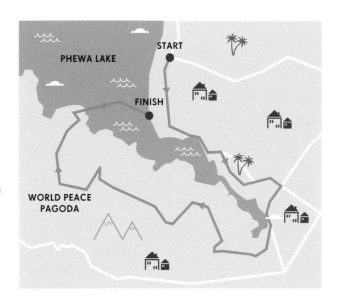

PHEWA LAKE

START

FINISH

WORLD PEACE
PAGODA

traffic, wilting heat and choking diesel fumes in places like Kathmandu. But there's also the pristine, glacier-cooled air of the Himalaya, waiting to fill your lungs the moment you vacate the country's urban sprawl. Pokhara is that tranquil basecamp for those headed deep into the Annapurna, either on a several-week walk through the region or a death-defying climb of the peaks themselves.

It's true that Nepal's tortuous topography gains elevation at a staggering rate, rising from just 194ft (59m) in the Terai plains to 29,072ft (8848m) at the summit of Sagarmatha (Mt Everest). And for super humans who are happy to trek for two weeks before running 26.2 miles at mountain-summit elevation, Nepal has a busy calendar of marathons and high-altitude ultras. But there are also some life-changing routes for ordinary runners, especially in Nepal's Middle Hills, the chain of forest and rice-terrace-covered ridges that abut the Himalaya.

Though there are many starting points for runs in the Middle Hills – even some on the outskirts of Kathmandu – few compare to those that begin in Pokhara, a town divided by just a single valley system from the rocky wall of the Annapurna mountain range. Destinations such as Sarangkot, Kahun Danda or the World Peace Pagoda are all easy detours from downtown Pokhara, offering a perfect primer for trekking up close to these spectacular summits. I decided to run up to the Peace Pagoda, one of dozens erected around the world by the Japanese Nipponzan-Myōhōji movement.

Pokhara itself is a country town with clean mountain air. You can start running from your hotel doorstep without having to worry about being mowed over by a phalanx of horn-honking trucks and mopeds. I picked up the pagoda trail by a small footbridge just south of the Phewa Dam on the outskirts of town. Energised by the crisp morning, I lifted my pace as the landscape opened up into flat rice fields to my left, with the forested mass of Ananda Hill rising to the right. As is often the case in Nepal, finding the exact path involved a few false starts. I eventually quizzed a local farmer, busy washing his hair at an outside tap. It didn't take long to locate the little Hindu shrine where the track veered into the forest and the fun began.

Running in Nepal is often a combination of stout hill efforts and head-scratching orienteering. Despite relying on occasional blazes, which cut into the trunks of trees to mark the trail, gaining the top of the ridge involved a certain amount of instinct and telepathy. But an air of calm descended as the path zig-zagged beneath a canopy of forest trees, which more than compensated for moments of doubt.

I saw no other humans as I skittered along the gravel path, but I did encounter a family of burly macaques, crashing noisily through the undergrowth. Although the gain in elevation was moderate by Nepali standards – about 1150ft (350m) – it was a mountain climb compared with my normal route back home, and I was thirsty and breathless when I finally gained the top of the ridge at a muddy saddle.

SECOND SUMMIT

Despite the proximity of the Annapurna range, Pokhara's most iconic summit is not one of the 8000m-plus peaks but. Machhapuchhare, a comparative tiddler at 22,943ft (6997m). From Pokhara, the mountain appears as a perfect pyramid of stone and ice, isolated from the surrounding peaks. The name – 'fish tail' in Nepalese – explains itself when you trek around the peak and the hidden second summit looms into view.

Clockwise from top: Pokhara's streets are quiet compared with Kathmandu; the run ends at Phewa Tal lake; chiya provides a pick-me-up. Previous page: the Peace Pagoda stands watch over Pokhara

"At the top of the ridge, the views I was running towards began to materialise – an amphitheatre of Himalayan peaks"

© Valdis Skudre | Shutterstock

© Jonas Gratzer | Getty Images

Here, the views I was running towards began to materialise. After some superhero-style leaps and bounds up the steep path, I emerged on the flat, open ridge-top in front of Pokhara's landmark Peace Pagoda. I sat down to catch my breath in front of an amphitheatre of Himalayan peaks, rising dramatically above the sprawling streets of the town and still-misty waters of Phewa Tal.

The mountains create their own micro-climate and views from the Peace Pagoda can be hit or miss, but on this occasion only a light brush-stroke of cloud hung over the Annapurna range, with the summit of the near-23,000ft (7000m) Machhapuchhare rising like an icy pyramid and stealing all the thunder from the peaks on either side. Even better, one of the small snack stands beside the pagoda was opening for business. I grabbed a hot cup of *chi-ya* to counteract the effects of the climb on my quads and calves.

After the journey uphill, the descent to Pokhara was a blissful trip, crashing rapidly down through the forest to the lakeshore on the north side of the ridge. I passed the first groups of walkers heading uphill to the pagoda via this shorter northern route as I reached the bank. I negotiated with a waiting boatman for a ride back to Pokhara in a doonga painted in primary playground colours.

There was one more treat in store. As we reached the centre of the Tal, I asked the boatman to pause, yanked off my shoes and socks, and stepped off the side of the boat, gasping for breath as I plunged into the icy coolness. To my mind, the purpose of running is to reconnect with your animal nature, and as I splashed around the lake, breathless and aching but undeniably refreshed, I was confident that my inner animal was very much alive. **JBS**

ORIENTATION

Start // Lakeside, Pokhara
End // Phewa Tal, Pokhara
Distance // 5 miles (8km), plus a 15-minute boat ride.
Getting there // Pokhara airport, 1.5 miles (3km) from Lakeside, is served by regular flights from Kathmandu; the trail to the pagoda starts on the southwest edge of town.
When to go // October to November or March to April.
Where to stay // Pokhara is packed with guesthouses and hotels, most in the neighbourhoods of Lakeside and Damside.
More info // www.welcomenepal.com/places-to-see/pokhara.html
Things to know // Early morning starts are best, before walkers start arriving from Pokhara; a little caution is needed as there have been muggings in the area in the past, though joggers have little to draw the attention of thieves.

MORE LIKE THIS
HIGH-ALTITUDE ADVENTURES

EVEREST MARATHON, NEPAL

Many think twice about walking the route
to Everest Base Camp; running it seems
like something only a masochist would
consider. But while it visits the camp
used by Everest mountaineers, perched
at 17,600ft (5380m) on the shoulder of
the world's tallest peak, the Himalayan
Marathon is tackled downhill, descending
the mountain to Namche Bazaar.
This means runners get two weeks to
acclimatise to the altitude while trekking
up to Base Camp, and a slap-up meal and
a cold beer in the Everest region's only
proper town at the end of the race. It's still
a serious undertaking that will challenge
any trail runner, with thousands of metres
of climbs as well as steep descents. As for
the 60km Himalayan Ultra...
Start // Everest Base Camp, Nepal
End // Namche Bazaar
Distance // 26.2 miles (42km)
More Info // www.everestmarathon.com

PARO TO TAKTSHANG GOEMBA, BHUTAN

Bhutan's most famous monastery was
reputedly founded by Guru Rinpoche,
who flew to this lofty retreat on the back
of a flying tiger. Taktshang is said to be
fixed to the rocky valley wall with the hair
of angels – getting here in running shoes
requires some grit and a fair bit of logistical
planning to ensure your guide meets you
at the right time for you to gain entrance
to the complex. But it's a delightful way
to explore the countryside around Paro.
Despite being home to Bhutan's only
international airport, Paro is a hamlet rather
than a city, so it's easy to escape into the
fields on minor tracks and follow the Paro
Chhu river northwest, before picking up the
hiking trail to Taktshang.
Start // Paro, Bhutan
End // Taktshang Goemba
Distance // 7.5 miles (12km)

LEH TO THIKSEY, INDIA

Perhaps the closest thing on earth to
Shangri-la, the mountain valleys of
Ladakh are criss-crossed by trails that
offer high-altitude training to make an
Olympic athlete slaver. The only challenge
is escaping Leh, with its ring-fence of busy
roads and military cantonments. Save
yourself the bother by riding a local bus to
Choglamsar, then leave the modern world
behind by running the rough farming tracks
that trace the banks of the Indus. Following
the river east, you can daisy-chain a string
of ancient Buddhist monasteries crowning
rocky outcrops along the riverbanks, before
hopping onto a Leh-bound bus for the
journey home. For something epic, run the
25-mile (40km) loop via the monasteries
at Shey, Thiksey, Stakna, Matho and Stok,
and gain some karma with your calorie burn.
Start/End // Leh (Choglamsar)
Distance // 6–25 miles (10–40km)

*Clockwise from above: runners catch
their breath at the start of the Everest
Marathon in Nepal; a porter performs
his own feat of endurance at Everest
Base Camp*

SEOUL'S HAN RIVER

It's not easy to find a city where runners are still a rare exotic bird. South Korea's capital is the place to witness the rise of a subculture.

Let's get one thing perfectly clear: it is not easy to go for a run in the heart of Seoul. But it is getting easier – and that's what makes it one of the most fascinating places for a runner right now.

Like a lot of large Asian capitals, Seoul is a huge, sprawling metropolis. More than 25 million people live in the region, with almst half of them, a total of more than 10 million, packed into its city limits. The city's density and layout of zig-zagging, non-linear roads, and its lack of expansive green space, make it tricky to navigate quickly on foot. It's also hard to put a route together, which is exactly what a visiting runner needs to do here, as there

is virtually no existing running culture to lead the way.

But South Korea is emerging as a global leader in technology, business, education and pop culture (depending on whether you think K-Pop counts as culture or not). And as societal norms shift from stoic, traditional and conservative to vibrant, youthful and forward-looking, running, too, is becoming a form of expression. In recent years, organised races, social fun runs and even running clubs have begun to pop up throughout the country.

I was in fact in South Korea to participate in a three-day trail running event adjacent to the Korean Demilitarized Zone, about 90 minutes northwest of Seoul. Having come here specifically to run, I

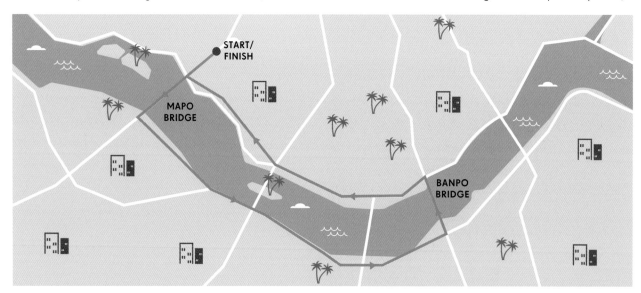

© Daniel Fung | Shutterstock

"The increased popularity of running may have something to do with the shift away from the six-day work and school week"

couldn't help but wonder what sort of opportunities there were – or weren't – in the capital itself.

Doing a little research on the plane, I came across a few blogs and a site for the Seoul Flyers Running Club, a group of local and expat runners who meet a few times a week. All signs pointed to the pathways along the Han River (known formally as the Hangang River). 'For flat runs of just about any length, head to the river, which runs east to west straight through the heart of the city, and has plenty of bathrooms and water fountains,' wrote American expat Joe Van Dorn, president of the Seoul Flyers Running Club. Still, I wondered whether I'd run into even a single other runner.

Just a few hours after disembarking my 11-hour flight from San Francisco, I was running towards the Han River. My goal was to run a simple loop from my hotel in the Mapo District. I headed south on Yeoui Ave with the intent of finding the pedestrian paths along the river. There were people everywhere but, early on, I mostly saw older men dressed in black, grey and navy business suits walking with purpose. But outside American chains such as Starbucks and McDonald's, younger men and women wearing casual colourful clothes, T-shirts and blue jeans, wore wireless pods in their ears and sipped iced coffee. As I passed traditional Korean barbecue and noodle restaurants, garlic and kimchi wafted through the air as workers prepared for the evening rush. Running through the streets, I felt as though I was witnessing South Korea's societal

changes up close. Meanwhile, as a runner I felt like I was also sort of participating in that change.

Within a few minutes, I was on a dedicated path that led me onto the Mapo Bridge, over the river, and down to the water. There were a handful of people on bicycles, but I had yet to see a single runner. Turns out, running has actually existed in Korean culture for a while. In fact, the Seoul International Marathon, also known as the Dong-A Ilbo Seoul Marathon, is the third oldest continuously held road race in Asia. But women were only allowed to participate in 1979 and even since then it has largely been a sport for older men. These days, 20- and 30-somethings are beginning to run for fitness, but also as a social activity, with 'run crews' that are sponsored by brands such as Nike, New Balance and Adidas. Some of this shift seems to have occurred circa 2004, on the heels of a shift away from six-day work and school weeks to five-days. 'Part of it was that Korea was pretty poor and no one had any time to do anything with one day off,' says Eunjin Choi, a 29-year-old graphic designer who has been running for six years and runs with the Seoul Flyers.

As I finally got into a consistent groove on the bridge over the river, I suddenly had expansive 180-degree views of the southwestern section of Seoul. High-rise buildings lined the river as far as I could see in either direction, aglow with the setting sun. I was surprised to see so many people out and about on a

JOIN THE CLUB

If you're visiting South Korea, consider joining the Seoul Flyers Running Club for a group run in the city or at Namsan Park, a hilly venue that offers great trail-run options and stunning views of the city below. A 'running club without boundaries', it boasts members from nearly 20 different countries, including teachers, diplomats, chefs, students and soldiers.

From left: Seoul street food; running is just taking off in South Korea; the water and light show of Banpo Bridge provides evening entertainment. Previous page: the Han River

Wednesday night. I encountered couples and groups walking and riding bikes, and many just relaxing on the grass at the river's edge. Some had even set up tents and appeared to be preparing to camp for the night. With dusk setting in and the light in the sky starting to fade, I headed east towards Banpo Hangang Park, one of the largest public green spaces along the river.

Even at nightfall, the park was alive with people. They come here to watch a dazzling light and water show on the Banpo Bridge, which had just started as I'd arrived. Moonlight Rainbow Fountain is the world's longest bridge fountain and comes to life as 10,000 LED lights and 380 water nozzles blast off. The 20-minute shows are set to music. The fountain was installed in 2009 under the leadership of then-mayor Oh Se-hoon, who believed it would highlight Seoul's eco-friendliness (the water is pumped directly from the river itself and continuously recycled).

Soaked from the fine mist of water hanging in the air all around me, I decided to begin looping back towards my hotel. As I crossed the bridge and started jogging, I finally saw a few other runners on the riverfront. I wound up running about 10 miles that evening and those were the only other runners I'd seen. The light and water show left the biggest impression, but I also often think about how few runners there were on such a pleasant late-summer night. I can only wonder how crowded those same river paths might be in a few years as running continues to boom. **BM**

ORIENTATION

Start/End // Mapo Bridge
Distance // 5–10 miles (8–16km)
Getting there // Incheon International Airport is about an hour from downtown Seoul via an express train, and 90 minutes via the subway system.
When to go // The best times to run are April–May and September–October when temperatures are more moderate.
Where to stay // The Mapo District has a lot of good options – like the Best Western Premier Seoul Garden Hotel – within striking distance of the river.
More info // www. seoulflyerstech.wixsite.com/seoulflyers
Things to know // Bukhansan National Park is an amazing park less than an hour from downtown Seoul, with more than 100 miles (160km) of trails and several high peaks.

MORE LIKE THIS
SOUTH KOREAN RUNS

DMZ TRAIL RUNS RUNNING FESTIVAL

Part of the DMZ Trail Runs running festival, the final 12 mile (20km) race of the three-day event (and the shorter 5.5 mile; 9km race held concurrently) is run along the edge of the Korean Demilitarized Zone that has separated South Korea and North Korea since the end of the Korean War in 1953. The mission of the event is to celebrate peace, life, communication and reconciliation for all Korean people. The 20K course is mostly flat for about six miles as it runs along the banks of the Imjin River, with views of sentry towers manned by South Korean soldiers armed with machine guns. It gets a bit hilly as it loops around two villages, through some rice fields and back to the river path before returning to the park that includes numerous monuments of peace and propaganda, and, oddly, an amusement park.

Start/End // Imjingak Park, Paju
Distance // 5.5–12 miles (9–20km)
More info // www.dmztrailrun.com

NAMSAN PARK, SEOUL

Namsan Park is a mountain running oasis located in the heart of Seoul, and the Wednesday night running destination of the Seoul Flyers Running Club. There are about six miles (10km) of paved paths through rolling terrain, including five different routes to the 86oft (262m) summit of South Mountain. The routes to the top are steep, but the amazing views of Seoul make it worth the effort. There are several historic sites inside the park, including the Mongmyeoksan Beacon Hill Site, a set of five brick beacons that were used to send smoke and fire signals to warn Seoul citizens of enemy invasions.

Start/End // Sungnyemun Gate
Distance // 6 miles (10km)

CHEONGGYECHEON STREAM, SEOUL

This concrete and stone pathway system follows Cheonggyecheon Stream as it flows west to east through Seoul, to a connection with the Jungnangcheon River. Opened in 2005 as an urban renewal project, it provided a public recreation space with clean water, natural habitats and historical markers in a place that was covered by concrete under an elevated highway. The stream passes several palaces, including Deoksugung Palace, Changdeokgung Palace and Changgyeonggung Palace, allowing the possibility of linking together a few historic sites during or just after a run.

Start // Cheonggye Plaza
End // Jungnancheon River
Distance // 7 miles (11km)

*From top: Seoul's
Cheonggyecheon Stream is
one of the city's newer urban
renewal projects; Namsan Park
is a favourite of the Seoul Flyers
Running Club*

A TIGHTROPE RUN ALONG THE AMALFI COAST

Southern Italy's cliff-side 'Path of the Gods' is becoming a trail-running mecca. Bring a head for heights and legs for brutal stair climbs.

I was a mere 1640ft (500m) above Bomerano's main piazza, but the scenery was already starting to look other-worldly. 'Sentiero degli Dei' announced the sign on a large stone monument high up in the mountains of Italy's Amalfi, a 30-mile (48km) stretch of spectacular coastline just south of Naples. I didn't need an English-Italian dictionary to work out what it meant. The aptly named 'Path of the Gods', pioneered and mythologised by the ancient Greeks, is well-known throughout the Italian peninsula for its heavenly vistas of terraced fields and hazy peaks.

Before I had even gone a dozen more paces I encountered another monumental sign, this one inscribed with quotes by Italo Calvino and DH Lawrence. I stopped momentarily to read the short poetic stanzas, wondering which other literary giants had passed this way. Had they walked the path? I mused. Or travelled by mule? Or, inspired by the Olympian spirit, had they attempted to run it, as I hoped to do? Glancing ahead at the narrow trail grafted into the cliffside, it looked as if running in the conventional sense was going to be a challenge, unless I grew wings on my feet and flew.

Italy's Amalfi is known for its lemons, ceramics, storied maritime history and style-conscious summer visitors. But that's only half the story. Beyond the tourist-mobbed towns is a paradise for runners who love hills. Backed by the precipitous slopes of the Monti

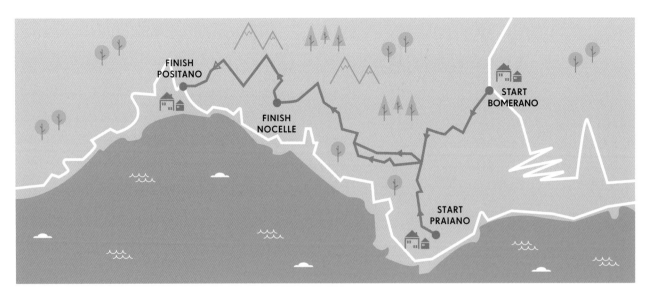

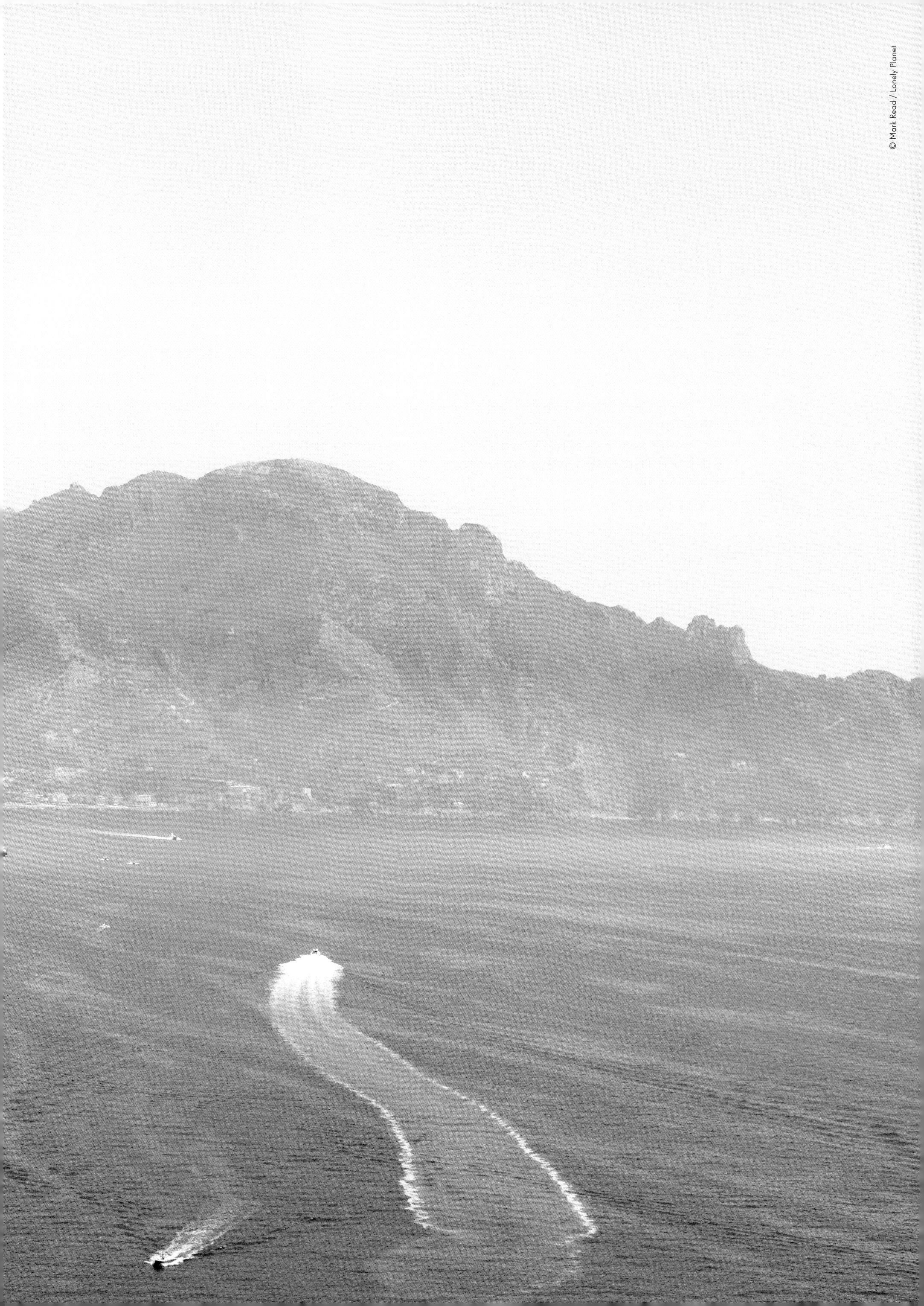

Lattari, there isn't much flat land in these parts. Instead, the steep hillsides have been tamed by well-built stone stairways, many of them dating back to medieval times. Iron leg muscles are a prerequisite, as are ultra-strong knee joints for the descents.

Though runners still aren't a common sight on the stairways, their numbers are increasing. These days, locals don't bat an eyelid as you canter past, although the resident dogs might raise a chorus of barking. In fact, if you're keen to compete, several ultra-runs have established themselves on the Amalfi Coast in the past few years, led by the Amalfi-Positano Ultra Trail, a 34-mile (55km) circuit that incorporates the Sentiero degli Dei.

When it comes to climbing, the Sentiero degli Dei is different from other Amalfi trails. Despite its location high above the winding coast road leading to and from the cliffside town of Positano, the trail itself is relatively flat, if you stick to the traditional route. This four-and-a-half-mile stretch traverses the lofty hillsides between the villages of Bomerano and Nocelle. This is trail running at its finest, a quick escape into a rugged mountainous realm: safe but a little edgy, tough but not too technical, and guaranteed to get your adrenaline flowing more than once.

A bus from Amalfi town had delivered me to the main plaza in the village of Bomerano. From here I jogged languidly down an attractive rural lane, negotiated a few undemanding steps, and quickly found myself beholding the two hard-to-miss welcome signs that mark the start of the official route.

Beyond the Lawrence-Calvino monument, foggy views of terraced fields and red-roofed farm buildings quickly unfolded as the path contoured around the mountain and passed beneath the overhanging Grotta del Biscotto (Biscuit Cave), a surreal natural feature where ruined houses are built right into the cliffs.

Fortuitously, I had chosen to run the trail in the morning before the hiking crowds hit. The sun was slowly burning off an ethereal mist as I tracked west, revealing a long, jagged coastline dotted with pinprick towns far below. The main challenge on the Sentiero degli Dei is the narrowness of the path and the intermittent rocky sections underfoot. Occasionally the trail becomes mildly exposed; periodically, it even disappears into small thickets of trees. Aspiring runners won't just need to have a head for heights, they'll also need to be suitably sure-footed and adept at sidestepping groups of hikers along the way.

The first landmark after the Grotta del Biscotto is an important junction at Colle Serra. Here, you get to choose between a low route or a high route. In search of sky-scraping views, I chose the high route, which ascended steadily past old lime kilns and abandoned farmhouses to a spectacular traverse with ever-present vistas of the azure Mediterranean, dotted with bobbing pleasure boats.

Just south of the Colle Serra, a path from the Sentiero degli Dei's alternative start in Praiano joins the main trail. Runners with masochistic tendencies will revel in this gruelling ascent. More redolent of a Stairmaster workout than a run, the path counts 1000 steps in a short thigh-pulverising climb.

ANCIENT AMALFI

The Amalfi Coast is laced with ancient footpaths, many of them dating back to the 10th and 11th centuries when this part of the coastline was an independent city state. Until the coastal road was built in the 1850s, the trails were the primary means of getting around. Italy's main hiking body, the CAI (Club Alpino Italiano) maintains a list of 124 numbered trails in the region, all marked with distinctive red-and-white paint. They measure out a total distance of 330 miles (530km).

Clockwise from top: the view towards Ravello; stairs leading to Positano; a welcome sign ushers runners and hikers onto the trails. Previous page: the oceanside perch of Amalfi town. Opening page: Positano at sunset

"I chose the high route with ever-present vistas of the azure Mediterranean, dotted with bobbing pleasure boats"

Both low and high routes meet again a mile west of Colle Serra. Invigorated by my lofty mountain traverse, I came galloping down from the high trail like a runaway mountain goat, still feeling relatively fresh. But there comes a point on the Sentiero degli Dei when you're forced to concede that this is no place to attempt a personal best. Aside from the jagged rocks, edgy drop-offs and traffic-jams of international tourists blocking your path, various lookouts along the way practically scream out at you to slow down and savour the moment.

So, slow down I did. In fact, I parked myself on a Hercules-sized boulder perched precariously on the hillside like an abandoned meteorite. From my bird's eye position above the crinkled mountains I gazed towards my destination: the steeply stacked houses of Positano, with the whale-like island of Capri winking beyond.

Around this point, the scenery radically changes, with dry Mediterranean scrub giving way to shady oak and chestnut forest. The main path tracks west toward Positano, kinks around some half-obscured *grotte* (caves) and descends into the Valle Grarelle, before climbing back up to the official finish point in the village of Nocelle.

A small kiosk serving cold drinks on a flowery terrace greeted me as I jogged into the village, but I resisted the temptation to indulge. In common with many Sentiero degli Dei hikers, I was determined to press on to the posh Amalfi resort of Positano, just 1500 steps further (all of them downhill). Why bother? Ice cream, a throat-warming glass of limoncello, a recuperative swim in the sea, and most importantly, a bus back to Amalfi town. **BS**

ORIENTATION

Start // Bomerano or Praiano
End // Nocelle or Positano
Distance // 4.5 miles (7km)
Getting there // Catch a SITA bus in Amalfi town for Agerola and get off in Bomerano's main square.
When to go // April to June, or September and October.
Where to stay // Positano is plush but expensive. Agerola and the towns to the east (Minori, Maiori, Cetara) offer better value with no significant drop in quality. Agriturismi (farm-stays) provide a more peaceful rural option.
More info // www.caimontilattari.it; the Club Alpino Italiano website (www.cai.it) has maps and descriptions for all Amalfi trails, including the 'Path of the Gods'.
Things to know // If you're too tired to walk from Nocelle to Positano, a local bus departs Nocelle 10 times a day.

Clockwise from top: the town of Vernazza along Italy's Cinque Terre; Cinque Terre signposting; a rugged undeveloped stretch of the area

MORE LIKE THIS
MEDITERRANEAN ESCAPES

CINQUE TERRE, ITALY

If there is one coastal trail in Italy that can rival the Path of the Gods for all-round seductiveness, it's the Sentiero Azzurro. Meandering for 7.5 miles (12km) across the Unesco-listed landscapes of Cinque Terre in the Liguria region east of Genoa, the Azzurro traverses windswept olive groves and seemingly impregnable vineyards before dipping serendipitously into the region's five ancient fishing villages, where plenty of historical distractions await. Protected in a national park, the trail charges a small fee (€7.50), but the investment is undoubtedly worth it. Adding to the allure, the trail is readily accessible by train, with a quintet of handy stations (one in each village) giving you the option to head back on public transport if you don't want to retrace your steps at the end.
Start // Riomaggiore
End // Monterosso al Mare
Distance // 7.4 miles (12km)
More info // www.cinqueterre.eu.com

CABO DE GATA, SPAIN

If you can find anyone old enough to remember the Costa del Sol before Spain's 1960s tourist boom, they'd probably say it looked a bit like Cabo de Gata. Some of the country's most beautiful and least crowded beaches are strung between the grand cliffs and capes east of Almería city, where dark volcanic hills tumble into a sparkling turquoise sea. Though Cabo de Gata is not undiscovered, it still has a wild, elemental feel, and its scattered fishing villages (remember those?) remain low-key. Running here is a solitary pleasure and particularly recommended off-season (October to April) when the weather remains mild, but the tourists stay away. You can run all the way along the coast in a multi-day run from Retamar in the west to Agua Amarga in the east (37 miles; 61km) or split the route into shorter segments, setting out from various towns en route. Whitewashed San José is the most convenient base.
Start // Retamar
End // Agua Amarga
Distance // 6–37 miles (10–61km)
More info // www.cabogataalmeria.com

GOLFO DI OROSEI, SARDINIA, ITALY

In a country with surprisingly few coastal trails, Sardinia's Golfo di Orosei adds a new dimension. This is the Mediterranean as modern tourists rarely see it: untamed, isolated and wonderfully untarnished. Whereas runners on Amalfi Coast and Cinque Terre trails require deft footwork to sidestep the steady streams of enthusiastic hikers, athletes in this roadless region have only sheep, eagles and the odd whistling farmer for company. The set of trails that run along Sardinia's east coast between the villages of Cala Gonone and Baunei are usually hiked in four days. But there's no reason why strong, adventurous, well-prepared runners can't complete the 28 miles (54km) in just one. Note the area's relative isolation and purchase a map, bring plenty of water and start early. Several beach restaurants and a *rifugio* provide various eating and sleeping options along the way.
Start // Cala Gonone
End // Baunei
Distance // 28 miles (45km)

TELEGRAFO

VOLASTRA

The Amalfi Coast

A SIGHTSEEING LAP AROUND EDINBURGH

Scotland's buzzing capital has trails, stairs, steep streets and narrow medieval lanes, making it the perfect city for a running tour.

We're standing at the Heart of Midlothian, a pavement mosaic halfway up Edinburgh's Royal Mile. 'This was the location of the notorious Old Tollbooth prison,' explains Nicole, my guide around the city. 'Prisoners were kept in appalling conditions and many were executed right here. So now it's good luck to spit on it as you walk by to show your disgust.' I take a hasty step backwards and bump into another tourist. A huge group is flowing towards us, presumably to hear the spitting story I've just heard. 'Best get moving,' Nicole smiles, and we run off, the crowd parting before our sweaty sports gear.

City tours and running make strange bedfellows. Yet, judging by their rise – there are more than 200 city running tours around the world, and their numbers grow each year – they are clearly finding an audience. The idea is simple: you get a knowledgeable city guide who is also a runner. They lead you on a run around their city. You get the double whammy of a great run and a fantastic

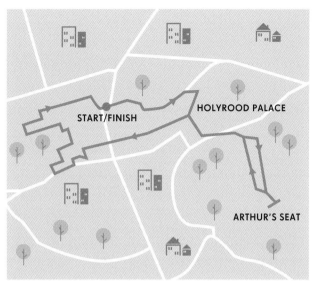

© Zbynek Strnad | 500px

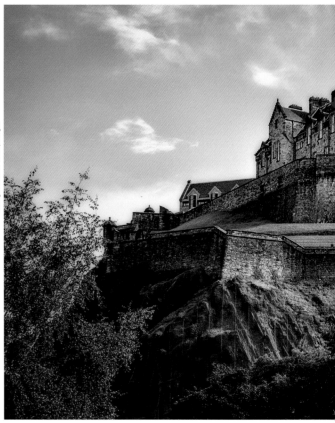

"We're covering way more ground than on a walking tour and the idea of a bus tour on these narrow streets is laughable"

tour of the sights. Some tours focus on the city's best sights, some focus on the best runs. The best ones – like my run around Scotland's capital – manage to deliver both.

I'd met Nicole that morning at the train station. She was easy to spot: an obvious runner among the thronging summer tourists, trim in purple and black leggings and, like city guides everywhere, plastered in logos advertising her business. In my running gear, surrounded by tourists, I felt curiously self-conscious and a little anxious. Which was I, a runner or a tourist? I wasn't sure.

But I had little time for an existential crisis. After the briefest of chats (plenty of shops and toilets along the way, pace not a problem), we were off, straight up the steps of Calton Hill.

From the top, it was easy to see why Edinburgh attracts more tourists than anywhere in the UK outside London. The city that inspired Hogwarts, Diagon Alley and so much of the Harry Potter world is ridiculously picturesque. On one low ridge lies the medieval Old Town, with its twisting alleyways, tall gothic buildings and the iconic castle above it all. Facing it on a parallel ridge is the 200-year-old New Town of elegant Georgian mansions, grand town squares and wide streets.

As if all that isn't enough, right at the bottom of the Royal Mile, dominating the skyline and, surely, making this the best city in the world for running, is a mountain. Arthur's Seat may only be 823ft (251m) high, but as Robert Louis Stevenson said, it's 'a hill for

magnitude, a mountain in virtue of its bold design'. The perfection of our route was laid out before us – up craggy Arthur's Seat, along the length of the Royal Mile from the Queen's residence at Holyrood Palace to the castle at the top, before looping back through the New Town. The best of Edinburgh in a 90-minute run.

It's at Holyrood Palace where I start to notice how I'm a tourist, but not a tourist. We stop at the gates and I hear about the history of the building. Another tourist sidles up to listen as Nicole tells me about the Queen's stay the previous week. She finishes her sentence and to our eavesdropper's surprise we both wordlessly run off.

Arthur's Seat doesn't feel wild, exactly – put a scenic peak in a city of half-a-million people and it's not going to be deserted – but it certainly doesn't feel like the city. We're on trails, not roads, and the steepness is such that we're fast-walking, not running. A few strategic questions from me keep Nicole talking so that I can concentrate on my breathing as we pull up to the rocky little summit.

As soon as we start our descent, Nicole picks up the pace. 'Come this way. We end up in the same place, but it's a much quieter path.' And we find ourselves running – really running now – down an empty grassy path, the city disappearing behind the crags in front of us, the tourists behind a ridge to our rear. For a few minutes we're a million miles away from the city, running fast and free, the only sound our lungs and our feet as we pound down the steep hillside.

NAKED AMBITION

The first recorded hill race took place in Scotland in 1064 when King Malcolm II was looking for the fastest messenger. The two elder MacGregor brothers – the race favourites – were neck-and-neck when their younger brother suddenly broke past. Apparently, one of them made a grab for him, getting a handful of kilt. The younger brother still finished first, but kilt-less.

From left: the city's famous Rat Race; Edinburgh Castle looms large; Previous page: Edinburgh Festival's famous big wheel comes to town in August

But it's later in the run, as we're pushing through the throngs at the entrance to the city's iconic castle, that I realise the real benefit of a running tour. We've climbed Calton Hill and Arthur's Seat. On our way up the Royal Mile we've ducked into a 17th-century garden, toured the inside of St Giles Cathedral, and slapped down the steep cobbles of Harry Potter's Diagon Alley (or at least, the street that inspired it). And we still have a quarter of the run to go – a whistle-stop tour of the elegant Georgian New Town. We are covering way more ground than we could on a walking tour. And the idea of taking a bus tour around these narrow medieval streets is laughable.

I suddenly understand what had made me anxious when I'd got off the train. I was worried that by combining running and city tours, I'd somehow ruin both – that I'd miss the workout and relaxation of an hour spent running, but that I'd also be moving too quickly to pay attention to what the city had to offer. But as we speed down the steep streets away from the castle, I'm a convert. At this pace, it feels like we can go anywhere, see anything.

'Who books these kinds of tours?' I ask Nicole, on a whim.

'The people who always throw their running shoes in their suitcase,' she replies. Then she gives voice to exactly what I'd been thinking. 'If you enjoy running, it's the best way to see the city. It's small groups, just you and me, exploring at our own pace. You see so much more if you're running.' **PP**

ORIENTATION

Start/End // Edinburgh Waverley railway station

Distance // 7 miles (11km)

When to go // Edinburgh is a year-round running destination. A benefit of city running is that winter runs in the dark are as spectacular as day runs.

Where to stay // A classy mid-range hotel is 2 Hillside Crescent (www.twohillsidecrescent.com), a Georgian town house tucked in the shadow of Calton Hill. Bargain-hunters won't do better than Edinburgh Central Youth Hostel (www.syha.org.uk), which has a great location and private rooms.

More info // www.edinburghruntours.com

Things to know // When choosing a guide, ask how big your group will be. A group of more than 2 or 3 people is more sociable, but necessarily slower. For tours in more than 100 cities worldwide, check out www.runningtours.net

MORE LIKE THIS
CITY RUNNING TOURS

AMSTERDAM, NETHERLANDS

If you really don't like hills, Amsterdam is the city for you. The capital of the Netherlands is as flat as a Dutch pancake. Built around a network of canals, its narrow streets favour bikes over cars and the only climbs are over the many bridges. There are as many variations on the route as there are backstreets in Amsterdam, but the goal is a loop linking the Rijksmuseum and Van Gogh Museum, over the Magere Brug past the Hermitage, across to Dam Square then Anne Frank's House. It's a very photo-friendly run, so allow longer than the short distance would suggest – this is a runner's city that rewards serendipity.
Start/End // Leidseplein bridge/station on the River Amstel (but this is a loop so it doesn't really matter).
Distance // 4.5 miles (7.1km)
More info // www.touristrunamsterdam. com

BANGKOK OLD TOWN, THAILAND

Due to its busy highways, narrow, potholed streets and endless crowds, Bangkok is hard work for the visiting runner. So a morning run tour is a great way to navigate this complex city. There are options that take in the famous sights of Old Town, or that explore the river and its web of canals. But why not try a more unusual route that delivers a triple-whammy of exercise, art and street food? This tour heads down Surawong Rd, taking you from some of the city's most chichi contemporary art galleries to Bangrak, where many of the best-known street artists in the world have left their mark. Then you head north past the Golden Buddha to Chinatown, where the street art runs out and the eating begins.
Start // Si Lom MRT station
End // Yaowarat Rd, Chinatown
Distance // 5 miles (8km)
More info // www.gorunningtours.com/ bangkok

MARRAKESH CITY WALLS, MOROCCO

The medieval medina of Marrakesh is known for its labyrinthine layout, the unrelenting heat of its daytime sun and streets so narrow that donkeys struggle to pass each other. So it might not seem an obvious choice for a run. But wake up early, before the sun gets too hot and the donkeys too ubiquitous, and run around the old city walls. It's difficult to get lost when you're following walls that are, in some places, 9m-high and 2m-thick. But nip in through the various *babs* (gates) along the way and you'll see the Saadian tombs at Bab Rob, skirt the stinking tanneries at Bab Debbagh and finish up running past the Koutoubia minaret to the fabled Djemaa El Fna, where the soothsayers, acrobats, musicians and water-sellers will just be setting up for the day.
Start/End // Djemaa El Fna
Distance // 8 miles (12.75km)
More info // www.runninginmorocco. com

From top: Amsterdam's canalside roads provide the perfect running track; it's hard not to be distracted by street snacks while running in Bangkok

AN ODE TO A CZECH RUNNING HERO

A little-known road race in the Czech Republic provides the ultimate lesson in true grit and spirit, and a renewed appreciation for the sport of running.

Epic is not the first word that comes to mind when you first arrive in the town of Kopřivnice, on the eastern edge of the Czech Republic. Grey, perhaps, or functional. The chimneys of an old car factory loom over one-size-fits-all concrete apartment blocks. A car-and-tractor museum is the main cultural attraction. It feels as grim as the Soviet era. However, Kopřivnice is, in fact, one of the most thrilling destinations a runner can visit.

Indeed, running romantics come here from all over the world, especially in September, when they come for a famous 14-mile (22.5km) road-race. What makes this race epic is its origin and its atmosphere. The clue is in the race's name: the Běh rodným krajem Emila Zátopka. Or, 'the run through the homeland of Emil Zátopek.' Zátopek is the greatest of all endurance runners. He won five Olympic medals, set 18 world records, broke once-unbreakable barriers at 5000m and 10000m. In 2013, *Runner's World* magazine declared him the best of all time – over any distance. He was born in Kopřivnice, in 1922.

From the moment you enter the bustling local school hall for registration, you realise that Zátopek's hometown is as warm as its exterior is grey. It feels as though every inhabitant wants to make your visit special. For you have come to honour their town's most famous son. Zátopek, who died in November 2000, would have been proud. Hospitality and warmth to strangers were, to him, the most sacred of duties, an essential part of his identity as a Moravian and as a runner. His wife Dana set up the race in his memory two years after his death.

The race is held on the nearest Saturday to his and Dana's shared birthday. Dana traditionally fires the starting gun, although the journey from her home in Prague is a long one for a woman in

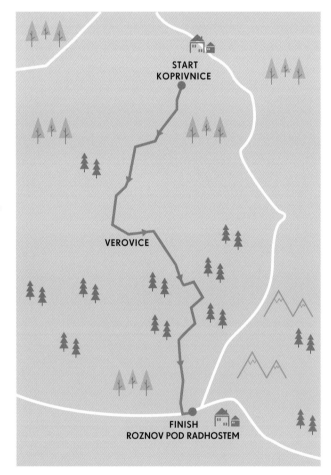

© John Wingfield/ Alamy Stock Photo

her mid-nineties. She is usually there at the end, too, when runners gather in Rožnov pod Radhoštěm's reconstruction of a traditional wooden Wallachian village for hot food and prizes. Zátopek is actually buried nearer the finish, next to a little wooden church. A wall of mountains – the Javorník Beskids – stands between the two towns. But what makes the race a must-try for lovers of running adventures is not the mountainous challenge of getting from start to finish, it is the thought of the footsteps you're running in.

The start of the race feels like a street party. By the time the town's outskirts are behind me, I am buzzing from the goodwill. The countryside beyond is quieter, with sloping grassland on either side of the tarmac and, usually, dark forests beyond. At times it feels disconcertingly empty. But the undulating miles pass quickly, and every now and then there's a village – Štramberk, Ženklava, Veřovice – where locals of all ages line the roadsides, offering treats, cheers, music and more.

In July 1952, Zátopek won three of his four Olympic golds in eight days: the only ever distance-running grand slam of 5000m, 10000m and a marathon. The latter was his first attempt at the distance. His only other marathon was at the Melbourne Olympics four years later, where he was injured and unfit, and the temperature was well over 80°F (30°C). 'Men,' he said at the startline, 'today we die a little...'

"Emil Zátopek's disregard for physical discomfort would have been shocking if it hadn't been so cheerful"

It's a quote I carry with me as, after about 6 miles, I exchange the main road for a lane-cum-track that climbs mercilessly for the next few miles. The forest here is thick and close; the track becomes rough, steep and winding. OK, I admit to myself, this is quite tough. The air grows colder as my gasps for it grow louder. Finally, at 2280ft (695m), I reach the saddle, a mile or so west of the holy mountain of Radhošt'. I am, at this point, crossing the 'spine' of Europe. Zátopek, running on this ridge as a young man, amused himself by stopping to urinate, aiming some to the north and some to the south.

Running the challenging terrain, I try to distract myself with thoughts of the challenges Zátopek himself faced. Born into grinding poverty, he had limited physical gifts. His running style was famously compared to 'a man wrestling an octopus on a conveyor belt'. He made himself the greatest athlete the world had seen through demented hard work. His disregard for physical discomfort would have been shocking if it hadn't been so cheerful.

© MARKA / Alamy Stock Photo

MYTH OF EMIL

Czech running
superstar Emil
Zátopek was
a glutton for
punishment. He
trained in rain and
darkness, on forests
and hills, in snow
and sand, in army
boots, anything to
make it harder –
and always with
a grimace of pain.
Every fan has a
Zátopek story: how
he trained while in
hospital; during a
plane flight; in the
bath; with his wife
on his back. And
most are true.

*From left: Emil Zátopek's gravestone;
a national hero at the 1952 Olympic
Games in Helsinki. Previous page:
Zátopek's hometown of Kopřivnice is
considered hallowed ground by many*

Meanwhile, his generosity matched his talent. Scorning the Cold War's divisions, he formed deep friendships with his fiercest rivals, chatting incessantly in races, in eight languages (mostly self-taught for that purpose). He was brave and charismatic: the Muhammad Ali of his day. When Warsaw Pact tanks invaded Czechoslovakia in 1968, crushing the experiment in 'socialism with a human face' known as the Prague Spring, Zátopek rallied protesters in Wenceslas Sq – and was cruelly punished for his courage.

In the final third of this race, the real fun begins: more than 4 miles of continuous descent. You can do most of it flat-out, if you dare, although the hairpin bends are challenging. If you can reach Rožnov pod Radhoštěm with anything left in your legs, apart from quivering jelly, you'll be doing better than I've done in my three attempts.

The first time I finished this race, in 2014, the local culture and language felt so alien to me that I could barely work out how to retrieve my kit afterwards. It is, despite the multinational field, a very Czech race. But the warmth and friendship transcend such barriers. I fell in love with it and kept coming back. By the third time, I felt so at home that I was toasting Emil's memory with his widow, Dana, the night before. That may account for the slightly below-par performance. **RA**

ORIENTATION

Start // Kopřivnice
End // Rožnov pod Radhoštěm.
Distance // 13.86 miles (22.3 km)
Getting there // Ostrava airport is half-an-hour's drive from Kopřivnice. A race-bus will get you back to Kopřivnice from Rožnov pod Radhoštěm.
When to go // The nearest Saturday to 19 September.
Where to stay // Kopřivnice is best for the pre-race atmosphere; Rožnov pod Radhoštěm for post-race. Rožnov is more scenic; Kopřivnice less touristy.
More info // www.beh-roznov.koprivnice.org; www.koprivnice.cz; www.roznov.cz
Things to know // If you're able to stay for a few days, try to fit in a hike up Radhošť (close to the mid-point of the race), central Europe's most famous holy mountain.

Ode to a Czech Running Hero

*Opposite: the cliffs of the Low
Tatras region in Slovakia*

MORE LIKE THIS
EASTERN EUROPEAN RACES

VELKÁ KUNRATICKÁ, PRAGUE, CZECH REPUBLIC

You might wonder what a race with a full course less than 2 miles long is doing in a list of 'epic' races. The answer is simple: hills – really steep ones; also mud and streams; and beautiful forest scenery; and the kind of weather you'd expect in central Europe on the first Sunday in November. The race takes place in the Krunatice Forest in Prague's Modřany district (where the great King Wenceslas IV died hunting in 1419). The full course involves three stream-crossings and three steep ascents, including the notorious Hrádek slope. First run in 1934, the race is considered such a classic that the president of the International Olympic Committee handed out medals for its 50th anniversary. Many categories cover only a shorter version of the route, and places in the full version are quickly taken. The record for the full course – 10:58.9 minutes – has stood since 1979.
Start/End // Kunratice Brook Valley
Distance // 2 miles (3km)
More info // www.velkakunraticka.cz

NON-STOP BEH HREBEŇOM NÍZKYCH TATIER, SLOVAKIA

This hard, exhilarating mountain race in the Low Tatras in Slovakia is held on the last Saturday of June. It's 30 miles (49km), with a total elevation of 7175ft (2187m). The theoretical base is the historic town of Banská Bystrica, but the start and finish – and everything in between – are deep in the adjoining national park. This is proper mountain-running: there's 2600ft (800m) to be climbed in the first 4 miles alone, from the start at Trangoška to the granite summit of Krupova Hoľa. But the views from on high are unforgettable, as is the descent from Veľká Chochuľa to Hiadeľské Sedlo. If you survive that the worst will be over, although it may not feel that way as you drag yourself over the final 6 miles. The near-vertical 720ft (220m) climb to Kozí Chrbát is a beast, but it all adds to the joy of the finish at Donovaly, where you can congratulate yourself on having completed one of central Europe's toughest mountain races.
Start/End // Low Tatras National Park
Distance // 30 miles (49km)
More info // www.nonstopbehnt.sk

TRANSYLVANIA BEAR RACE, ROMANIA

You couldn't call this an easy race: it's an ultra distance of hilly Romanian countryside, with 5577ft (1700m) of ascent and descent, culminating in a monster climb (including 176 steps of covered wooden stairway) to the medieval citadel of Sighişoara. Sighişoara is a Unesco-listed heritage site, a distinction it shares with the start, the old Saxon village of Viscri. In between lie miles of undulating trails, through ancient forests and occasional open pastures. The local wildlife, described by the organisers as 'vibrant', includes plentiful wolves and brown bears. But no competitor has yet been devoured mid-race, so there's a good chance you'll survive for that final climb. And if that isn't enough to worry you, keep in mind that Sighişoara was the birthplace of Vlad III Dracul, the 15th-century 'Impaler' and alleged vampire.
Start //Viscri
End //Sighişoara
Distance //31–50 miles (50–80km)
More info // www.transylvanian bearrace.com

A PORTAL TO THE PAST IN PEMBROKESHIRE

Wales' westernmost point sits in one of Britain's most beautiful national parks. This world-class trail run is a race through time as it passes stunning ancient monuments.

The southwest tip of Wales is a geologist's playground where rock scars and layered cliffs leave striking clues about our past. Some of this rock dates right back to the Precambrian era, before multi-cellular life first emerged. With its remnants of ancient civilisations littering the coastline, this edge of Wales is also heaven for history lovers, as Britain's earliest architects had a penchant for north Pembrokeshire rock (Stonehenge was built from bluestones found in nearby hills). And yet to my mind this stretch of cliffs and beaches holds something even more exciting than all of that: one of the most beautiful trail runs in all of Britain.

Over the years I've compiled a fat file of runs in Wales, and this 13-miler (21km) skirting the country's westernmost peninsula remains my favourite. It begins off-road along the Pembrokeshire Coast Path and completes the loop on country lanes. Indeed, the in-your-face history and geological beauty are inspiring, but the natural flow, isolation and ruggedness make it feel as though it was built for early morning half-marathons.

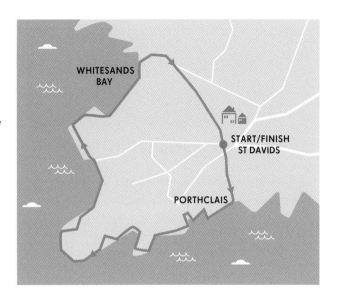

WHITESANDS BAY

START/FINISH
ST DAVIDS

PORTHCLAIS

© Sarahstirling.com

"I can just make out the banks and ditches of the Iron Age fort here, which is slowly being dismantled by the sea"

Immediately upon setting off, I feel the freedom and exhilaration of the path. It's rocky in places but rarely awkward enough to demand my gaze. The rock all around me, however, is hard to ignore. Colourful cliffs rise around me, some of the faces a deep purple, others a shade of rose. Red-and-white striped pebbles on the beach resemble boiled sweets. The cliffs jutting into the sea seem primeval and alive. The path ahead rolls into the distance, bursting with wildflowers in pink, blue and gold.

Today – and every time I run here – there seems to be a deeply spiritual vibe. But it's only if you really tune into the environment that you begin to trip over the ghosts of Welsh mythology. The area has been so lightly touched by modern man that you'll pass by forgotten Stone Age monuments, crumbling Bronze Age roundhouses, the ramparts of an Iron Age fort, Dark Age chapel ruins and even a hidden medieval cathedral. But it's not as simple as scanning the landscape as you jog. You have to run mindfully, and even explore off the path a little to spot the ruins among the rocks and earth that have begun to hide them.

Most importantly, there is hardly anyone else here. In fact, it feels as though hardly anyone has ever been here. Thankfully, the ribbons of frustrating country lanes, slow tractors and sheep between Pembrokeshire and the rest of the world defend this corner from all but the determined few. Even if the crowds do discover it someday, I take solace in the fact that it will always enjoy some level of protection, thanks to its status as a national park. It was in fact one of Britain's very first national parks – designated way back in 1952 – and remains the only coastal one.

I power along the clifftop to a promontory at the end of Caerfai Bay, then pause to look back. Opposite is another piece of land jutting out, connected by a narrow natural bridge. I can just make out the banks and ditches of the Iron Age fort here, which is slowly being dismantled by the sea. Legend has it King Arthur roamed these parts during this era, fighting raiding tribes from overseas. What emerged is the idea of Wales itself. The Anglo-Saxons who began to dominate England called the Celts 'Wealhs' – foreigners.

Just a half-mile in and my feet start to fly as I settle into the flow of the path. I leap over a few tendrils of scratchy gorse bushes to reach the stone ruins of St Non's Chapel. Thought to be one of Wales' oldest Christian buildings, it is said to mark the birthplace of David, patron saint of Wales. In 1081, William the Conqueror himself made a pilgrimage to the monastery. Not long after, work on St Davids Cathedral began, on the site of the monastery. Two pilgrimages to this cathedral were then declared equal to one made to Rome.

I trot carefully downhill towards a deep inlet with a tiny picturesque 12th-century stone harbour known as Porthclais. Originally used for importing coal and timber, these days it's a great place to launch a kayak. In fact, it's here that I feel as though I leave the ancient world behind and step into this park's future, as adventurous daytrippers are launching colourful boats into the bay and I can hear the jangle of rock climbers placing gear into the cliffs. As I carry on, the chatter of swimmers rises up from Porthlysgi Bay; soon I will see surfers riding the waves in Whitesands Bay.

Reaching Pen Dal-aderyn, the westernmost tip of mainland

NATURE'S CALL

Between April and
September, the
islands around
the Pembrokeshire
coastline become
loud, noisy cities of
sex-mad birds in the
height of mating
season. The best
island to visit during
the wildlife love-fest
is Skomer, home to
the largest Atlantic
puffin colony in
southern Britain.
There are 21,000 of
them, all remarkably
unbothered by
tourists so watch
your step. There
are also 23,000
guillemots and
7000 razorbills!

*From left: St Davids Cathedral; a
member of Pembrokeshire's impressive
puffin colony; a trail-runner's dream.
Previous page: where the Irish Sea
meets Wales*

Wales, I sit down to bite into a sandwich. This is a good place
to spot seals and dolphins. I can see a boat in the water, taking
tourists out for a closer look at the sealife and to spot puffins
waddling on the nearby islands. Thinking about what a peaceful
natural playground this place is today, I can't help but wonder
what the ghosts of the Pembrokeshire coast make of all the brightly
coloured Gore-Tex and Lycra.

The next stretch is a clifftop blast that rewards you with views of
Whitesand Bay's vast beach. Beyond the beach, the rocky top of
Carn Llidi pokes up through the hill's green flanks. On its hillside
stands the oldest monuments on this run: a lichen-covered 20ft
slab, hefted into place in the late Stone Age, around 3000 BC, to
mark a tomb. Nearby are several low, circular stone walls – once
Bronze Age roundhouses – along with ancient animal enclosures.
I like to veer off-trail to explore these, somehow drawn to enter the
gaps that were doors and gateways, even though the tumbled
walls are low enough to step over.

Heading south on country lanes, there's no avoiding civilisation
as I enter the village of St Davids, which, because of the
aforementioned cathedral, claims to be Britain's smallest 'city'. It
may be small but this village is well aware of its natural assets.
From regular beach clean-ups to carbon neutrality, St Davids is
known for its progressive thinking when it comes to saving the
environment. This forward-thinking community is hell-bent on
preserving this coastline, allowing the Stone Age men, warriors,
saints, kings and medieval pilgrims haunting the clifftops to
continue their business unbothered. **SS**

ORIENTATION

Start/End // St Davids
Distance // 13 miles (21km)
Getting there // St Davids is 16 miles (26km) from the
nearest train station, which is in Haverfordwest.
When to go // Spring and summer are the seasons for
spectacular wildflower shows. Autumn and winter promise
big surf and the ultimate peace and quiet.
Where to stay // You'll get a warm Celtic welcome at
the well-kept Ty Boia B&B (www.ty-boia.co.uk). Or there's
camping at Caerfai Farm (www.caerfaifarm.co.uk).
More info // www.pembrokeshirecoast.wales
Things to know // Be sure to top off your run with a Celtic
Crunch ice cream at Gianni's.

MORE LIKE THIS
WILD WELSH HEADLANDS

THE LLYN PENINSULA

The Llŷn Peninsula extends into the sea
west of Snowdonia. It is a particularly
rural, quaint and quiet spot at the very
fingertip of the peninsula, where a huge
carpet of white sand is laid out in front
of the village of Aberdaron. Head west,
following the coastal path round to
Pen y Cil, the southwestern point of the
headland, looking out for dolphins and
seals. Continue north to Braich y Pwll, the
westernmost point on the North Walian
mainland, admiring Bardsey Island with its
19th-century lighthouse (the tallest square-
towered one in the UK), and imagining
medieval pilgrims rowing across to visit the
1500-year-old monastery. Archaeological
finds prove that the island has been
inhabited for at least 4000 years. Now
either retrace your steps or follow the minor
road back.
Start/End // Aberdaron
Distance // 6 miles (9.6km)
More info // www.llyn.info

HOLY ISLAND

Just beyond the west coast of Anglesey
lies a much smaller island, connected by
a bridge. The quartzite rocks of its highest
summit, Holyhead Mountain (722ft;
220m), can be seen from miles around; in
summer the lower slopes are cushioned
with purple heather. Around these lower
slopes, and elsewhere on the island, there
are a number of standing stones and burial
chambers, hence the name Holy Island.
From South Stack car park, follow the coast
path up past the photogenic lighthouse,
which clings to an offshore islet. In spring,
guillemots and puffins breed and chatter
noisily on these cliffs, and you can see
choughs all year round. Follow the path
round to North Stack before scrambling up
to the summit of Holyhead Mountain for
more views. Descend west to return to the
car park.
Start/End // South Stack
Distance // 4.5 miles (7.2km)
More info // www.visitanglesey.co.uk

THE GOWER PENINSULA

This tongue of land jutting into the sea
just west of Swansea was designated an
'Area of Outstanding Natural Beauty'
back in 1956, and it hasn't changed
much since. Right at the tip lies a 3-mile
(4.8km) strip of pure butterscotch beach
with the spine of Rhossili Down behind
it. Run along the beach, then follow the
path up and along the top of the low cliffs
that mark the northern end of the Gower
Peninsula. Continue round Foxhole Point,
before picking up footpaths and slogging
up and along the dunes behind the beach
to reach The Beacon (633ft; 193m). There
are spectacular views down to the village
of Rhossili and Worms Head beyond. The
latter is a narrow tail of land that dips into
the sea and then rises again to a little
headland. Scramble down steeply to return
to the car park.
Start/End // Rhossili
Distance // 9.5 miles (15km)
More info // www.explore-gower.co.uk

*Clockwise from top: the desolate beach of
Aberdaron on the Llŷn Peninsula; South Stack
lighthouse on Holy Island; Rhossili Bay beach on
the Gower Peninsula*

A Portal to the Past in Pembrokeshire

BARCELONA'S
SEA-TO-SUMMIT

*Forget the Gothic Quarter – one of Europe's best city runs connects
Barcelona's lively Mediterranean seafront with its soaring scenic hilltop.*

Just two short minutes into my run along Barcelona's wide shoreline, I catch sight of Frank Gehry's *El Peix* (The Fish), the huge rooftop sculpture shimmering in the first rays of an early September morning. The sun is just rising over the Mediterranean as I slow my pace and attempt to take it all in. The 183ft (56m)-long work, with its scale-like façade, is an emphatic introduction to the seaside district of Barceloneta, the city's old fishing quarter. Happy to be out before the heat arrives, I turn for one last glimpse of the bronze sculpture then speed out onto Barcelona's grand waterfront promenade perched over the golden sands below.

Before me stretches an open expanse of palm-lined pathway; beyond that, a brilliant 4.5-mile (7km) run that will take me from Barceloneta, skirting the edge of the busy Gothic Quarter, before turning inland and heading through Poble Sec to the hilltop heights of Montjuïc. The starting and ending points of my journey will spin me back a few centuries as I go from the city's old seaside district

(revitalised in preparation for the 1992 Olympics) up to a 300-year-old fortress looming some 590ft (180m) above the docks.

Though famed for its medieval lanes and art nouveau architecture, Barcelona's dense city centre can be a challenging running environment amid the winding cobblestone lanes and crowded narrow sidewalks. Yet just a short distance from medieval neighbourhoods like El Born you'll find gorgeous wide flat stretches along the seaside that are perfect for stepping on the gas.

Combine all this with a quad-burning ascent up the city's iconic hill – not to mention the photogenic public art, leafy gardens and iconic monuments that make this one of the most livable cities in the world – and you have the makings of one of the best urban runs in all of Europe. Best of all, it ends with a knee-friendly descent on the aerial gondola, back to the waterfront.

As I settle into a rhythm, I find myself among other runners, power-walkers and assorted other early risers on this popular route that traces the coastline. To my left, the deep blue Mediterranean laps against golden beaches, with a few barefooted runners plodding along the sands. To my right, a wispy line of palm trees stretches skyward backed by low-rise buildings set off from the road.

"Far below is the bustling port, with huge ships and ferries bound for the Balearic Islands, Genoa and Tangier"

After moving on from Gehry's fish, I catch a glimpse of the grid-like lanes, impossibly narrow alleys and densely populated apartment blocks of Barceloneta leading off to my right. Jutting from tiny balconies, lines of laundry and red-and-yellow-striped Catalan flags flap in the breeze. Although empty at this hour, by lunchtime Barceloneta's neighbourhood eateries will be packed with locals feasting on plates of grilled squid, tender razor clams and other delicacies 'del mar'. Barceloneta has a legendary maritime connection dating back more than 200 years, and there's no better place in the city for fresh seafood.

For the moment, though, I must banish all thoughts of freshly shucked oysters and shift into a higher gear. Buoyed by a light breeze at my back, I keep up a steady pace until I reach a towering sculpture which appears to teeter over the seaside. The 10m-high *L'Estel Ferit* (The Wounded Shooting Star), is yet another of the many public sculptures so loved by locals in this corner of the city. Designed by the German artist Rebecca Horn, these four stacked metal and glass cubes, seemingly balanced on top of one another, pay homage to the *xiringuitos* (boxy, shack-like eateries) that once lined Barceloneta's shoreline.

Public art was an essential part of Barcelona's revitalisation in the early 1990s, and it has slowly become an integral part of the waterfront neighbourhood in the eyes of most locals. This run also takes me past pop artist Roy Lichtenstein's 15m-high *El Cap de*

Barcelona, a brilliantly colourful mosaic-covered work in honour of Barcelona's most famous native son, Antoni Gaudí.

The masts of huge sailboats bob along beside me as I round the Plaça del Mar and run the length of the city's picturesque marina. For the next mile, I try to maintain a solid cadence, as it will be the last flat pavement before I cross the southern end of La Rambla and begin the uphill climb through Poble Sec, a less touristy village-like neighbourhood of tapas bars, outdoor cafes and bohemian drinking dens.

But by the time I reach the Mirador del Poble Sec, the wheels start to fall off. My pace slows to a hobbling jog as I huff my way further uphill, the road seeming to get steeper with every step. I feel as if I'm running on a backwards-moving treadmill as I grind out the next 500m of pavement. At long last, an overlook greets me just off a small traffic circle (the Plaça de Carlos Ibáñez). The views stretch across the expansive city to the distant mountains beyond. I'd like to linger, but I force myself to press on – or up, rather.

My calves are burning as I follow Avenida Miramar and head into the Jardins de Joan Brossa. The climb takes me past towering cypress trees, thick-trunked palms and fragrant pine trees. Near the top, cable cars glide effortlessly overhead, providing speedy transport links to the city below for passengers who'd rather not hoof it up the slopes of Montjuïc.

Exiting the park I tackle the final stretch of the run. Though

UNDERGROUND BUNKERS

During the Spanish Civil War Barcelona suffered devastating bombing raids, forcing locals to construct hundreds of bomb shelters around the city, including a massive one built into the lower slopes of Montjuïc. One of Barcelona's best preserved air-raid shelters, Refugi 307 was dug by locals in 1937 and has around 1300ft (400m) of tunnels.

From left: hitting the hills above Barcelona; the famous Sagrada Familia cathedral; Port Vell's pedestrian zone. Previous page: the city's harbour at night

relatively short (400m or so), it's quite steep, and I'm moving at a snail's pace by the time the Castell de Montjuïc rises into view. Dating from the 18th century, the imposing fortress looks quite inhospitable with its stout brickwork, shadowy embrasures (once bristling with cannons) and wide (but currently waterless) moat. For many Catalans, the fort remains a symbol of the darkest days under Franco, when it was used as a political prison. I pass the arched bridge leading into the thick walls, and my run ends at a small lookout facing south.

Far below is the bustling port, a whirl of activity with its huge container ships and ferries bound for the Balearic Islands, Genoa and Tangier. I linger until I begin to feel the cool breeze tingling against my damp clothes, then walk downhill to the teleférico station. There, I climb into one of the old-fashioned red gondolas, which carries me back down to the waterfront.

Along the way, the city spreads wide, taking in the beachfront, harbour and hillside. Soaring above the city centre, cranes hover beside the towers of Gaudi's still unfinished masterpiece of the Sagrada Familia, while further out, densely packed boulevards race off towards the green slopes of the Serra de Collserola.

It also offers a fine overview of the morning's run – and of future runs. This northern fringe of Barcelona, with forests still home to wild boar, has some magnificent off-road options – an inviting outing for another day and another time. **RS**

ORIENTATION

Start // Waterfront promenade near Casino Barcelona (Carrer de la Marina 19)
End // Castell de Montjuïc (off Carrer del Castell)
Distance // 5 miles (8km) one way
Getting there // Barcelona's international Aeroport del Prat is 8 miles (13km) southwest of the city.
When to go // Year-round.
Where to stay // Lodging near Barceloneta makes a convenient base both for running and for exploring the Gothic quarter nearby. The comfy Hotel del Mar has rooms overlooking the waterfront (doubles from €85).
Things to know // Once you finish near the Castell de Montjuïc, you can take a cable car down to Estació Parc Montjuïc, where you can transfer to a funicular railway that descends Montjuïc and connects to the metro.

*Opposite: Lyon, France from
the Fourvière cathedral*

MORE LIKE THIS
CITY SEA-TO-SUMMITS

LYON, FRANCE

Lyon has two picturesque rivers (the Rhone and the Saône) set beneath strategic heights where the city was founded circa 43 BC. A memorable route combines waterfront scenery with a rewarding (but challenging) climb up Fourvière hill to a stunning lookout near the city's magnificent basilica. Start on the east bank of the Rhone, just north of the Pont Winston Churchill, cross the river at the Pont de la Guillotière and cut through the grand Place Bellecour, Lyon's biggest plaza, en route to the pedestrian-only Passerelle St-Georges which traverses the Saône. Run up the west bank of the Saône. After passing three bridges, turn left at the fourth and follow Montée St-Barthélémy as it climbs uphill. Take the entrance to Parc des Hauteurs and wind your way to the top. You'll emerge at the base of the Basilique Notre Dame de Fourvière, with sublime views over one of France's loveliest cities.
Start // Pont Winston Churchill
End // Basilique Notre Dame de Fourvière
Distance // 3.7 miles (6km)

PERTH, AUSTRALIA

Famed for its pretty beaches, verdant parkland and sparkling riverfront, Perth offers seemingly limitless options for memorable running routes. One fantastic route takes you along the south shore of the Swan River, crosses the Narrows Bridge and heads into leafy Kings Park for the ascent up Mt Eliza. The run starts on the waterside running/biking path near Optus Stadium. Curve along the shoreline, with the city skyline just across the river. The views keep getting better as you cross the Narrows Bridge. Once on the river's north side, head towards the lush expanse of Kings Park, then the small Kennedy Fountain on the north side of the road. The ascent begins here, running up the 150 steps of the Kokoda Track, built to commemorate the Australian soldiers who fought along the gruelling Kokoda Track in Papua New Guinea. Once at the top, it's only a few hundred metres east to the State War Memorial.
Start // Optus Stadium
End // State War Memorial
Distance // 4.3 miles (7km)

SEATTLE, WASHINGTON, USA

A runner's paradise, Seattle offers a beguiling mix of waterfront, challenging hills and sublime views of both the Olympic Mountains to the west and soaring Mt Rainier to the southwest. Lake Union is a favourite destination, in part because it's nearly a perfect 6-mile (9.6km) loop. However, for some variety, you can run half the lake, then throw in some climbing up Capitol Hill for a well-rounded 3.7 miles (6km). Starting on Fremont Ave N, cross the Fremont Bridge and cut down to Westlake Ave. Follow the running/ biking path south to Lake Union Park, then loop north along Fairview Ave. Turn right onto E Blaine St for a slow, steady climb up Capitol Hill. Head up the stairs and continue along E Blaine and keep climbing until you reach Federal Ave. One block further, turn onto E Galer St, this leads into leafy Volunteer Park, with fine views of the Space Needle, Elliott Bay and (if the weather gods are cooperating) Mt Rainier.
Start // Fremont Ave
End // Volunteer Park
Distance // 3.7 miles (6km)

A CLASSIC ROUND IN THE LAKE DISTRICT

In the spiritual home of British trail running, this accessible section of the notorious Bob Graham Round – with an exciting add-on – is the best of the lot.

As I lay in bed on Sunday night I couldn't get the Bob Graham Round out of my head. I was exhausted from a long weekend of work competing in two big races in England's World Heritage-listed Lake District National Park. The last thing I needed before a long drive home was an early alarm, let alone more running. But I don't get to the Lakes often and trail-running history – or fell running, as it's known here, a remnant of the Norse word for hill – looms larger in these parts than anywhere else in the UK. The ghosts of fell running legends wouldn't stop whispering in my ear until I finally set my alarm for 6am.

While organised trail races were popping up in the States as early as 1905 (see The Dipsea Trail Race), fell running was also becoming a thing in the UK. Races were usually part of village fairs and sports days, where wiry mountain guides would compete against each other. Around these parts, say the names Joss Naylor, Billy Bland or Nicky Spinks – all modern multi-record-breaking fell-running luminaries – and the words seem to echo around the dales.

In 1932, to celebrate his 42nd birthday, a Keswick hotelier named Bob Graham ran a circuit of 42 summits inside 24 hours and the Bob Graham Round was born. The 'BG' is a folkloric challenge in which runners must travel 66 miles (106km) to tag all 42 summits, with 27,000ft (8230m) of ascent, inside 24 hours. Some 2000 people have joined the exclusive Bob Graham Club since its creation, but it's commonly thought that at least that number have tried but failed. I'm actually one of those 2000 to have run a BG – back in 2016 – but it never gets old. In fact, it becomes something of an addiction.

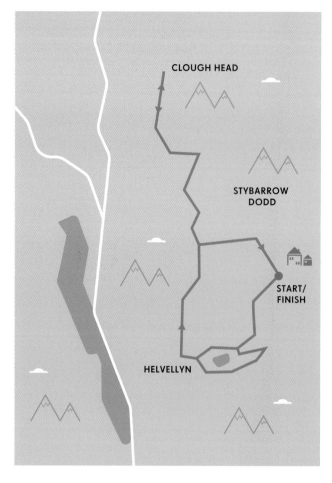

CLOUGH HEAD

STYBARROW DODD

START/ FINISH

HELVELLYN

After my smartphone shocked me semi-awake, I tumbled down the stairs, into my Inov-8 X-Talons and out the door into the drizzle before my body could realise what was happening. My plans were loose. I only had a few hours to spare so I planned to just hit Leg 2 of the BG, in the Helvellyn range. This would require accessing it via the notorious Striding Edge, a Grade 1 knife-edge scramble, with life insurance-invoking drop-offs either side.

The drizzle helped wake me, as did the stiff ascent. The terrain was fun: rocky and grassy in places, but largely on good stony trails. Soon, I could feel big thrilling areas of space either side of me, filled with swirling mists and dreamy possibilities. When the first large rock appeared out of the clag, blocking my path, I knew I was at the start of Striding Edge.

There's little conventional running to be done on Striding Edge itself, especially in the wet. In fact, it looks impassable from afar, but each time you get close to the next rock, there's a clear way over or around it. That said, three points of contact is always recommended. My hands are less accustomed to being relied upon like this and I wished I'd brought gloves.

On the other side, the terrain became easier but it also got steeper. After one more slog I was on the rounded summit of the volcanic behemoth known as Helvellyn, the third highest point in

"After Great Dodd, my sixth top of the day, it was satisfying to pick off several more summits with comparative ease"

England, where the trail officially joins the Bob Graham route.

Most people run this route clockwise. But having spent so long trying to get up high, I didn't want to yield my hard-earned advantage just yet, so I headed northwest, staying high, then north to the summit of Lower Man. Once up here, the hard work done, you can run fast and tick off fells, as you glide over the terrain.

In general, the peaks up here aren't large in world terms. England's biggest, Scafell Pike, also in the Lakes, is just a hair over 3,200ft (978m) tall. The Lakes gets lots of rain too. So the mountains are often green, with rocky heads. From here, it felt good to switch over to autopilot as I tagged top after top.

Ever so briefly, but oh so gloriously, the clouds parted to my left. Through a letter-box gap I spied the world of Wordsworth and Alfred Wainwright, and the much mythologised lumpy green and yellow fells, the vast lakes and ancient woods, all swathed in a special damp timelessness. And then, of course, it was gone again, as if it never happened.

BOB WHO?

Bob Graham wasn't a natural athlete. He was short and stocky, teetotal and vegetarian, but he had excellent knowledge of the Lakeland fells. In preparation for his first 'round', he walked each fell in bare feet, to both toughen up his skin and save his gym shoes. He walked the uphills and ran the downhills, with extraordinary speed, wearing tennis shoes, shorts and, apparently, a 'pyjama jacket'.

This page: the Lake District's hulking Helvellyn Range. Previous page: the airy traverse along Striding Edge

After Stybarrow Dodd, I followed the barely detectable curved drop-off to my right, round to the summit of Great Dodd, my sixth of the day. It was satisfying to tick off several more peaks with comparative ease. In the clouds, each looks familiar but with subtle differences, bigger cairns, broader plateaus, different levels of playful hostility.

About 10 miles in, I had time for one last summit, Clough Head, before a reluctant volte-face. The three hours of running had been tiring, but satisfying. I retraced my invisible steps, hoping for another glimpse of the Lake District landscape. But no, instead I got 'classic' Lake District views, which is just another way of saying no view at all. It was damp, windy and drizzly, but bulging with the sort of wildness and edginess that makes a simple run here feel like an expedition.

As I reached the col before Raise Fell, I was out of time. Eight summits in three hours and it was time to descend and get on the road. I took a good, easy-going path back down into the quiet village of Glenridding, where I'd begun. It's a fast-flowing trail that quickly lowered me beneath the weather and far away from those lovely big lumps.

Once down, I knew I had just enough of a post-adventure glow to last me through my long drive on the motorway back home. **DH**

ORIENTATION

Start/End // YHA Helvellyn, Glenridding
Distance // 16 miles (25km)
Getting there // The Lake District can be tricky to get around without a private car. If you do take the train, aim for Ambleside, then take a taxi to YHA Helvellyn.
When to go // February to November. Striding Edge in mid-winter can be treacherous.
Where to stay // The local youth hostels in the Lake District are basically HQ for all visiting outdoorsy folks. YHA Helvellyn is the start and end of this run (www.yha.org.uk/hostel/yha-helvellyn).
More info // www.lakedistrict.gov.uk
Things to know // Because of the wet, a route like this requires good grippy trail-running shoes.

*Opposite: easy does it on
Blencathra's Sharp Edge*

MORE LIKE THIS
UK LAKE DISTRICT CLASSICS

BLENCATHRA

Multi-headed Blencathra (2848ft; 868m)
is the third summit on most Bob Graham
Rounds and a cult favourite with locals.
This is also a classic Lake District fell run
in that the distance isn't big, but with
2500ft (773m) of ascent, it'll take some
time and your legs will feel it. A testing
climb up Mousthwaite Comb soon rewards
with big views. From Scales Beck there's a
choice of the thrilling Sharp Edge or the
more relaxed, direct route to the summit,
where you'll be rewarded with huge views
of the Lakes in all their glory (weather
allowing). Then tighten your shoelaces
for an exhilaratingly speedy descent via
Scales Fell.
Start/End // White Horse Inn, Scales
Distance // 4.5 miles (7km)
More info // www.lakedistrict.gov.uk

GREAT GABLE AND GLARAMARA

In good weather, Great Gable (a BG
summit) allows huge 360-degree views of
the Lakes. It takes some hard yak to get up
there and not many will run all the way, but
it's well worth it. Sourmilk Ghyll waterfall
can be an astonishing sight after heavy
rain fall. Green Gable, too, experienced
just beforehand, is a BG summit and you'll
learn the hard way how Windy Gap got
its name. It's a steep descent from Great
Gable to Styhead, but Allen Crags has
some fun ridge-running and the gradual
long descent back to Seathwaite is the stuff
of trail-running daydreams. This route may
be only 7 miles (12km), but allow a couple
of hours to complete it.
Start/End // Seathwaite
Distance // 7 miles (12km)
More info // www.lakedistrict.gov.uk

YEWBARROW, RED PIKE, SCOTT FELL, PILLAR, KIRK FELL

For something a bit more challenging and
to taste perhaps the most spectacular
section of the BG, leave remote Wasdale
Head and slog it up mighty Yewbarrow
(the sight of which has been known to end
BG attempts). Follow the ridgeline down
to More Head and climb to tag Red Pike.
If you're feeling adventurous there's an
out-and-back to craggy Steeple. Continue
round to Pillar to catch a lovely gradual
descent – which is fun running – that will
carry you to Black Sail Pass, followed by a
hearty slog up Kirk Fell and a steep, knee-
shuddering descent back to Wasdale.
Start/End // Wasdale Head
Distance // 9 miles (15km)
More info // www.lakedistrict.gov.uk

BERLIN'S GREATEST HITS

The home of the world's fastest major marathon is a city where the increased speed allows you to tour Tiergarten, follow the Wall and see everything in between.

Berlin's boulevards are famed for being flat and fast – indeed, more marathon world records have been set in this city than in any other in the world. It's a city I had long wanted to visit and, as a runner, I couldn't help but plan a quick tour that somehow involved some of the famed race stretches. It just so happens they also pass by many of Berlin's greatest sights – the Reichstag, Brandenburg Gate and, of course, the Berlin Wall – making it one of the great running cities in Europe.

The friends I was visiting for the weekend live in the central area of Schöneberg, just south of the Tiergarten, one of Europe's largest urban green spaces. The park itself teems with runners and would be the perfect place to start. From there, I could run east through the heart of the city to the Spree River which, like all great city rivers, links many great historic buildings and monuments, and provides easy cruising terrain. Other than that, my intended route was intentionally loose, with no set distance, designed to allow for spontaneous detours.

I ran the day I arrived – a hot and sunny Friday afternoon in May – as a sort of speed-tour to help me get my bearings for the rest of my visit. Once I reached the U-Bahn station of

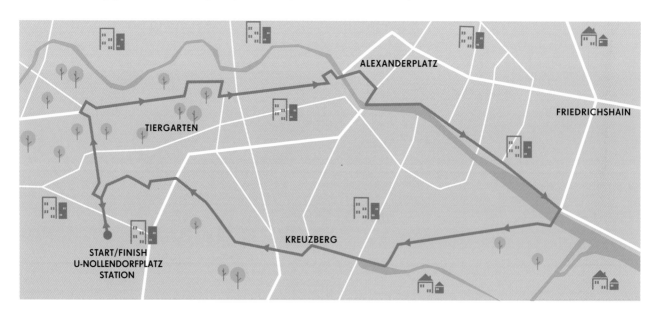

Nollendorfplatz, I headed straight for the park. I broke into my stride just as I left the street pavements and entered the garden pathways. I left Berlin's city streets behind and enjoyed warming up on the pleasant tree-covered trails of the Tiergarten. The air even chilled slightly. My first mile marker was the 220ft (67m)-tall Siegessäule, which rises from the centre of the Grosser Stern roundabout. This Victory Column – crowned by a gilded statue of the goddess Victoria to commemorate a Prussian win in the Danish-Prussian war – provides inspiration to the thousands who run past it at the start of the marathon each year.

Suitably energised, I continued into the depths of Tiergarten. I've always loved city parks like this one that make you feel as if you're exploring a countryside forest. It wasn't long before I popped out of the urban wilderness and caught my first glimpse of the Reichstag building and its sparkling glass Norman Foster-designed dome.

I turned south to Brandenburger Tor (Brandenburg Gate), another historic structure, but with more modern connotations. Since the fall of the Berlin Wall 30 years ago, this historic gate has become the focal point of celebration for a reunified Germany. Running beneath its arches actually sent a chill down my spine. I contemplated returning one day to compete in the marathon, and imagined what it must be like to cross the finish line here.

As I sped down Unter den Linden, in what was once East Berlin, I enjoyed the subtle differences in architecture. Looming on the horizon was one of the former German Democratic Republic's most impressive structures, the 1207ft (368m)-high Fernsehturm TV tower. And, after crossing the western arm of the Spree, onto Museum Island, I was taken by the copper domes of the Berliner Dom (Berlin Cathedral). It looked so marvellous that I made an indulgent loop of the adjacent Lustgarten's lawn for a better look.

After being thwarted by a construction site while heading south on the eastern arm of the Spree, I quickly weaved east onto Spandauer Straße, which put me face to face with the Rotes Rathaus (Red Town Hall), with its distinctive neo-Renaissance-style red-brick tower and history-telling terracotta frieze. While I knew that I needed to somehow find my way back to the Spree, I was enjoying not knowing where I was or where I was headed for a few moments. Zig-zagging the streets in search of a seam, my pace felt quicker.

Eventually, I hit the cobbles of Rolandufer and another scenic stretch of the Spree. But I had one important area to cover before heading home. Turning onto Holzmarktstraße, my surroundings became grittier as I passed several derelict buildings and industrial sites. Then I hit the Wall – literally. Here I was at a famed stretch of the historic landmark known as the East Side Gallery, a one-mile section that in 1990 became the canvas for 105 murals, each a monument to that incredible moment in history when East joined West.

Running along this stretch it felt as though a giant picture book's pages were being turned as I passed by. My mind was racing as

FOLLOW THE WALL

When running or walking through Berlin keep an eye out for a double row of cobbles running along the ground, with the occasional plaque reading 'Berliner Mauer 1961–1989'. This marks the original route of the entire Wall and will remain, thanks to a local government initiative to maintain its zig-zagging path, even where it veers across streets and through parking spots. It is a poignant – if subtle – reminder of how much this city has changed in just half a century.

Clockwise from top: the marathon finish at Brandenburg Gate; empty lanes along the River Spree; the Fernsehturm tower pierces the skyline. Previous page: Berlin's fast, flat streets make for great runs

© SCC Events | Camera4

© Matthias Haker | 500px

fast as my legs at that point: I pondered the public's initial reaction to Dmitri Vrubel's painting of Erich Honecker and Leonid Brezhnev passionately kissing; I marvelled at the heavy, swirly strokes of Peter Russell in *Himmel und Sucher*; and I warmed to the colourful cartoon heads laid down by Thierry Noir.

Eventually, I reached a break in the Wall, where I nipped through to find the new East Side Park, a lovingly landscaped, grassy confine on the river. It had a couple of paved paths that allowed me to add another pleasant little detour loop. Just before leaving the park, I spotted Oberbaumbrücke, a quaint red-brick bridge with two fairy-tale towers. I excitedly took a hard right and ran over to get a closer look.

Seven miles in, I had reached the U-Bahn station of Schlesisches Tor, which would be a perfect spot to call it quits and catch a lift home. But I was feeling energised from the easy running so I chose instead to carry on west towards the Landwehr Canal. After a few more miles of residential streets and urban boulevards, I hit the canal and its leafy respite. By the time I had returned to the Nollendorfplatz U Bahn station, I had run nearly 12 miles (19km).

Being able to cover so much ground had a slightly different result than expected. I was amazed at how many of the big landmarks I was able to see in such a short time. But more memorable were all the things in-between the major sights – the things I wasn't expecting to see, the neighbourhoods that weren't on my route and the vantage points that put well-known sights in a different perspective. **MP**

ORIENTATION

Start/End // U-Nollendorfplatz station, Schöneberg

Distance // 12 miles (19km)

Getting there // Berlin's public transport system (U-Bahn, S-Bahn, buses and trams) is extensive and efficient, extending all the way to the airport.

When to go // May, June, September and October are warm and dry. July and August are warmer but wetter.

Where to stay // Das Stue (www.das-stue.com) is a boutique hotel set in a 1930s Danish diplomatic outpost. The Tiergarten is its front yard, and the hotel's pool, sauna and spa are perfect for soothing sore legs.

More info // www.visitberlin.de/en

Things to know // Even though it's fun to get lost, Berlin is big – carry a map or smartphone to keep you on track, and money to pay for public transport in case you need it.

MORE LIKE THIS
CITY CENTRE SIGHTSEEING

LONDON, UK

The River Thames makes for a great guide to help you get the best of London. It flows through the heart of the city and past some of its most famous landmarks. And its lesser-known canals travel through backwaters so peaceful it's hard to believe they are part of the capital. An ambitious 18-mile (29km) route takes in both, along with four beautiful Royal Parks. The start is Big Ben, before continuing east along the Thames' north bank, with views of St Paul's, the Shard, Tate Modern and Tower Bridge. At Limehouse Basin, turn left to follow the atmospheric Regent's Canal north and eventually west. Not long after skirting Regent's Park, the canal-side path arrives at Little Venice. From here, it's south on roadside pavements to Hyde Park and a pleasant run along the edge of the Serpentine. The final stretch takes in Green Park, St James's Park and Horse Guards Parade, from where Big Ben is a short sprint away.
Start/End // Big Ben
Distance // 18 miles (29km)

PARIS, FRANCE

Starting atop the Jardin des Plantes, this 5.5-mile (9km) route cuts through the historic botanical gardens before popping out onto the Left Bank of the Seine, with its lamp-lit bridges, lined with striking buildings of cream-coloured Lutetian limestone. From here a cobbled riverside path heads west past the Cathédrale Notre-Dame de Paris and Île de la Cité. Then, elegant pedestrian bridges of Pont des Arts and Passerelle Léopold-Sédar-Senghor allow a detour to the Right Bank and back for a look at the Louvre and its glass pyramids. Continuing round a bend in the Seine, the path runs beneath the shadow of the Eiffel Tower before allowing you to cross the river again on Pont d'Iéna. From there it's an uphill climb through Jardins du Trocadéro to the finish line at the Arc de Triomphe.
Start // Jardin des Plantes
End // Arc de Triomphe
Distance // 5.5 miles (9km)

MELBOURNE, AUSTRALIA

Melbourne's tranquil Yarra River twists and turns its way past the city's central business district and out through sections of quiet forested parkland. This 9-mile (15km) route starts at the architectural wonder of Webb Bridge on the north side of the river, then follows the water beneath skyscrapers, along the promenades of South Wharf, Yarra and Southbank, before hitting the Main Yarra Trail. This tree-lined path skirts the Royal Botanic Gardens and then circuitously weaves past Herring Island, Como Park North and Winifred Crescent Reserve. After crossing MacRobertson Bridge, the route passes through Loy's Paddock Reserve then heads back towards the city centre along the Main Yarra Trail, parts of which float on the river itself. Once back in the CBD, it follows Flinders Walk to Princes Bridge and the finish line at Flinders Street Station.
Start // Webb Bridge
End // Flinders Street Station
Distance // 9 miles (15km)

Clockwise from top: London's Tower Bridge spans the River Thames; Melbourne's Royal Exhibition building; the Eiffel Tower in Paris

THE LONDON MARATHON

One day a year, Londoners crack a smile and break out in spontaneous joy to cheer on runners during the city's beloved annual race.

I am a Londoner, born and bred. But I have a confession: I've never watched the London Marathon. I've seen some TV coverage, but I've never taken to the streets to witness first-hand that malcoordinated conga line of runners passing by in a blur of high fives and technicolour charity vests. So when I found myself on the startline to run it in 2014, I had no idea what to expect.

Mo Farah was debuting, so I thought perhaps that would draw a few running fans. I knew the finish outside Buckingham Palace would be a little rowdy. But the 26.2 miles before that? Meh. It was a balmy spring Sunday – surely Londoners would rather be picnicking in parks, drinking in pub gardens, or watching football. I was wrong. Very wrong.

Turns out, London is a city transformed on marathon day. The near-professional level of cynicism, lack of eye contact and effective ban on talking to strangers disappears. On the crowded train towards the start in Greenwich, I scanned the carriage for other runners. They were everywhere. I nervously chatted with a man who, like me, had a spiderweb of 'KT tape' on his leg. Finding the start is a simple matter of letting yourself get carried by the stream of runners flocking towards the three large coloured blimps that float above Greenwich Park and Blackheath.

After collecting under the arch, we were underway. The first few miles were in fact eerily quiet, as we navigated the sleepy streets of south-east London. All I could hear was the thud-thud-thud of thousands of trainers hitting tarmac. Eventually, a man running beside me introduced himself – to anyone who would listen, really —and began detailing his race plans, his hopes and dreams. His name was Neil. A few runners chatted back, but most of us were still 'Londoners' at this point, having not quite covered enough ground for that race-day transformation.

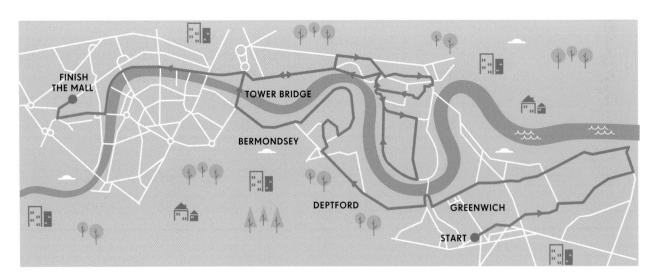

After a loop out to Woolwich Arsenal and back to Greenwich again we rounded a corner to face the most incongruous sight: the 150-year-old Cutty Sark clipper, one of London's most famous tourist sights. It's a ship straight out of a film set, all wooden elegance, masts and bowsprit. I wasn't quite sure why I was so taken aback but I found myself wondering aloud: 'Is that really there the other 364 days of the year?'

Of course, London is a city rich in history and the marathon tours the whole lot. Bermondsey is in the Domesday Book, Rotherhithe was a place of Elizabethan dockyards, and Brunel's Thames Tunnel was the very first underwater passage in the world.

By mile 10, the runners had gone a bit quiet, but the crowd was now revving up. Many were shouting Neil's name, which made me wonder if I should have put my name on my vest, too. Tower Bridge is clearly the beginning of something entirely different. It's a gauntlet of screaming spectators, cameras and marshals, all within touching distance. It's so overwhelming I was almost relieved to be spat out the other side, and to the halfway point.

This also signals the start of the marathon that I remember. At what's known as 'the highway', running clubs are gathered – including my own – to wave club banners and flags, to cheer on their own and boost morale. My entire club screamed my name and, of course, I waved back like a lunatic. Seeing them was like taking an energy shot, felt for at least the next half-mile. This must

be what it's like to be Neil all the time, I thought.

I'd been warned that Canary Wharf is a part of the course that sucks you in but is reluctant to spit you out again. Even your GPS watch goes a little haywire, they say. The crowds, however, were so full and deep, and enthusiastic, that I lost myself in the atmosphere. I can only remember a blur of reflected sunlight and mirrored glass. I was still alongside Neil at this point, though we had developed a sibling-like love-hate relationship. I appreciated the odd, breathless, 'Great work!' and 'Stay with me!', but I was also beginning to dread hearing his name being shouted from the sidelines.

By mile 24, I would have given a kidney to get away from Neil – his name now just a peculiar torturous sound. At Birdcage Walk, there was just half a mile to go. More importantly, I knew my kids were on the sidelines here. This last stretch was an intensely emotional experience. My brain couldn't comprehend the cheers. It was a wall of sound, willing us to the finish line. I recognised the voice of a club mate: 'Go Kate!' And yes, I still had Neil by my side.

We rounded the corner towards the finish. I could see Buckingham Palace and the beautiful Tudor bricks of St James's Palace. Then I was over the line. I was handed a goodie bag, food, water and, of course, a medal. I was on empty but I did have one solitary thought running through my mind: 'I'm doing that again. My GOD, but I'm doing that again.'

That, and 'Where's Neil? How is Neil?' **KC**

WACKY WORLD RECORDS

The London Marathon is one of the biggest fundraising events in the world, and competing in fancy dress has become an integral part of that. Each year sees a team of Guinness World Record adjudicators on the course, checking costumes and verifying records, including the first time a pencil, a poo emoji, Paddington Bear and a knight in full armour all completed the race.

From left: London comes alive on marathon day; runners pass Big Ben; the Tower of London on the River Thames. Previous page: London long-distance legend Mo Farah

ORIENTATION

Start // Greenwich or Blackheath, London
End // The Mall, London
Distance // 26.2 miles
Getting there // London's roads are closed for the race so don't even try to drive. The nearest Tube stations are Blackheath, Maze Hill or Greenwich, depending on which colour start you are (blue, red or green). Each is about a 20-minute walk from the start.
Where to stay // There's a lot of new accommodation around King's Cross and it's a very well-connected base.
More info // www.virginmoneylondonmarathon.com
Things to know // London Marathon runs a ballot system, but you need to be quick, because it's only open for a few days after the previous year's race. It's also very oversubscribed.

Opposite: Berlin's Spree River

MORE LIKE THIS
MAJOR EURO-MARATHONS

BERLIN MARATHON, GERMANY

Berlin has one of the fastest courses in the world, which is why the last six men's marathon world records have been set on the wide, pancake-flat streets of the German capital. Like London, it is one of the 'big six' that make up the World Major Marathons series, with around 40,000 runners pounding those *straßes*. The flat course makes it perfect for both PB-chasers and first-timers. The race starts in Tiergarten and winds through central Mitte before heading out to the leafy suburbs and back. The highlight for many is running under the Brandenberg Gate.

Start // Tiergarten park
End // Brandenburg Gate
Distance // 26.2 miles (42km)
More info // www.bmw-berlin-marathon.com

AMSTERDAM MARATHON, NETHERLANDS

The Amsterdam course starts at the Olympic Stadium (built for the 1928 games), heads towards town, then takes you on a long 'out-and-back' along the Amstel River. It's a flat and fast course, with a smaller field than London or Berlin, though there's still plenty of support from local residents and musical bands en route. There's also a 13-mile (21km) half marathon and a 5-mile (8km) option, as well as a kids' fun run. And Amsterdam's famous apple pie surely makes the perfect recovery food.

Start/End // Olympic Stadium
Distance // 26.2 miles (42km)
More info // www.tcsamsterdam marathon.nl

PRAGUE MARATHON, CZECH REPUBLIC

Flat, fast and exceptionally beautiful, the Prague Marathon is also an IAAF Gold Label event, which means it's extremely well organised. In fact, all seven of the races put on by the RunCzech organisation get this label, more than any other country in the world. After carb-loading on dumplings the day before, runners gather for the start in the stunning cobbled Old Town Square, Staroměstské náměstí. Breaking out from the narrow streets, the race crosses the famous Charles Bridge to the sound of traditional Czech music. Like the city itself, the course hugs the Vlatava River, crossing at various points before finally ending back in the Old Town Square.

Start/End // Staroměstské náměstí
Distance // 26.2 miles (42km)
More info // www.runczech.com

A QUIET RUN
IN ROME

*Connect with ancient history by heading out into
the stillness of a car-free dawn in Italy's capital.*

It's dawn and the streets of Rome are silent and still. In other words, the city is unrecognisable. The pavements are empty, the cafes are closed and the cascading ruins, lit bright against the ink-blue sky, stand in silence. It's my time to run.

In Rome, significant sights have not been quarantined with vast parks built around them, they have not been put onto a high shelf for study from afar. The sights *are* the city, in your face and part of the everyday landscape. Thus, even iconic Roman features such as Vespas and crowded outdoor gelato cafes can sometimes kill the fantasy.

At dawn, it's easy to imagine the triumphs and travails brought forward by the longest-lasting empire in our history, a religion that would transform men and nations, and the renaissance that came to redefine art and culture as we know it today. We can of course also thank the Romans for some of those modern-day treasures such as bucatini all'amatriciana and the three-hour lunch, but I'll leave those things for after my workout.

I often like to start my runs with a heart-pounding climb, and so after setting off from my cosy hotel in the Aventino district, I begin with an ascent of the cobblestoned side streets of Aventino Hill. At the top, the perfectly manicured Giardino degli Aranci park offers up great views across the sleeping city. From this vantage point, at this time of day, the city feels pure, clean, closer to its romantic roots. Modernity and chaos are cloaked in darkness. All that remains is history.

As I look across the city, there is something missing, of course: no honking Fiats or motorinos, no crowds waiting to take a picture with a 'real-life' gladiator in front of the Colosseum, no vendors, no clogged pavement cafes. It's only as the rest of the city is

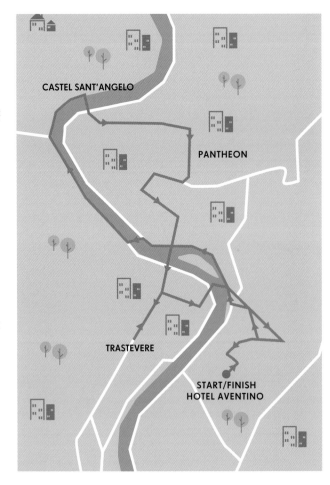

still dreaming that I myself daydream about Romulus and Remus abandoned on the shoreline of the Tiber that sits below me. I imagine Roman ships delivering grain across the empire and armies triumphantly returning with vast stashes of looted gold.

Once I reach Giardino degli Aranci park, my legs are warm and my run still feels playful. Down I go at breakneck pace as I rocket past sleeping cops and a doting couple getting in their last kisses before they have to sneak back into their parents' houses, before the sun breaks the horizon. I careen down the hill with the abandon of a four-year-old and finally find my way to the Tiber River.

There are dozens of bridges across the Tiber – both ancient and modern – as it snakes its way through Rome. I like to make it a point to cross the river at least once during my journey, sometimes a few times. Running in Rome any time of day can be challenging with all its stops and starts, but there's a nice trail down along the Tiber that provides an escape. I descend to get in a few miles of cruising time, passing the Ponte Sisto bridge, with its circular oculus, the sort of architecture so unique to this empire.

As I pad along the river in silence, history is coming to life. I see the corners of Vatican City and the circular fortress of Castel Sant'Angelo. One of my favourite things to do is get over to the

> "In Circus Maximus I push as hard as I can, imagining the thundering chariots being pulled by sinewy thoroughbreds"

other side of the river to explore the twisted narrow streets that carve up the heart of central Rome. So I cross the Sant'Angelo bridge and head down into the maze to get lost amid the *piazze* and palaces that are normally far too packed to even walk through, let alone gallop.

Eventually, I always seem to end up at the Pantheon, as if by gravitational pull. It certainly is massive and has a cosmic power, dating back to 118 AD. Inside is the tomb of the Renaissance master Raphael. I slow down here to take a breath below the oculus, and to contemplate the genius behind its design and construction. As I catch my breath, the sun is just breaking the horizon and I feel as though I've come here to worship at the feet of the great Roman gods. I imagine Mercury himself lifting me up and delivering me to the end of my journey.

Alas, I'm on my own to finish the run. I head down through

IMPORTANT FORT

Near the Vatican is the Castel Sant'Angelo, former mausoleum of Hadrian and once the tallest building in Rome. Inside are weapons used to protect the castle back in the day. A 13th-century passageway connects the castle to the Vatican. Many a pope has taken refuge here, including Pope Clemente VI, who hid here in the 1527 Sack of Rome.

Clockwise from left: Circus Maximus marks the end of the run; runners on marathon day; you'll spot the Basilica di Santa Sabina on route. Previous page: morning calm at the Colosseum

more neighbourhoods that are just waking up now. I make my way to Campo de' Fiori, where a few vendors are setting up. Without the tourists the piazza feels vast, more grand, and even more enchanting. Then I cross the Tiber once again, aiming for Trastevere. Passing the various ristorantes and trattorias, it's hard not to begin thinking about lunch, as I stare up from narrow alleyways at the hanging gardens.

The easy way home from here is back up and over the Aventino Hill, where a warm shower and breakfast cornetto await. Instead, I decide to end my run with a little foot race. I cross the Tiber one more time and head to the Circus Maximus, where, in ancient times, chariot races were held. I amp up my pace and push as hard as I can across the vast arena, imagining roaring crowds and thundering wagons being pulled by sinewy thoroughbreds. Here, I deplete every last ounce of energy I have left before walking back to Aventino.

As I walk back, I feel inspired to explore even more, though I am spent. The truth is, Rome at any time of day has a powerful aura, dripping with history. But to experience it devoid of its usual sights and sounds, what is normally just a backdrop comes alive and creates a canvas for your imagination to run wild. **GB**

ORIENTATION

Start // Hotel Aventino
End // Castel Sant'Angelo
Distance // 6.2 miles (10km)
Getting there // The start of this run is near Rome metro station Circo Massimo.
When to go // Summers are hot, but running is pleasant all year round.
Where to stay // Aventino has wonderful hotels, including the Aventino Hotel and Hotel San Anselmo. Staying across the way in Trastevere is also quite nice.
More info // www.lonelyplanet.com/italy/rome
Things to know // They often clean the streets with water at night, so some areas can be slick at dawn. Generally, the streets of Rome are safe at dawn, but remain aware during this less crowded time.

Opposite: St Mark's Square kicks off
a waterfront run in Venice

MORE LIKE THIS
ROMANTIC CITY RUNS

VENICE, ITALY

Running in Venice is no easy feat. But if you get up early enough to beat the crowds, a trot from St Mark's Square along the Riva degli Schiavoni waterfront to the gardens at the Giardini Pubblici is a fantastic way to start your day. The nexus and plexus of Venice, St Mark's Square is crowned by its gorgeous eponymous cathedral. Though you can't go in wearing running duds, check out the outside mosaics before you set off. From there, head towards the waterfront, past the gothic-style Palazzo Ducale and onto the Riva degli Schiavoni waterfront walkway. Here's where you can pick up some speed, heading east past the 18th-century Church of Pietà and several historic buildings and scenic bridges before you arrive at the Giardini Pubblici. The cruise around the park is a fantastic way to start your day, before heading back for a warm cornetto and cappuccino near St Mark's Square.
Start // St Mark's Square
End // Giardini Pubblici (and back)
Distance // 2.5 miles (4km)

MADRID, SPAIN

With its grand architecture, tapas tavernas, abundant sunshine and a love of life, Madrid has amazing runs right in its historic downtown. Start at the Prado Museum and continue along the Paseo del Prado – the eternally pulsating main vein of life, culture and politics for the Spanish capital. From there, check out the fantastic Neptuno, Apolo and Cibeles fountains, before leaving the Prado to head to the vast system of paths, gardens and monumental architecture found in the Parque de El Retiro. Don't miss the Palacio de Cristal, a gorgeous metal and glass structure that houses occasional art exhibitions.
Start/End // Prado Museum
Distance // 3.7 miles (6km)

MUNICH, GERMANY

Much like Paris' Seine and Rome's Tiber, Munich's Isar River provides the perfect handrail for a tour of Germany's most beautiful city. A popular out-and-back starts on the east side of Max-Joseph-Brücke and heads south, through many of the city's impressive green spaces. Along the way you'll pass the golden angel statue *Friedensengel*, the parliament building and, finally, the zoo at the southernmost tip of the route. But you can also make short detours along the way to see Vienna Square and Mariahilfplatz, with its impressive church. Unfortunately, you'll have to cross the river to access the busier city centre and its stunning St Peter's Church – and the most famous beer gardens – but the views from this side of the river highlight just how picturesque the Bavarian capital is.
Start/End // Max-Joseph-Brücke
Distance // 6.2 miles (10km)

DUBLIN'S WILD AND WINDSWEPT PENINSULA

A little slice of wilderness in Ireland's capital, Howth Head's coastal cliffs and sweeping views offer urban trail runners an easy escape.

Framing the northern side of Dublin Bay, rocky Howth Head has featured prominently in Irish folklore, poetry and literature since ancient times. It's the site of a 5000-year-old grave thought to be a portal to another world; it was a landing point for Viking marauders; and the place where Leopold Bloom proposed to Molly in James Joyce's *Ulysses*. The rugged terrain, steep cliffs and sense of isolation give it an undeniable allure for runners looking to get off road without having to travel miles beyond the city.

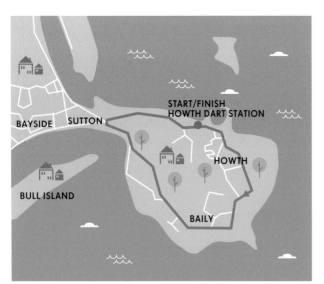

Today, Howth is also one of the most sought-after addresses in Dublin, home to many of the city's rich and famous. Imposing houses fan out from a quaint little village with a host of colourful restaurants and lively pubs, a farmers' market and an upmarket fishmonger. Its residents, however, rigorously protect its untouched headland and enough of the wilderness remains to make it a glorious retreat from the city.

Just hop on the DART train anywhere in central Dublin and head north – in 25 minutes you'll be running out of the station gate and following the sounds of wires clinking against masts in Howth's little marina. Minutes later you'll be heading up the road by the east pier and straight out of town towards the edge of Ireland.

One weekend morning it was early enough that I had the trail largely to myself. A typical loop is just over 6 miles (10km) of almost deserted paths weaving along cliff tops, dipping into hollows and pulling up over blind peaks that lead to uninterrupted views of the sea.

Before me lay an undulating ribbon of freedom, most of it off road, with no major ascents – it was enough of a challenge to keep my mind and body fully engaged on the rolling terrain. But it's the sense of isolation that I love most here. Dún Laoghaire and Killiney on the south side of the city are also top Dublin runs, often crowded with weekend warriors but still very urban. Howth is a surprise and it makes the city-based trail-runner's heart soar.

I ran up the hill past the little beach at Balscadden Bay, where above me was a sturdy Martello Tower, one of many built in the 19th century to defend against invasion by France. I didn't

stop to look; there are far grander sights ahead. Soon the road narrowed, the trees closed in and I left the town behind. A break in the foliage revealed Ireland's Eye, a small island just off shore. On a clear day I've even had a view all the way to the Mourne Mountains in County Down.

On this day, though, dark clouds gathered ominously. It was one of those theatrical skies where the sun picks out every detail on the island but the backdrop is a deep, slate grey. My legs were warming up and despite the gentle incline my pace increased in anticipation of the glories ahead. I was keen to swap tarmac for rutted path and a little more of a challenge.

I continued on past Balscadden House, the childhood home of WB Yeats, where the road gently ascends to Kilrock car park and a gravel path leads up onto the headland proper. As if on cue, the clouds parted and the grey morning became gloriously sunny.

I hopped, skipped and leapt over roots and ruts in the trail, jumped over wayward brambles and launched myself into the landscape. It's my favourite section of the run: the big skies and sweeping views, the city far behind me. I selfishly bided my time while another lone runner up ahead made their way round a bend and out of sight.

This is a run I prefer to do alone, even though I was not entirely alone – birds screeched and squalled, the wind rustled in the gorse, seals basked on rocks as waves crashed. I was about 164ft (50m) above the sea now with steep cliffs dropping into the glittering water while gulls, guillemots and razorbills flittered about.

Inland, the headland rises sharply to a rocky peak, its slopes swathed in yellow gorse, purple heather and lush bracken. I headed on, making my way along the rutted, bumpy track over rocks and roughly hewn steps, concentrating on the view as much as the trail will allow. The trail undulates gently but the prospect of a lengthy fall if you stray too far from the path keeps the mind alert with every footfall.

Eventually I reached a point where all that was in front of me was open sea. I paused to take it in and, of course, that's when the heavens opened. They always do here – it's not a matter of if, but when. But I enjoyed it. Bad weather always makes things feel like so much more of an adventure. The rain dripped down my face. I blew out of my mouth to get the drops off the end of my nose, but I felt invincible as I picked my way along the path.

Then, as quickly as the rain came down, it stopped; the sun was out, the smell of heather and gorse and sea hung in the air. Here, I got my first view of Wicklow on the far side of Dublin Bay, a concertina of peaks dipping into the sea beyond.

Ahead, the more than 200-year-old Baily Lighthouse appeared on a nose of rock jutting out into the sea. Here, the trail changes again, the vegetation thickens and tames, trees begin to overshadow the path, pebbly beaches lie in little coves and garden fences ebb and flow.

I scrabbled over rocks and up some steps as the city came into view. Strung out along the bay and set against the backdrop

IRISH PIRATE LORE

Legendary pirate queen Gráinne Mhaol (Grace O'Malley) controlled the west coast of Ireland in the late 16th century. She famously met with Queen Elizabeth in London and then stopped to rest at Howth Castle on her return, but found the gates closed. Furious, she kidnapped Lord Howth's son and said she would only return him if the castle gates were left open and an extra place was set for dinner; it's a tradition that continues today.

Clockwise from top: sea thrift flowers on Howth Head; coastal paths make for great running; the bucolic headland is less than half an hour from Dublin. Previous page: Howth Head's Old Baily Lighthouse at land's end

"Howth residents rigorously protect its headland and enough wilderness remains to make a glorious retreat from the city"

© Jon Sparks / Alamy Stock Photo

© Max Rooney

of the Wicklow Mountains, Dublin looked like something from a glossy tourist brochure. It was beautiful, though I liked how far away it felt. I was also glad to leave it behind, turn inland and get out of the wind.

Purple arrows mark the route here as the trail weaves between high walls of gorse, creeping steadily upwards. As I climbed out of the trees I was treated to yet another panoramic view of the capital. I paused for breath, my smugness replaced by a quiet sense of euphoria.

This is why I run, I thought to myself. It's not just that sense of elation from considered effort; it's that no matter how bad the weather or how lazy I feel, I've yet to ever regret a run here. Finally, I picked my way through the greens, feeling very out of place before emerging onto the wonderfully named Bog of Frogs.

Despite the sense of elation, my legs were starting to smart and my breathing had become heavy. I was paying the price for my over confidence on the lower section of the hill. But I was still climbing, and eventually emerged onto high gorse and heather moorland just beneath Black Linn, at 560ft (171m), the headland's highest point.

From here, I started my descent, gathering pace as the hill yielded to my feet, my body making a thousand minor adjustments with every step. Then, like that, I unceremoniously popped out in a nondescript housing estate and onto the roads that would carry me downhill back to the station in Howth, and back to reality. **EO**

ORIENTATION

Start/End // Howth DART station
Distance // 7.4 miles (12km)
Getting there // DART to Howth from Dublin city centre.
When to go // Early morning and late evening are best. Weekend afternoons can be busy with walkers and the trail is narrow so it's frustrating trying to get past.
Where to stay // Stay anywhere in the centre of Dublin and you can easily hop on the DART out to Howth.
More info // www.irishtrails.ie
Things to know // Run in a clockwise direction for the best views. If you're stuck for time, peel off early onto the challenging Black Linn Loop that leads up over the summit and back to the village. If you've got more time, continue along the coast path rather than turning inland once you see the city. You'll arrive in affluent Sutton and can hop on the DART back into town from there.

MORE LIKE THIS
OFF-ROAD RUNS IN IRELAND

CLIFFS OF MOHER COASTAL TRAIL, CO CLARE

Ireland's most dramatic cliffs drop more than 1650ft (200m) into the Atlantic on the west coast of Co Clare, in a mesmerising series of headlands carved out of dark limestone. Understandably, they attract hordes of visitors. While a trip to the main viewing point is marred by tour buses and crowds, a run along the coastal trail from Liscannor to Doolin provides all the glorious isolation you could wish for. The trail winds along the cliff tops through fields of livestock, offering views of the glittering expanse of Galway Bay framed by cliffs, rock arches and sea stacks. Puffins, kittiwakes and fulmars nest here and, if you're lucky, you may see whale sharks in the inky depths below. There's no barrier so don't stray too close to the edge but do leave time for a visit to Doolin's legendary pubs, where live traditional music is almost guaranteed.
Start // Liscannor, Co Clare
End // Doolin, Co Clare
Distance // 12 miles (20km)
More info // www.cliffsofmoher.ie

OLD KENMARE RD, KILLARNEY NATIONAL PARK, KERRY, CO KERRY

As part of the longer Kerry Way, the Old Kenmare Rd is a well-marked track through moss-draped oak woods, open moorland and mountain uplands. It meanders through Ireland's most popular national park but sits far from the crowds that throng Killarney and its scenic slate-grey lakes. Starting at the head of gushing Torc Waterfall, you'll keep a steady ascent through lush and twisted woods as you follow the course of the Owengarriff River between Torc and Mangerton Mountains. With views of Ireland's highest peak, Carrantuohil (3408ft; 1039m) in the Macgillycuddy's Reeks, deep russet hillsides and the scenic lakelands, you'll cross open bog on raised boardwalks before reaching Eskanamucky Glen and the route's highest point at Windy Gap.
Start // Upper Car Park, Torc, Co Kerry
End // Kenmare, Co Kerry
Distance // 10 miles (16km)
More Info // www.killarneyguide.ie/old-kenmare-road

PORTBALLINTRAE CAUSEWAY LOOP

Not all runs take in a Unesco World Heritage Site. This short outing along Antrim's Causeway Coast takes you along windswept beaches and dunes to the otherworldly Giant's Causeway, an expanse of hexagonal stone columns that blanket the coast here. This Causeway is a tourist honeypot, but take to the coastal path and run early or late in the day and you may just get the place to yourself. The route starts on the beach in workaday Portballintrae, crossing the Bush River (which feeds the rill at the Bushmills Distillery just upstream) before you get to the soft sands of Bushfoot Strand. Then follow a cliff-top path to the Giant's Causeway, dropping down to sea level as you run between the outcrops of weirdly regular rock. Bear right by 'The Organ' and up the steep steps of the Shepherds Path to loop back towards Portballintrae, following the coastal railway and dunes.
Start/End // Beach Rd, Portballintrae, Co Antrim
Distance // 5.5 miles (9km)
More info // www.walkni.com

*Clockwise from top: County Clare's
Cliffs of Moher; a waterfall in
Killarney National Park; the ruins of
Dunluce Castle near Portballintrae*

THE ATHENS MARATHON

Racing along the original epic route from Marathon to Athens gives a sense of what distance running was all about long before aid stations and bib numbers.

egend has it, back around 490 BC, a Greek soldier named Pheidippides ran about 25 miles, from the town of Marathon to Athens, to inform top brass that the Greek military had heroically defeated the vastly larger Persian army. He then dropped dead from exhaustion. As I myself awaited the start of the Authentic Athens Marathon a few years ago – mingling, hydrating and stretching among the 10,000 other runners – I'm sure I wasn't the only one contemplating how this impressive act of athleticism and heroism inspired the very race we were about to run, as well as all modern marathons around the world.

The route of the first modern-day Olympic marathon in Greece in 1896 is said to be a direct historical nod towards Pheidippides' run centuries earlier (fittingly, the very first gold-medal winner of the modern Olympic event, Spyridon Louis, was a Greek national). Of course, much has changed in this city over the past few thousand years – especially in the past few decades – but with ancient monuments everywhere you turn, it's still easy to imagine the route as it looked when Pheidippides himself ran it.

In high school I was not only an active mid-distance runner, but I had also been fascinated by Pheidippides' story ever since Mr Hennessy's history class. When I finally decided that I wanted to do a marathon before my 30th birthday, I knew this was the race for me. I enlisted my close friend, Tom, to join me. He had also done athletics in school and sat right beside me in Mr Hennessy's history class.

As the sun rose over the hills surrounding Marathon, I sat on the dry grass beneath a stadium which, while not particularly impressive in an aesthetic sense, had a strong aura of history, made even more

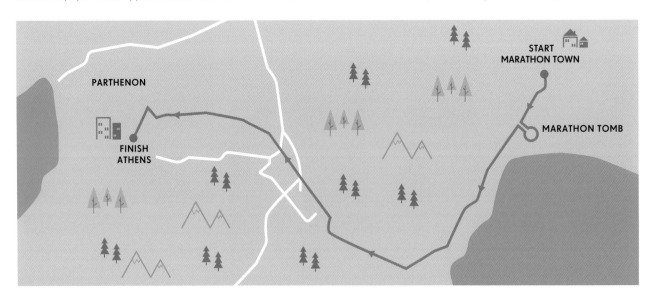

dramatic by its flickering flame cauldron. The story of Pheidippides loomed large here as I tried to control my nerves. I became only slightly less terrified when I noticed several runners were dressed up in faux bronze breastplates and Hellenistic-style armour.

Packed in like sardines on the startline, Tom and I both smiled broadly as 'Zorba's Dance' began blaring over the loudspeakers. The ancient and the modern collided awkwardly as we awaited the starting signal.

The Athens Authentic Marathon began with a long section along Marathonos Ave, before following mostly main roads almost all the way to the heart of the capital. Around the first water stop in Nea Makri, several Greek grandmothers held out olive branches, and clapped us on with warm encouragement, cheering, 'Bravo! Bravo!'

Though there are no steep hills on this course, it does climb gradually for a full 13 miles (21km), beginning just after the 6-mile (9.5km) mark. During the slog, I focused on finding a rhythm. Except for the cypress trees, the dusty whitewashed landscape felt a lot like that of my home state of Victoria, Australia. Further along, we entered more urban stretches with small roadside churches, gritty shopfronts, half-built apartment blocks, a few historical statues and the occasional red poppy. It certainly wasn't the Greece you see on postcards, but rather the Greece that hard-working locals see every day.

At the halfway mark I was feeling surprisingly good. I noticed

"Greek grandmothers held out olive branches and clapped us on with warm encouragement, cheering, 'Bravo! Bravo!'"

a runner to my right, who was either an Orthodox priest or just dressed as one. Decked in traditional black garb and matching black trainers, he had a few decades on me and, yet, was easily keeping pace. Heavily bearded – and beaded – the priest got a huge cheer every time he ran past a crowd.

But then, as genuine lactic fatigue began to set in, Tom and I passed a table beneath some pine trees, full of carefully laid out chopped banana. It doesn't sound like much but after hurriedly mushing it into my mouth, I once again felt as though Heracles, the god of strength, was pushing me along. I began to dial up my pace along the built-up Mesogeion Ave, which led us right into the heart of Ancient Attica – the cradle of Western civilisation. My confidence grew as I realised I had busted through that horrifying stage known as 'the wall'.

Near the end, every single muscle in my body began to tighten. But the spectators were now thick and vocal as I ran past honey-hued urban sprawl leading straight up to the looming Acropolis, high on the horizon. But as soon as I could see the Panathenaic

ORIGIN STORY

Though the Panathenaic Stadium may be the original home of the 'modern-day' Olympics, the original Olympics (776 BC) is on the Peloponnese peninsula, at the ancient site of Olympia. There were a number of historical buildings here, most famously the Temple of Zeus. The Olympic flame is still lit here, and it's where the official torch relay begins.

From left: glory in Greece; the finish line at Panathenaic Stadium; those who make it pick up a medal. Previous page: Lykavittos Hill over Athens

Stadium, my energy reserves plummeted and I ran the last downhill stretch near the ritzy Hrodou Attikou St grimacing with pain and muttering profanities under my breath.

Thankfully, as I got closer, I couldn't help but think of Pheidippides once again, shouting 'Victory!' to his comrades as he arrived in central Athens. Built entirely of marble in 566 BC, the ancient arena is open at one end, making it feel like the final stretch of a racecourse (which it was back in 330 BC). Hence, even before you hit the final straight you can see others passing under the finish line arch, arms raised in glory. It gave me just the encouragement I needed for the final push. Inspired by both past and present, I thought about Pheidippides, but also the capacity all humans have to force themselves to their very limits.

I'd love to say that as I took my final strides across the finish line, I, too, cut the figure of a running warrior. But the truth is I was just an exhausted, sweaty mess. Jelly-legged, I waited in the recovery area, stretching and gulping water as if I'd just been rescued from the Sahara. Tom finished looking just as exhausted as I felt.

Despite having zero energy left, it was impossible not to be overwhelmed by the experience of having just retraced ancient running history. Hobbling away from the stadium, we took a photo for posterity, with the magnificent Parthenon in the background. We then turned our attention to something far more important: debating where we would stuff our faces with lamb souvlakis. **SN**

ORIENTATION

Start // Marathon
End // Athens
Distance // 26.2 miles (42km)
Getting there // The Authentic Athens Marathon event provides a bus to the start from various parts of the city.
When to go // November.
Where to stay // Staying in or near central Monastiraki is convenient and offers a little buzz for when you want to celebrate after the race.
More info // www.athensauthenticmarathon.gr
Things to know // If your schedule permits, a great place for a mini-trip from Athens to wind down after the race is the island of Hydra (where there are no cars). A dip in the ocean could be just what your body needs. Be sure to check ferry times.

*From top: the 100km Pharaonic Race
outside Cairo; the finish line at the
Kosice Peace Marathon in Slovakia*

MORE LIKE THIS
HISTORIC RACES

THE CARTHAGE RACE, TUNISIA

After nearly a decade of stymied tourism due to safety concerns, now is the time to return to Tunisia, especially if you're into historical ruins without the crowds. Imbued with Phoenician heritage, this February marathon starts in Carthage at the Roman amphitheatre, and loops through both Sidi Bou Said (a blue and white town in northern Tunisia not far from the capital) and La Marsa (a coastal spot, popular with affluent Tunisians for holidaying). The course is relatively flat, hence perhaps a good option if aiming for a PB. The event also offers a half-marathon distance and a 6-mile (9.5km) route, if you don't feel like committing to the full 26.2 miles.
Start/End // **Amphithéâtre de Carthage, Carthage**
Distance // **26.2 miles (42km)**
More info // **www.the-carthage-race. com**

100KM PHARAONIC RACE, EGYPT

Inspired by a race between a pack of soldiers that took place in the time of an Egyptian king around 690–660 BC, the 62-mile (100km) Pharaonic Race happens in November, a few months before the official Egyptian Marathon. An ultra distance like this isn't for the faint-hearted. The race starts about two hours' drive outside of Cairo at the Hawara Pyramid, tracing around various other pyramids before finishing in the ancient burial ground of Saqqara. The route is a mixture of road and desert, with unpaved sections along the way.
Start // **Hawara Pyramid, Al Fayoum**
End // **Pyramid of Djoser, Saqqara**
Distance // **62 miles (100km)**
More info // **www.egyptian marathon.com**

KOŠICE MARATHON, SLOVAKIA

This race takes places in Slovakia's 'second city' and is one of the oldest marathons in Europe, dating back to the 1920s. The first time it was ever held only eight runners took part, but nowadays it's a popular event and regarded as one of the fastest marathon routes in the world due to its flat roads. Also known as the International Peace Marathon, the course snakes through various examples of gothic and Soviet architecture. These days, the event aims to raise money for Slovakian children living with cancer.
Start/End // **Hlavná Street, Košice**
Distance // **26.2 miles (42km)**
More info // **www.kosicemarathon.com**

ARRANCABIRRA

The Alps are home to some of the most serious trail runs in the world. Once a year, thousands take them less seriously, running this boozy 18k in the silliest costumes they can find.

The dramatic Alpine landscapes of Courmayeur, in the Aosta Valley on the Italian side of Mt Blanc, is an area well-known to skiers and trail runners. As an avid ultrarunner I had always associated Courmayeur with extremely competitive and serious mountain ultramarathons such as Tor des Géants and the legendary Ultra-Trail du Mt Blanc, both of which I've run. But the Aosta Valley is also home to a lesser known race that in many ways is more memorable: the Arrancabirra, a beer-soaked costume party set against the rugged backdrop of the Italian Alps.

In a sport that's often characterised by rigid diets, strict training regimes and early mornings, I've come to learn how important it is to seize opportunities like this to let loose. The Arrancabirra, at the end of the European race season in October, provides a sort of release valve for the pressure cooker of accumulative lactic threshold training. It actually follows a few of the same trails as the more iconic races, but the local vibe keeps Arrancabirra much more low key.

The race is still largely unknown to runners outside of Aosta Valley, yet it is fiercely popular among locals, and the 1500 registration spots sell out within days. I was warned by some Italian friends to put the June registration date in my calendar or risk missing out. Launched in 2006, the Arrancabirra has slowly built a following, but even the crowd remains predominantly Italian. However, it's important not to let the party atmosphere fool you. At 11 miles (18km), and with over 4590ft (1400m) of climbing, the terrain is as challenging as any trail race out there.

While my typical pre-race ritual usually involves things like studying the course profile to help shape my training, for the Arrancabirra it's the race theme that dictates how much preparation is required. Neither costumes nor beer drinking are mandatory for the race, but I was wisely advised that both were encouraged. More to the point, you will stand out like a sore thumb here if not decked out and slightly buzzed. In fact, it was those runners who crossed the finish line most dishevelled and inebriated who got the biggest cheers. Making good time, stone cold sober, might even get you booed here.

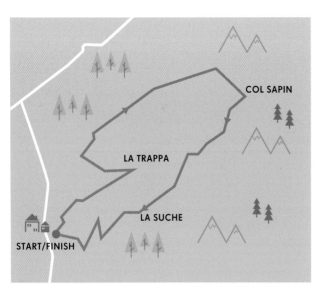

COL SAPIN

LA TRAPPA

LA SUCHE

START/FINISH

As I waited at the start, I was glad I had been warned. The theme was 'Rio Samba' and I showed up dressed in a frilly cloud of yellow and green fabric, complete with a feather headdress. Any first-timer fears I had about overdressing immediately evaporated when I saw one man with a kayak on his back, two others in leotards and blond wigs, and an entire mixed-gender team in tutus.

At the crack of 10am, we all set off down the main pedestrian street of Courmayeur, before turning up the road towards the mountains. I jogged alongside a man dressed as a cardinal on one side and a woman covered in red feathers on the other. It was only a matter of minutes before we had reached the first beer stop at the start of the trail that led up to a mountain hut known as the Bertone refuge. I chugged the first warm beer enthusiastically. As soon as I took my last gulp, a volunteer marked my bib to signify my accomplishment. I took off, chasing the cardinal up the path.

The trail up to Bertone winds several hundred metres through the trees until reaching a clearing at 6560ft (2000m) elevation. I had passed through Bertone many times before in training and in racing, and so I was delighted to take the time to stop and take in the view this time with another beer in hand.

From Bertone, the course took us up another few hundred metres along a ridgeline, providing an unobstructed view of the Val Ferret and the Mt Blanc Massif. It was surreal to have this backdrop of some of the most imposing peaks of the Alps, as brightly coloured carnival-clad runners bounced along the jagged skyline.

As I reached the top of the climb, race volunteers were on hand offering water and warm tea instead of beer. I was actually disappointed at first. Until I glanced down at the rocky descent that unfolded in front of me. The feathers on my head were still intact and in place and I was determined to finish that way. I hiked up my long skirt with one hand and held my hiking poles in

COSTUME PARTY

Being the fastest doesn't get you the most cheers here. It's the runners who have the most fun and wear the loudest costumes that garner favour (runners who take themselves too seriously have even been booed!). So even if you are the competitive type, focus on having the best costume, rather than the best finishing time. Past race themes have included 'Arranca Wars' (the Italian version of *Star Wars*) and 'Gara Goliardica' (Lord of the Drinks).

Clockwise from above: alcohol instead of aid stations at Arrancabirra; rule no1 – don't take yourself too seriously; the Alpine ascents still hurt. Previous page: every madman (and dog) for himself at the start

the other, trying to steady myself on the uneven ground.

In fact, I felt as though I was beginning to sober up as I reached the third checkpoint on the other side of the valley. Naturally, I swigged yet another beer alongside a few racers who had stopped to chow down barbecued sausages and another wearing a black afro wig and dancing around, shaking rainbow maracas.

By the time I arrived at the fourth stop at La Suche, a collection of mountain huts at the top of the final descent, I was happy to have most of the technical trail behind me. La Suche is a place I could spend hours taking in the full panoramic mountain views. However, I began to worry that the longer I stayed, the more time the beer would have to soak into my bloodstream so I got a move on.

Taking extra care over the tree roots and rocks, I picked my way down to the fifth and final beer stop, before joining the road that led to the finish line – and more beer, of course. I flopped down on the grass outside of the finish-line tent, watching the other competitors arriving in varying states of disarray.

It was the perfect way to end my European race season. After clocking hundreds of miles in intense competitions throughout the year, I was heading towards mental burnout, and I had started questioning my motivation for racing at all. The Arrancabirra was the answer. This race ensures that you don't take yourself too seriously. It reminded me as to why I got into running in the first place. It wasn't to chase podium spots or record the fastest times. It was to experience a bit of magic out on the trails, surrounded by other runners who were equally crazy for running.

As for the after-party? Well, let's just say that what happens at the Arrancabirra, stays at the Arrancabirra. **SC**

ORIENTATION

Start/End // Courmayeur, Italy
Distance // 11 miles (18km)
Getting there // Fly to Turin, take public buses to Courmayeur. Alternatively, fly to Geneva Airport, rent a car or take an airport shuttle to Chamonix and a public bus from Chamonix Sud through the Mt Blanc to Courmayeur.
When to go // The race is in October (registration opens in June and it often sells out within days).
Where to stay // Hotel Croux is centrally located, reasonably priced, and the owners run one of the checkpoints at La Suche – they can advise both on the race itself and the after-party options.
More info // www.arrancabirra.it/en
Things to know // While outlandish costumes are encouraged, wear one that is flexible enough for the variable weather conditions in Aosta Valley, and for the climbs, which can be difficult to navigate after a few beers.

Opposite: the vineyards of Pauillac
provide the backdrop for the Marathon
du Médoc in Bordeaux

MORE LIKE THIS
BOOZY RACES

LE MARATHON DES CHÂTEAUX DU MÉDOC, BORDEAUX, FRANCE

This marathon, held every September in France's Bordeaux wine region, has been combining running, booze and costumes since 1985. Over the course of 26.2 miles, 8500 runners are invited to taste up to 23 different wines along the way, accompanied by music, food and other festivities. Do not expect the typical marathon snacks at the aid stations though – here, it's fresh oysters. Winners receive their weight in Medoc wines. It's not the lactic acid you need to worry about after this race, it's the hangover.
Start/End // Pauillac
Distance // 26.2 miles (42km)
More info // www.marathondumedoc. com/en

THE BACCHUS MARATHON, DORKING, UK

The British version of Marathon du Médoc offers 12 wine and food stations along the 26.2-mile loop (six for the half marathon distance; one for the 5-mile event). Each September, a couple of thousand people – mostly in costume – run through the Denbies Vineyard wine estate and into the adjacent National Trust land in the Surrey countryside, enjoying numerous bands stationed along the course and sampling wine along the way. Don't get too distracted though: there is a strict time cutoff of 2 hours and 20 minutes for the first loop, which represents the half marathon distance, and marathon runners must be capable of finishing two loops within 5 hours.
Start/End // Denbies Vineyard, Dorking
Distance // 26.2 miles (42km)
More info // www.runbacchus.com

BEER LOVERS' MARATHON, LIÈGE, BELGIUM

If wine isn't your thing, sign up for the Beer Lovers' Marathon, held every May, through the streets of the historic city of Liège in the French speaking Wallonia region. It provides 15 different Belgian beers along the route, as well as food and water checkpoints every 3 miles (5km). This relatively young race has a generous cutoff time of 6.5 hours, which means you could even walk it if you end up having a little too much fun. Watch out for the last four miles, though, which contain a beer stop every mile.
Start/End // Place St Lambert, Liège
Distance // 26.2 miles (42km)
More info // www.beerlover marathon.be

THE NORTH POLE MARATHON

Not a lot of people on this planet can say they've been to the North Pole — even fewer have run a marathon here. Those who have the cash can kill two epic birds with one stone.

In its 15-year history, the North Pole Marathon has only been cancelled once because of weather. Which is funny considering the conditions — every year the life- and limb-threatening cold are enough to shut down any other marathon, anywhere else on the planet. And that's exactly what kept me awake at night for a full week before the race. I hate being cold. I actually get a little stressed if I know I'll be racing in temperatures below 60°F (15°C). But a race around the Arctic also sounded like nothing I had experienced in my running career. It was 2014 and I was about to turn 40. It seemed like a good excuse to do something extreme.

Despite the danger, the North Pole is beautiful and otherworldly. While you inherently know you shouldn't be there, it captivates your complete attention and respect, much the same way a remote desert does. To this day it remains one of the most memorable races I've ever competed in — despite being one of my slowest marathons ever — and it's certainly one of the most stunning places I've ever visited. And the running is only a small part of the experience.

As I made my way towards Norway that spring, it became clear why it costs €16k (£14,000) to run this race. As a sponsored runner I was lucky enough to have my expenses covered, but I couldn't help but wonder who could afford it. In many ways, it's who you would expect: investment bankers and hedge fund managers, charity runners, and a few professional athletes like me, all from a dozen or so countries. But I was surprised by the shared lust for

adventure. Everyone I met had a passion for collecting unique experiences like this one, and it was inspiring. This event is particularly popular with runners who have completed a marathon on every continent and want to add a bonus race to their CV.

Once in Oslo, I boarded a connecting flight to Svalbard, the northernmost year-round settlement on earth. Here, runners and support crew sit and wait for a break in the weather so they can

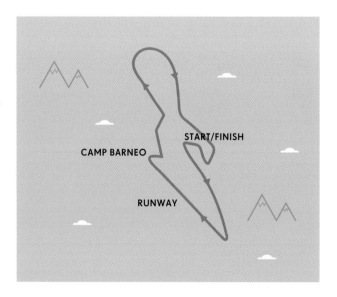

© Mark Conlon | North Pole Marathon

© Mark Conlon | North Pole Marathon

"The tight course keeps us within screaming distance of camp, which is extremely comforting in a place where losing a glove could have life-changing consequences"

board a past-its-prime Russian plane to fly them a further 650 miles (1045km) to the Pole itself.

From the air, the white is blinding. Against the featureless terrain is Camp Barneo, a makeshift headquarters and landing strip, carved out of the ice flow by Russian paratroopers, specifically for the race. As we came in for a bumpy landing, the only sign of humanity is this small cluster of blue tents against an endless expanse of nothingness. It's a stark sight, for sure. But it's only once you step off the plane into the dry stinging cold that you feel the North Pole.

The tiny runway is surrounded by sleeping quarters, a mess hall and an outhouse. Though outhouse in this context just means a large bucket lined with a heavy rubbish bag and topped with a polystyrene toilet seat (if it were made of anything else it might freeze to your skin). I quickly found my cot, stowed my gear and met my 'roommate' Kolja, a German Formula One sponsor scout. We exchanged pleasantries, but all I kept wondering was how the hell I'd be able to run here.

The race itself takes place atop a thick layer of ice and crusty snow that shifts beneath your feet. Temperatures range from -13°F (-25°C) to -41°F (-41°C). The race course is actually just a giant loop that competitors run five times to hit 26.2 miles. It feels like kind of a gimmick at first – running in a giant circle over and over – until I learn why it's done this way. For one, breaking trail here is a serious

undertaking and the ploughed and flattened areas of camp are easier on the legs. More importantly, the tight course keeps us within screaming distance of help. This is extremely comforting – the North Pole is not a place where one wants to be miles away from camp. Even being far out front or far behind the pack here is unnerving. If you were to lose a glove or, worse, punch through the ice, the consequences could be life-changing, if not life ending.

On the second day, the marathon began with little fanfare. There were no spectators – except the gun-toting Russians guarding against stalking polar bears – and the silence is amplified by the sound-deadening ice. Instead, I began to tune into the sounds of the Arctic. As we started our first frosty loop, I could hear the snow crunch and crack beneath me. The firm surface gave slightly under my weight with each step.

During the second lap, runners stay in the lanes created during the first lap in order to avoid having to break trail all over again. I, however, had a slightly different challenge. I was here to set a record and, therefore, had to take the lead for most of the run. In order to pass people, I would often have to pass them by going off trail, sometimes venturing into knee-deep snow.

As the course became more and more travelled, the laps began to pass quickly. Before I knew it, I had covered 18 miles (30km). And once you get past the cold, which you eventually do, the true beauty begins to sink in. With two thirds of the race behind me, I

DAILY DRIFT

There is no land beneath the ice mass of the Arctic. North Pole Marathon runners are essentially running on an ocean. The ice is between 6ft (1.8m) and 12ft (3.6m) thick atop a 12,000ft (3600m)-deep ocean. Because the ice shifts, it is unlikely the course will pass over the Pole itself, which is why race organisers have a helicopter standing by to drop runners at the Pole afterwards.

From left: Greece's Argyrios Papathanasopoulos claims victory at 2018's North Pole Marathon; competitors tackle the Arctic wilderness. Previous page: the right running gear is essential for survival

needed more fuel to carry me through the back nine. I stopped to scarf down an energy gel. This would normally be a pretty quick pit stop, but I was wearing so many layers I burned precious minutes just exposing enough skin to eat. Once my hands were free, I tried to loosen my facemask. But it wouldn't budge: it was frozen to my face from the sweat and exhalation moisture. My eyelashes had also frozen together and I could barely see, and I couldn't pull any of the layers away from my skin without severe pain. I had no choice but to duck into a dining hall to warm up for several minutes. Many who do this race duck into the shelters after every lap in order to warm up and refuel.

As I stepped back into the cold, I was blinded by the glare. My vision slowly returned as I began my final few laps. I still couldn't feel much, but I could feel myself smiling as I cruised the final third of the race, now plodding along well-trodden lanes.

My official time was a little over four hours – officially my slowest marathon. The next finisher came in an hour after me. Understandably, there is no hard cutoff at this race. If you've made the effort to get here – and paid for it – they'll let you run for as long as you like, within reason, until you finish. Despite my slow time, it was a course record. But another race record was not the only thing I brought home from the Arctic. It's a landscape I'll never forget. The North Pole marathon also recalibrated my idea of cold – I ran the Antarctica Marathon just three years later. **MW**

ORIENTATION

Start/End // Camp Barneo
Distance // 26.2 miles (42km)
Getting there // Fly to Oslo (OSL) then Svalbard (LYR) then travel by chartered plane to the North Pole.
When to go // The race is held in April.
Where to stay // The blue tents at Camp Barneo are your only option.
More info // www.npmarathon.com
Things to know // Sweat is the enemy in the Arctic. The goal is to be cold at the start of the race – like really cold – so that when you start running you stay just under the point of sweating. Gear wise, a facemask is a must (I like the Cold Avenger) and be sure to bring trail-running shoes that are a full size bigger than what you normally wear to accommodate two pairs of thick socks.

MORE LIKE THIS
ICE-COLD RUNS

THE ICE MARATHON, ANTARCTICA

This sister race to the North Pole Marathon is the southernmost footrace in the world, as recognised by Guinness. Union Glacier is remote, situated in the Heritage mountain range. The conditions are extreme with temperatures ranging from 0°F to (-18°C) to -40°F (-40°C). Expect to see nothing living, no animals, no insects, no birds (the penguins live closer to the coast here). The race takes place among a landscape of white snow, ice and mountains, in a part of the wold where the sun does something different and the light plays across the desolation.
Start/End // Union Glacier, Antarctica
Distance // 26.2 miles (42km)
More info // www.icemarathon.com

THE POLAR CIRCLE MARATHON, GREENLAND

The Polar-Circle Marathon is not as lifeless as other similar races. For one, you may spot an arctic fox or musk ox, or even a dog from the nearby town of Kangerlussuaq, just north of the Polar Circle itself. The race takes place mostly on gravel roads, with forays onto the ice sheet, but it affords great views of glaciers and Arctic lakes. The course has a substantial climb in the first few miles, but after that it's mostly rolling downhill to the finish. The temperatures can range from -5°F (-20°C) up to a balmy 50°F (10°C).
Start/End // Kangerlussuaq, Greenland
Distance // 26.2 miles (42km)
More info // www.polar-circle-marathon.com

THE LAUGAVEGUR ULTRAMARATHON, ICELAND

The Laugavegur Ultramarathon traces the most popular hiking trail in Iceland. Most people hike this trail in four days but ultra runners will cover the entire thing for this one event. Short but steep hills and shockingly cold water crossings make this a challenging course. But steaming volcanoes, black sand riverbeds and mountains provide plenty of motivation to go the distance. Plus, the race organisation is Icelandic so you can expect things to be pretty dialled in.
Start // Landmannalaugar, Iceland
End // Þórsmörk, Iceland
Distance // 34 miles (55km)
More info // www.marathon.is.laugavegur

From top: the Ice Marathon
in Antarctica; Iceland's
Laugavegur ultramarathon

THE GREAT OCEAN ROAD MARATHON

Australia's most scenic drive is also the venue for one of the world's most beautiful marathons. And when you run it, you don't have to keep your eyes on the road.

The first time I ran the Great Ocean Road Marathon I spent most of the time looking at, well, the Great Ocean Road. Don't get me wrong, the road is in pretty good nick, considering the ridiculous number of cars that travel it every year. But it's certainly not worthy of such a study. Out of the corner of my eye I saw others absorbing the views, looking at the amazing trees and out towards lonely driftwood-littered beaches. But I just kept looking down.

That marathon – at 27 miles (44km) it's actually technically an ultra – was to be my longest run ever. And, looking back, I now see that idea weighed me down. So when I went back for another go, I made a promise to myself at the startline. No matter what, I would keep my head up. I would look out at the ocean. Soak up the visual splendour, the road clinging to the edge of the wild ocean, hugging huge rock cliffs and sandy beaches. I'd be one of the ones looking out.

One thing I had learned the first time around is there's no point checking the weather in advance for the Great Ocean Road Marathon. Nature's probably going to throw it all at you, no matter what the forecast says, and during my second go it was no different. The race is held in western Victoria, about two hours' drive from Melbourne, in mid-May – the cusp of Austral autumn and winter, when the cold is arriving. The Great Ocean is actually Bass Strait. Apparently, explorer Matthew Flinders said of this area: 'I have seldom seen a more fearful section of coastline.'

As I queue up to use the toilets before the start of the race in the resort town of Lorne, I gaze out at the water. Along this stretch, forest meets the sea, as eucalyptus trees come right to the road. It's a sparsely populated area, with the occasional

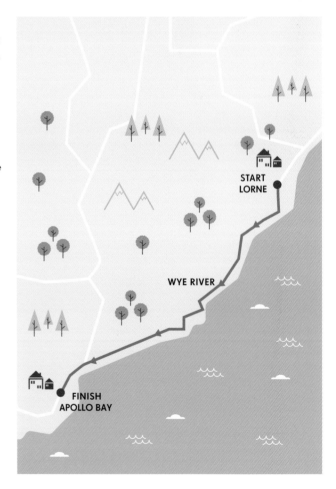

timber home perched on the side of a cliff. These are mostly everyone-knows-everyone towns.

I actually lived along here once, long before I was a runner. I've driven tourists along this stretch, cycled it in events and even researched the winding strip for guidebooks. But the Great Ocean Road only closes twice a year and the marathon is one of those times. No matter how many times I'd driven it, it feels like a rare, wonderful privilege to travel it car-free.

When we finally set off from Lorne, all I hear is the rumble of feet hitting the road. In fact, it almost drowns out a chorus of white and yellow cockatoos screeching their way through life on balconies. We leave the surfers bobbing in the water to the left of us, pass the new and improved Lorne pier, then Lorne Fisheries Co-Operative. The Grand Pacific Hotel, circa 1875, is on our right. Guests in full motorcycling gear cheer us on – they can't go anywhere until we've gone.

Then, there's nothing. The nothing's always a shock. This is not a remote run – far from it. But, as the runners find their paces and thin out, I find my place and my pace. I also find solitude. It's just me and the road, really, and the blue of the water, the green and grey of the trees. This race has actually morphed into a weekend-long Running Festival with a range of events, and there are almost 8000 people running in one or more of the races. Yet

"A chorus of white and yellow cockatoos screech from balconies as surfers bob in the ocean to the left of us"

somehow, the thousands of other marathoners disappear.

I mark my progress on the run by the towns I pass through, such as Wye River, which is now surrounded by blackened trees and bare land from a bushfire that wiped out many of its houses in 2015. Remarkably, the Wye River General Store was spared – it's a great place for a coffee.

I had vowed to open my eyes to the sights, but I'm realising the scents change quickly, too, on the Great Ocean Road. Sea mist hangs in the air and there are patches where shaded rocky cliffs drip water, bringing the deep smell of the forest. Cuttingly cold wind can spring from nowhere. Last time, on reaching the top of one of the hills (the route has a 1600ft; 488m elevation gain), my feet were even lifted from under me by a gust.

Just over halfway through the marathon, at Kennett River, I remember to look up towards the local koala population that sits in the eucalyptus trees above. I don't see any, so I look at my phone to see the time. I realise that the winner has probably already finished.

Yeah, I'm slow. I don't always train. I get the dregs at the aid

BUILT BY HAND

The Great Ocean Road was carved into land between the ocean and farms and forests by about 3000 returned WWI soldiers. They finished the job in 1932 and it became a toll road (it's free now). Enjoy the retro charm of the over-the-road memorial arch on your way to Lorne – it celebrates the diggers who built it. In Kennett River, look up to spot koalas lazing and grazing in the gum trees.

Clockwise from left: the Great Ocean Road is closed to cars only twice a year; cockatoos roost on balconies along the way; one of the marathon's many rugged stretches. Previous page: Apollo Bay signals the last stretch of the race

stations – the last slimy jelly snake. People are tired of cheering us on by the time I come through. I run with fit-looking people and feel good about myself – until we chat and I realise that they're injured. No matter, things are going to plan, my plan of just taking it all in.

Once we join the coast again, I see big white-froth-topped waves. It must be freezing out there, I think. Still, surfers persist in popular spots up and down this coastline. I always look out past the breakers to see if I can spot any blowhole spray on the horizon. No whales today. But there is a rainbow. And, of course, dark clouds out towards Apollo Bay way.

I feel good. The excitement of the start hasn't diminished much, and the excitement of finishing is building. Still, my challenge with the Great Ocean Road Marathon is that the timing mat is under the cypress trees that line the entrance to Apollo Bay. You run over it, hear the beep, see your time (5:18 – told you I was slow). But there's still over a mile (1800m) to go. It's raining. If I'd run faster, I'd have stayed dry. Instead, I have to run faster just to get through it.

I wrap myself in a race towel, grab a finish-line banana and, with a couple of tears of success in my eyes, start searching for the bus that'll take me back to Lorne. I get to travel the Great Ocean Road one more time today. **JD**

ORIENTATION

Start // Lorne
End // Apollo Bay
Distance // 27 miles (44km)
Getting there // Lorne is 90 miles (145km) from Melbourne. The closest domestic airport, Avalon, is 55 miles (89km) away.
When to go // The third Sunday in May.
Where to stay // Great Ocean Road Cottages (www.greatoceanroadcottages.com) has great in-the-trees cottages as well as dorm-style rooms with cheap doubles.
More info // www.greatoceanroadrunfest.com.au
Things to know // Standard warm-weather running gear should suffice, but gloves may help you get through a chilly morning. A drop bag filled with a warm change of clothes is a good idea for the finish.

MORE LIKE THIS
COASTAL MARATHONS

SURF COAST TRAIL MARATHON, TORQUAY, AUSTRALIA

This fun trail marathon takes runners alongside the stretch of the Great Ocean Road closer to Melbourne. Beginning on the beach in surf-loving Torquay, it follows the Surf Coast Walk to Fairhaven, 42km away. It passes by world-famous surf break Bells Beach, heads inland into the scrub at Point Addis, and includes plenty of sand running. At Point Addis, marathoners meet up with their half marathoner friends and continue on through the beachside towns of Anglesea and, finally, Aireys Inlet. It's hard to stay dry with river crossings at high tide and some running at the edge of the sea. As you close in on the finish line, there's the stunning Split Point Lighthouse to run towards before a sandy finish at Fairhaven Surf Lifesaving Club.
Start // Torquay
End // Fairhaven
Distance // 26.2 miles (42km)
More info // www.
surfcoasttrailmarathon.com.au

BERMUDA MARATHON

Bermuda Marathon runners start in Hamilton, alongside the half marathoners. But when the latter are coming in to finish, the marathoners keep going and do another lap – but it's not your usual lap: the route takes you from the start, past the Botanic Gardens, along the South Rd beside Bermuda's south coast, past Harrington Sound, clear to Bermuda's north coast. Bermuda's pretty small – think 20 miles by 2 miles – so you sort of feel like you've run the whole country! Runners can expect a rolling course with pastel-coloured houses and mansions dotting the route. It's a tropical location where you can stop to sniff the frangipani and bougainvillea. Fit folks can take on the Bermuda Triangle Challenge, which involves three races in three days.
Start/End // Hamilton
Distance // 26.2 miles (42km)
More info // www.
bermudaraceweekend.com/race-info

DINGLE MARATHON, IRELAND

You may recognise this craggy wave-scoured spot in southwest Ireland from *Star Wars: Episode VII*. And the filmset, since dismantled, could even be seen from Slea Head Dr, which forms part of the Dingle Marathon route. Regardless, if you run this race, you'll be one of the lucky ducks who get to experience some of the most breathtakingly tall and rugged sea cliffs on the one day of the year that it is completely *sans* traffic. The run starts in the marina of the picturesque fishing/tourist town and gives you views of the Blasket Islands, ancient forts, anxiety-inducing cliffs and a lot of Atlantic Ocean.
Start/End // Dingle
Distance // 26.2 miles (42km)
More info // www.dinglemarathon.ie

From top: Horseshoe Bay Beach,
Bermuda; Ireland's Dingle Marathon
stretches from the country roads of
County Kerry to stunning sea cliffs

MELBOURNE'S
MUST-DO PARK RUN

*The 'Tan' is a legendary little loop that has everything a great
city run should, and some wildlife that makes it one of a kind.*

Runners have become a fixture in city parks the world over, whether they're competing in an organised event or simply sneaking in a workout around office hours. At dawn we come out by the million, chasing an early morning high or seeking some zone 2 meditation. For some, a park run is an exercise in escapism, a chance to breathe more deeply or get a little further away from the exhaust fumes. For others, it's all about PBs and Strava splits. Nowhere offers a more striking snapshot of this diverse congregation than Melbourne's de facto trail-running temple: the 'Tan'.

This two-mile route loops around the city's impressive Botanic Gardens, in the shadows of skyscrapers north of the river, out towards the trendy 'hoods of South Yarra and St Kilda. Some locals do a lap every day; others might mooch around once in a blue moon. I run it every chance I get and am here once again this morning, with a head full of thoughts about how the Tan symbolises so much about the city.

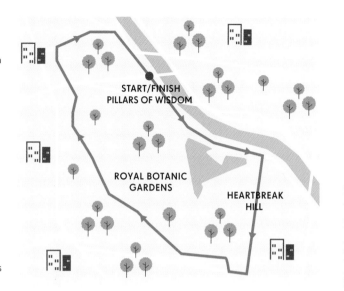

START/FINISH
PILLARS OF WISDOM

ROYAL BOTANIC
GARDENS

HEARTBREAK
HILL

© Takatoshi Kurikawa | Alamy Stock Photo

© Timothy Christiant | Shutterstock

"The Tan is a running nerd's nirvana, with distance markers every 250m, digital clocks and lights that keep it navigable until the witching hour"

You can join the loop wherever you like, but the 'official' start point of a traditional lap of the Tan is the Pillars of Wisdom, on the south bank of the river, opposite Swan Street Bridge. From here, I like to set off clockwise along Alexandra Avenue, with the Yarra to my left and the ornamental lake on my right.

Melbourne is a truly multilayered metropolis. Obsessed with the arts, it's a place where suits, students and skaters share the graffiti-tattooed alleyways and craft-coffee joints. But it's also a city where every road seems to lead to a green space. Unsurprisingly, for a city steeped in sport of all kinds, the Victorian capital has perfected the park run concept, offering a route to suit every boot. Indeed, nearly 5-million square metres of grassy gardens and trail-striped public spaces punctuate the concrete jungle here.

But the Tan tops the lot. Named after either the tanbark used for the original horse track built in the early 1900s, or as a shortening of the word Botanical – nobody can agree on which – the Tan is mostly on gravel with a bit of asphalt thrown in. So popular is the track that sometimes it looks as though a river of runners flows around this 94-acre (38-hectare) corner of semi-cultivated nature, cuddled by a bend in the Yarra River. The Tan is a running nerd's nirvana, with distance markers every 250m and digital clocks, and it is well-lit until the witching hour.

But I mostly come here to break a sweat. The circuit's sternest challenge comes quickly with the ascent of Anderson St, aka

'Heartbreak Hill'. It gets the blood pumping around my muscles, which are still protesting the early start. The peak of this pinch point, though, reveals a sunrise-illuminated view across the serpentine coil of the Yarra and into the high-rises beyond. Next, I follow the track as it wends northwest, parallel to Birdswood Avenue, passing the Children's Garden on the right and the solemn World War I memorial, Shrine of Remembrance, on the left.

I once ran the Tan with elite American ultrarunner and mountain man Anton Krupicka, famous for his flowing locks, bushy beard and hoofing around the roof of the Rockies with next-to-nothing on. The terrain and busy trail couldn't have been much further removed from his usual stomping grounds in the high, lonely peaks of Colorado. But ever-affable Anton seemed genuinely excited about the number of runners out on an ordinary workday morning. It was a privilege to share such an iconic track with a genuine star of the trail-running cosmos. But, to be honest, my most pleasurable runs here have all been much like this one, a few minutes past daybreak, just me and the trees, birds and beasts that call the Botanical Gardens home.

There's something persistently wild about this run. Despite the digital timers and lights, the gardens are home to night herons, flying foxes and other nocturnal species, as well as thousands of birds and animals, including marsupial possums, as common here as squirrels are in the parks of London or New York.

PARK RECORD

On 21 December 2006, Australian 5000m specialist and four-time Olympian Craig Mottram set the current record for running the Tan with a time of 10 minutes and eight seconds. Mottram completed this run with players from the nearby Richmond Football Club – he gave the professional Australian Rules footballers a two-and-a-half minute head start, but still thrashed them.

From left: urban wildlife patrols the Royal Botanic Gardens; the Shrine of Remembrance war memorial. Previous page: plentiful parks make Melbourne one of the most runnable cities in the world

Once beyond the Sidney Myer Music Bowl, I trace the track as it elbows back to Alexandra Ave to return to the Pillars of Wisdom. Here, a stone plinth celebrates the fastest Tan times ever recorded, with entries including bling-winning Olympians from Australia, Kenya and North America. I'll never get anywhere near these times, but I couldn't care less. In these precious dawn moments, as the earth spins and the southern city turns to face the sun, its towering steel-and-glass edifices are set aglitter with a magical light, and the birds of the Botanical Gardens twitter as they change shift.

They're a noisy bunch, making a bewildering series of sounds, from the R2D2-esque wolf-whistle-come-fart of the white-plumed honeyeater to the low beatbox bass hum of the tawny frogmouth. Ever the tourist – despite a decade-and-a-half of habitual running visits to the park – I'm always most tickled by the kaleidoscopic clouds of rainbow lorikeets and rosellas that rampage through, as cacophonous as they are colourful. I can never understand how some of my fellow runners cut out this part of the experience with earphones.

And when the sounds of the city are drowned out by the noise of nature – be it dawn chorus or evensong – you can run right back into the Aussie outback here, even though you're on the cusp of Melbourne's CBD. Which is what makes this one of the world's very best park runs. **PK**

ORIENTATION

Start/End // Pillars of Wisdom, near the junction of Alexandra Ave and Olympic Blvd
Distance // 2.4 miles (3.8km)
Getting There // The Botanic Gardens are a short walk from the city centre. Tram stop 19, at the Shrine of Remembrance/St Kilda Rd, will get you closest.
When to go // The Tan is mild all year round. Sunrise and sunset are prime times.
Where to stay // 'Burbs such as South Yarra, Prahran, Middle Park or St Kilda East, which are all close to the Tan.
More info // www.rbg.vic.gov.au
www.onlymelbourne.com.au/tan-track
Things to know // Coffee has been elevated to an art form in Melbourne. Grab a post-run caffeine hit near the Tan at spots such as St Ali Coffee Roasters.

MORE LIKE THIS
ICONIC PARK RUNS

PHOENIX PARK, DUBLIN, IRELAND

One of the largest walled green spaces in Europe, history-heavy 1,750-acre (708-hectare) Phoenix Park is home to a herd of wild fallow deer and multiple flocks of free-range runners. There's no particular prescribed route to follow – joggers just follow their underfoot preferences, with road runners sticking to the tarmac tracks and trailhounds seeking out the softer and more technical pathways that wend between the trees. A lap of the park running parallel to the perimeter wall is 6.6 miles (10.5km), but there are many more interesting routes to explore, looping around sites such as Áras an Uachtaráin (official residence of the President of Ireland), Dublin Zoo, Wellington Monument and the 15th-century Ashtown Castle.
Start/End // Chesterfield Ave (route of Great Ireland Run)
Distance // 6 miles (10km)
More info // www.phoenixpark.ie

ALBERT PARK, MELBOURNE, AUSTRALIA

Among the dozens of great urban runs to explore around Melbourne is one that gets people legging around the Formula 1 Grand Prix circuit in Albert Park. This grassy space sits between the city, St Kilda and Port Phillip Bay. A circumnavigation of Albert Park Lake is just a shade under 3 miles (5km), and this has become a popular place to set a PB, not least because of the weekly mass-participation park run event that happens every Saturday morning. The terrain is a rich mix of concrete, gravel and sandy paths, but by far the biggest hazard are the resident black swans, who don't like to get out of the way for anyone. The course record is 14:29, although Michael Schumacher got around it in 1:24 in 2004.
Start/End // Melbourne Sports and Aquatic Centre (MSAC)
Distance // 3 miles (5km)
More info // www.parkweb.vic.gov.au;
www.parkrun.com.au/albert-melbourne

BUSHY PARK, TEDDINGTON, LONDON, UK

Having begun as a brilliantly simple concept – a non-competitive, ultra-inclusive, timed, free, weekly 5km run in a public space – Parkrun is now a fully fledged global phenomenon, embraced by millions. And it all started here, when the 13 original apostles of Parkrun jogged around Bushy Park on 2 October 2004. Parkrun tourists travel around countries and continents ticking off new courses, and Bushy – as the epicentre of a running revolution – always tops their to-do list. Hundreds of Parkrun pilgrims visit every Saturday from all over the world, to run anticlockwise around the famous route. More than 1700 ran the 10th-anniversary event, and guest gallopers have included Mo Farah.
Start/End // Diana Fountain/Heron Pond, Bushy Park
Distance // 3 miles (5km)
More info // www.parkrun.org.uk/bushy

Clockwise from top: a fun run in
London's Bushy Park; Dublin's
Phoenix Park is one of Europe's largest

Melbourne's Park Run

THE ORMISTON GORGE POUND LOOP

This bite-sized offshoot of northern Australia's famed long-distance Larapinta Trail could very well be the best short trail run on the continent.

The late, great Aboriginal artist Albert Namatjira painted thousands of canvases depicting his exquisite backyard subject: the mesmerising Tjoritja, or West MacDonnell Ranges, in the Northern Territory of Australia. Famous for their rugged landscapes, Namatjira's watercolours drip with light and colour, featuring stark white gum trees and the twisted scrubland that epitomises the harsh yet inviting outback. Never could Namatjira have imagined that his works would also act as a seed of inspiration for trail runners.

Flush with high escarpments and dramatic valleys ripe for exploration, Namatjira's painting *Near Ormiston Gorge* was in fact the pictorial signpost that pointed me toward the West MacDonnell Ranges. Mile-for-mile, the Ormiston Gorge and Pound Loop is the best short run in Australia, period. At a bite-sized 5.6 miles (9km), this circular offshoot of the renowned Larapinta Trail – which stretches a full 140 miles (223km) and is a common multi-day walk or ultra-distance run – leaves straight from the Ormiston Gorge car park, offering an accessible, richly distilled taste of what it's like to run the arid zone landscapes of Australia's iconic Red Centre.

Indeed, my own first encounter with this single track came at the end of a 20.5-mile (33km) run under a skin-crinkling solar glare: my energy registered as bone dry as my hydration pack. I was leading a group of runners on a multi-day trail-running

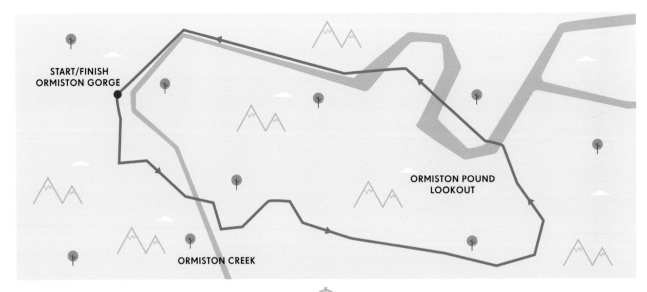

START/FINISH ORMISTON GORGE

ORMISTON POUND LOOKOUT

ORMISTON CREEK

"We hit the water's edge and the trail disappeared into its depths. We waded in, run packs high above our heads"

mission along the main Larapinta Trail. It had been a sturdy six hours of climbing high ridges and descending into gorges. But even beauty takes its toll when the environment is riddled with sharp rocks underfoot, thorny bushes to brush past and the odd King Brown snake to leap over.

Our group was halfway through an east to west tour and the idea of tacking on an extra five miles to capture the Ormiston Gorge and Pound loop was a nonstarter as we made a beeline for the air-conditioned confines of the car park's kiosk and the ice cream for sale inside. We then hit the nearby swimming hole. However, after a soothing dip in the chilled waters of the gorge, the call of yet another potentially great run was too great. In fact, the thought of a mellow warm-down was even starting to sound like a good idea. And so, with legs sufficiently iced (we may be in the desert, but waterhole temperatures here remain stubbornly freezing), we set off.

Running back out of the car park – the route can be done in either direction, but counter clockwise is suggested so you finish off with a highlight water-crossing in the gorge – we picked up a trail we had ignored earlier. After crossing the dead-dry Ormiston Creek, it led northeast, away from the Larapinta Trail, gently meandering up an exposed valley.

It's easy to imagine – even for Antipodeans – that a run through the 'Dead Heart' of Down Under would be characterised by trackless sand dunes, baked by a searing desert heat. As it turns out, central Australia is not so bereft of life, nor as harsh a place to run as one would envisage. Indeed, the trails of Tjoritja are teeming with wild creatures, watery oases and giant mountain ridgelines that loom large over enchanting slot canyons and gaping prehistoric valleys, packed with exotic flora. Views are akin to imaginings of a Martian landscape, as sharp red and orange rocks glower at you from either side of a well-packed down trail.

As the orchestra of anticipation rose in volume, we reached a small saddle, where a short switchback deviation took us onto an exposed lookout. The reward was an astounding view that Namatjira would surely have judged worthy of a month sitting at the easel.

Before us sprawled 'the Pound', an immense bowl fringed by steep-sided mountains jutting up out of the flat, sandy floor. To the north is the majestic Bowmans Gap, a chasm that splits the final act of the Chewings Range, marking the northern boundary. To the east, the eyeline draws back to the dominant peak of Mt Giles (4557ft; 1389m), which stands sentry approximately 10kms away as the crow flies, at the eastern end of the crater-like enclosure. Both escarpments tower over Ormiston Creek and its dry tributaries,

The fastest known time running west to east along the entire 140-mile (223km)-long Larapinta Trail – which encompasses 13,000ft (3965m) elevation gain – is 58 hours and 48 minutes. It was set by Simon Duke and Rohan Rowling in 2018. Chris Macaskill-Hants holds the FKT east to west (61hrs 32mins, 2014), which is believed to be the more challenging route.

From left: native spinifex plant; trails often disappear into the drink. Previous page: Ormiston Gorge's terrain is stunning but steep

along with an abundance of spinifex, ever-present white ghost gums and a solitary winding trail that funnels into Ormiston Gorge itself.

The northern wall felt immense once we were up close. Formed when one gargantuan block of quartzite slid atop another, in a powerful display of geological creation, it is a fortress-like monolith. Running into the gorge's depths, the trail turns to sand before offering up some rock hopping, and a test of core strength and balance. The shadow of the cliff above was edging ever closer to engulfing us.

Eventually, we hit the water's edge and the trail disappeared directly into its depths. There was no option other than to wade in up to our waist in the frigid waters, holding our run packs high above our heads.

From the crossing, we had a choice to remain low, rock hopping back around the waterway towards the sandy riverbank beach and campsite, or go high on the Ghost Gum Walk. The view was too much to resist so we went high. We reached a lookout over the gorge, and back up the chasm we'd just run. One lone ghost gum overlooks the gorge's snaking crevice here: if only I had the talent of Namatjira and a canvas in my pack, I might have stopped to paint the scene. Instead, a second ice cream awaits in the kiosk below. **CO**

ORIENTATION

Start/End // Ormiston Pound car park
Distance // 5.6 miles (9km)
Getting there // The Ormiston Pound car park and camping site is 84 miles (135km) west from Alice Springs, Northern Territory.
When to go // May–October.
Where to stay // Camping and van sites at Ormiston Pound with attendant kiosk.
More info // www.nt.gov.au/leisure/parks-reserves
Things to know // Take care when crossing the water body towards the end of the counterclockwise loop, it can reach up to your waist or so. Once you have crossed the water, you can choose to take the low or high route to return to the Ormiston Pound car park.

Opposite: Australia's 140-mile-long Larapinta Trail is one of the continent's most famous multi-day runs

MORE LIKE THIS
OFF-ROAD RUNS IN OZ

CARNARVON GORGE, QUEENSLAND

Carnarvon Gorge is a hidden gem worth the long journey inland to access it. The national park features towering sandstone cliffs, gorges aplenty, spurs and ridgelines, sweeping table lands, diverse flora and fauna and an abundance of Aboriginal rock art. The main 54-mile (87km) circuit can be run in sections – there are five campsites en route. We suggest a 2–3 day run mission carrying all you need to be self-sufficient. Or stick with short out-and-backs on trails ranging from 1 mile to 12 miles, return. The gorge is home to a range of significant plant species including remnant rainforest in sheltered gorges, endemic Carnarvon fan palms, ancient cycads, ferns, flowering shrubs and gum trees. The ochre stencils, rock engravings and freehand paintings are regarded as some of the finest Aboriginal rock art in Australia.
Start/End // Carnarvon Gorge Visitor Area
Distance // 1–54 miles (1.5–87km)
More info // www.npsr.qld.gov.au/ parks/carnarvon-gorge

FLINDERS RANGES INCLUDING WILPENA POUND, SOUTH AUSTRALIA

Located a few hundred miles north of Adelaide, South Australia's largest mountain range plays host to the iconic natural amphitheatre that is Ikara (Wilpena Pound), along with the Heysen Range, and Brachina and Bunyeroo gorges. It is a beacon for arid-zone trail running. Artist Albert Namatjira made the West MacDonnell Ranges famous, so too the Flinders Ranges were popularised by the works of German painter Sir Hans Heysen. Rugged mountain scenery, gorges, plentiful wildlife and flora can all be explored via more than two dozen primary walking tracks, including our favourite, the St Mary's Peak Loop. But options are endless along the 750-mile (1200km) Heysen Trail, which stretches all the way south to Cape Jervis.
Start/End // Wilpena Pound
Distance // 12 miles (19km)
More info // www.heysentrail.asn.au

LARAPINTA TRAIL, NORTHERN TERRITORY

If you want more than a taste and are trained up enough for the main course, then hit longer sections – or all of – the Larapinta Trail. You can run it in either direction, although many runners prefer to go from east (Alice Springs) to west (Redbank Gorge), so as to reward themselves at the end with the 10-mile (16km) out-and-back up to Mt Sonder, best completed at sunrise. It can be done self-sufficiently if you fastpack with food drops or use local transport companies. Better yet, there are trail-run tour companies that can guide you along highlight sections. You can also enter the Run Larapinta multi-day event for four section highlights amid a friendly but competitive environment.
Start // Alice Springs
End // Rebank Gorge (Mt Sonder)
Distance // 140 miles (223km)
More info // www.larapintatrail.com.au

THE KEPLER TRACK

Carrying you across mountaintops and along some of the world's most stunning ridgelines,
New Zealand's 'Great Walk' seems far more suited to ambitious trail runners.

The wind had been howling like an aggrieved banshee from the moment we set out along the 36-mile (58km) Kepler Track. But it wasn't the elements that literally floored me. It was overexcitement – and a little stupidity – as I stopped concentrating on the rock-strewn path in front of me and attempted to take a mid-stride photo of my running buddies legging it straight into a scene from a dream. The Kepler Track is indeed the sort of dream a trail runner might experience after scoffing too much cheese just before bedtime, having nodded off while fantasising over photos of wild singletrack, forest trails and knife-like ridgeline routes. Thankfully, I was not dreaming. This was

the real deal. But face-diving the trail woke me up to a certain reality: if I didn't watch my step, I might take a tumble right off the side of this rocky ridge and not even live long enough to brag about my accomplishment.

It's no fluke that New Zealand breeds legendary adventure athletes such as Richard Ussher and Anna Frost. Dangling at the bottom of the globe, with a national population half the size of London's, the Land of the Long White Cloud is also the home of countless long trail-running routes. These are tracks as lonely as they are lovely, snaking across terrain so varied it feels as though it can't possibly all belong to the same planet, let alone a single country.

Active volcanoes, ancient rainforests, titanic fjords, heaving glaciers, perpetual waterfalls, bubbling mud fields, snowcapped peaks and empty ocean-stroked beaches – all just everyday wallpaper for spoilt Kiwi trail runners. Nine of New Zealand's tracks are so exceptional they've officially been bestowed with the appellation Great Walk. But any trail that can be tramped can also be trotted, as I discovered during an expedition where – with two fleet-footed friends – I was running the full list.

The Milford Track is often touted as New Zealand's very best trail, partly because it inspired the Great Walks concept, but also because it's an undeniably sensational journey through the otherworldly surrounds of the South Island's Fiordland National Park. For me, though, having jogged the job lot, the Kepler Track offers the ultimate challenge for trail runners looking to explore the country's rough-edged riches.

For starters, it's a circular route, which makes logistics much easier, and you can decide which way to go according to conditions on the day. But whichever direction you take, it's the

LAKE TE ANAU

START/FINISH

LAKE MANAPOURI

stunning variety of the terrain that elevates it to epic status. You travel from calm, tree-fringed lowland singletracks that skirt the lake to the exposed, wind-blasted and blade-shaped ridgeline across Mt Luxmore.

We decided to run anti-clockwise, leaving Lake Te Anau trailhead along a track that shadows the shoreline of Australasia's biggest freshwater puddle. This short stretch is flat and pretty, wending through beech forest and giant ferns. But after Brod Bay the path abruptly reared like an angry snake as the ascent of Mt Luxmore began. Threading through tight tunnels in-between imposing limestone bluffs, the track climbed mercilessly, scaling more than 1500ft (450m) in nearly two miles (3km) before popping out of the treeline, exposing us to a wicked westerly wind that forced a decision to pause and layer-up.

We had the path to ourselves, but in a couple of months the Kepler Challenge would see hundreds of competitors tackle the 37-mile (60km) route, some finishing with sub-5-hour times. Plenty of people will take twice that time, though, and this is an ultra-distance run that anyone with mid-level experience and fitness can realistically do, if they approach it sensibly. Or, if the whole-loop length is too intimidating, it can also be tackled in stages, with overnight rest stops in excellent huts, allowing time to explore super-interesting side attractions (including caves near Luxmore Hut and a wonderful waterfall close to Iris Burns Hut).

Most of those who have just a day turn around at Luxmore Hut to wend and descend back to the trailhead. This 17-mile (27km) out-and-back is the route of the Luxmore Grunt, a race held annually on the same day as the Challenge. While these events feature on many a runner's bucket-list, I prefer to meet my mountains minus the crowds — and the conditions that accompanied our Kepler canter were ensuring just that.

'Dress to stay warm and windproof.' This was the sage advice scrawled by 'Ranger Peter' on the whiteboard in Luxmore Hut. He had used the double O in 'windprOOf' to form a pair of eyes in a grinning cartoon face. Then, in a more serious font, *sans* smiley anything, he suddenly segued into business mode: 'Northwest winds rising to severe gales in exposed places. Snow to 1100m overnight.' This forecast was one reason we met only one other human during our adventure, which would be unthinkable on the perennially popular Milford Track, whatever the weather.

After refuelling on trail mix we pushed on and, following a brief climb to the brow of 4829ft (1472m) Mt Luxmore, received a reward in the shape of some top-shelf ridgeline running. Charging along 7 miles (12km) of flowing summit-hugging singletrack, we peered down through the clouds at Te Anau's sprawling South Fiord and gazed across the range to the snow-dusted Murchison Mountains.

At Hanging Valley emergency shelter we hid from the wind for a quick lunch, jealously protecting precious rations from a couple of keas, the tenacious mountain parrots that boldly boss the highlands of Te Wāhipounamu. And then it was time to stop fighting gravity, and to surf it instead, starting with a dramatic drop down Iris Burn.

COMPETE ON THE KEPLER

One of the world's great mountain races, the Kepler Challenge has been run annually since 1988, three years after the Kepler Track opened. The field is limited to 450 competitors, and entries always sellout within five minutes of opening. The record for the full 37-mile (60km) course is a staggering four-and-a-half hours, set by Martin Dent in 2013. If you're up for the challenge (of getting a place, let alone finishing), visit www. keplerchallenge. co.nz

Clockwise from top: easy terrain is the exception; runners ready for the start of the Kepler Challenge; it's a bucket-list ultramarathon. Previous page: ridgelines keep things interesting

"We jealously protected precious rations from tenacious keas, the mountain parrots that boss the Te Wahipounamu highlands"

The track swept around a seemingly endless section of sharp-elbowed switchbacks to the eponymous hut, from where the long, largely level 20-mile (32km) run-out begins. Quickly this became a race — us versus our nearest star — as we sought to complete our feat before the sun hit the horizon. Dropping through a gorge, we scaled the scar of an earlier avalanche and entered the protection of a podocarp forest before reaching Moturau Hut, which is perched on the beautiful banks of Lake Manapouri.

From the swing bridge at Rainbow Reach, the Waiau River took us to the trailhead and we finished with just enough light left in the day to read the sign we'd rushed past 10 hours earlier. It waxed lyrical about the Kepler being a Great Walk. We agree. But, arguably, it's an even greater run. **PK**

ORIENTATION

Start/Finish // Kepler Track Car Park on Lake Te Anau
Distance // 37 miles (60km)
Getting there // The best access to the trailhead is via Queenstown or Te Anau.
When to go // The Great Walks season runs from late October to late April, during which time the track might be busy. Outside of this period, conditions can be harsh – potentially deadly – and not great for running.
Where to stay // Te Anau is the gateway town for Fiordland and has a broad range of options (www.fiordland.org.nz).
More info // www.doc.govt.nz/keplertrack
Things to know // Always check the forecast carefully, no matter how clear the conditions look. Things change quickly in New Zealand. And pack more than you think you'll need: waterproof and windproof outer shells, calories (you will burn them big time on the climb).

*Opposite: 28,169ft (8586m)
Kanchenjunga towers in the distance
during India's Himalaya Run & Trek*

MORE LIKE THIS
OFF-ROAD RIDGELINES

DODO RUN, MAURITIUS

Sitting pretty in the midst of the Indian Ocean, Mauritius is known for its famed-but-long-extinct flightless bird, flashy weddings and beautiful beaches. But there are also gritty trails and sweaty runners. Indeed, a strong running culture exists here and – as veterans of the Dodo Trail (an event named after that aforementioned flightless bird) will attest – the tropical island offers myriad sensational sky running routes. The most epic of these traces the course of the Xtreme race, rollercoastering across the ridgeline of the Black River Range. It starts at the foot of Le Morne Brabant and scales Piton de La Prairie (550m), Piton du Fouge (660m), Montagne la Porte (550m) and Piton Canot (550m) to reach the roof of the island, le Piton de la Rivière Noire at 2716ft (828m), before descending via Black River Gorges and finishing at Tamarin.
**Start // Le Morne Brabant
End // Riverland Sports Centre, Tamarin
Distance // 30 miles (50km)
More info // www.dodotrail.com**

THE RAZORBACK, VICTORIA, AUSTRALIA

Mt Feathertop (6306ft; 1922m) is far from Australia's highest peak, but it holds the country's classic alpine challenge – known as the Razorback – with the route between its peak and nearby Mt Hotham (6105ft; 1861m) commonly considered one of the southern continent's best ridgeline runs. Sitting in Victoria's stunning Alpine National Park, it offers several variations to match your fitness, ranging from a 40-mile (64km) ultra to the 13.6-mile (22km) short-course ridge run. Sitting between these, the 24-mile (40km) Razorback Circuit is an excellent option for those wanting to taste the cream of the Victorian High Country, with the route running up Bungalow Spur, traversing the Razorback and crossing to Diamantina Spur, before heading down Bon Accord Spur.
**Start/End // Harrietville Caravan Park or Diamantina Hut
Distance // 24 miles (40km)
More info // www.runningwild.net.au**

HIMALAYA RUN & TREK, INDIA

One of the world's oldest annual trail-running events, the Himalaya Run & Trek (HRT), is a five-day epic that begins in the tea plantations near the sky town of Darjeeling in West Bengal, and runs a ring route through the clouds, tracing the vertiginous border between India and Nepal. The views along the 100-mile (160km) route, which for several days features five of the world's six highest peaks (Everest, Kanchenjunga, Makalu, Lhotse and Cho Oyu) take away any breath the altitude might have left in your lungs. If five days of running sounds too much, the middle day can be done as a standalone 26-mile challenge. It travels from the Himalayan eyrie of Sandakphu to the river-side settlement of Rimbik, under the eyes of the planet's most famous mountain range and through stunningly pretty flower-bedecked valleys and villages. This is arguably the world's most beautiful marathon.
**Start/End // Maneybhanjang (full five-day circuit)
Distance // 100 miles (160km)
More info // www.himalayan.com**

SYDNEY'S SPECTACULAR SEAFRONT

The famous ocean-hugging track between Bondi and Coogee beaches is stunning. But an annual outdoor art-show holds its own in competing for your attention.

As if the coastal views from the cliff tops overlooking Sydney's Tamarama Beach aren't stimulating enough, someone has seen fit to exercise my imagination even more with some seriously abstract alfresco art along the way. During a dawn run, I've come across a mob of man-shaped figures, who fail to return my g'day as I gallop past.

Turns out, this gang of eyeless effigies, staring out across the Southern Ocean, is part of Sculpture by the Sea, the world's largest free public art installation. Spread out over a little more than a mile, beyond Bondi, this annual two-and-a-half-week festival features works by Aussie and international artists, some of which can be mind-meltingly modern, others pleasingly thought-provoking. Once a year, far from the confines of a gallery, these free-range artworks are let loose along the first part of a 4.2-mile (7km) trail between Bondi and Coogee beaches in Sydney's southern suburbs.

This same stretch also holds the distinction of being one of the most famous seaside strolls in the southern hemisphere. Tracing the

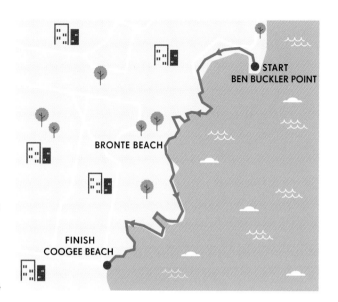

START
BEN BUCKLER POINT

BRONTE BEACH

FINISH
COOGEE BEACH

© stevecoleimages | Getty Images

"At Clovelly Beach, home to one of the oldest surf lifesaving clubs, a school group is taking board-riding lessons – how different this is to my own PE education"

epic coastline, and linking the beautiful beaches that help make Sydney one of the most desirable and liveable cities on earth, this suburban pathway is a constant reminder for locals about how bloody blessed they are, with or without world-class art as a sideshow.

But as popular as this path is, in the hours either side of daybreak it's much more of a running route than it is a walkway. Long before the ramblers, amblers, backpackers and tourists take to the track, runners bowl through in both directions, on cobweb-clearing morning missions.

I catch the first bus to Bondi with my gear already on, not expecting to gallop around an art show. Instead, I am merely looking forward to a run in the early morning sun, around some of the most spectacular shoreline on the planet. Bondi is, of course, well known beyond Australia, but the truth is, it's only the launch pad for a journey that takes in much better spots.

From Ben Buckler Point in North Bondi I run around the curve of the famous beach and past a monument to Black Sunday, a dark day in 1938 when a series of monstrous waves washed hundreds of people into the sea, drowning five of them. Such scenes are hard to imagine on a calm bluebird morning, but I soon see powerful surf sending spray surging into the saltwater pool at Bondi Icebergs Club, an iconic ocean-fed swimming spot on Notts Ave. It's here that the path begins toward Coogee.

As tempting as the water looks, I continue cantering south on the doubletrack concrete waterfront walkway as it drops between the rocks and then rises to round Mackenzies Point, where a newly restored ancient Aboriginal rock carving of a giant ray can be seen. This landscape has been inspiring artists for centuries – maybe millennia. Some of the 225-million-year-old sandstone cliffs around here are topped by rocks decorated with ancient indigenous carvings depicting marine animals.

This morning, much more modern and totally transitory artwork lines the trail. Here's a giant mirrored igloo-like thing. A few paces further I find a pile of precariously balanced boulders, spilling across the grass of Marks Park. And then there's the gang of silent statues, encountered as I round Mackenzies Bay and meet Tamarama Beach, where hundreds of bikini-wearing, budgie-smuggling sun-worshipers will give my silent featureless friends something to stare at soon enough. Surely there's a sign explaining all this somewhere, but those are for the walkers. I simply carry on past, happily applying a narrative layer of my own conjecture to the strange scene. Which is what such art is all about, surely.

What follows is a sort of greatest hits of Sydney's beaches and coves. I bid the sculptures adieu and bound on to Bronte, the best of the beaches in my humble opinion thanks to barbecues in the verdant park, beautiful body-boarding conditions and a free-to-use tide-fed pool for swimming laps. I then trace the track south,

HISTORY MYSTERY

One non-indigenous rock carving above the ocean in North Bondi is believed by some historians to depict a Spanish sailing ship, accompanied by Roman-style lettering interpreted as an assertion of conquest. It's a controversial belief, as it would mean the Spanish beat Captain Cook to Australia's east coast by some 200 years.

From left: Mackenzies Bay; the path from Bondi to Coogee; 'Red Trumpet Red Table' by Philip Spelman, part of Sculpture by the Sea, 2014. Previous page: Sydney's famous Bondi Beach

past Calga Reserve and into Waverley, to wend along the famous boardwalk that skirts a cemetery with killer views of a restless ocean

Beyond the boardwalk, after a little hook round Shark Point, I run round the corner into Clovelly, another cracking beach cuddled in the arms of a yet another cove and home to one of the world's oldest surf lifesaving clubs. This morning, a school group is taking to the waves for a board-riding lesson, giving me pause for thought about how very different this is to PE lessons during my own education. I hope these kids appreciate how lucky they are.

I'm feeling pretty fortunate myself, though, feet floating on freshly released endorphins, until Cliffbrook Parade brings me back down to earth. This passage, linking Clovelly to Gordons Bay, is a quads crusher, but it all feels worthwhile when I pop out the other side into a beautiful bay accessible only by boat and foot. I can see snorkellers and divers are already taking to the gin-clear water for an early morning aquatic adventure.

The chill of the dawn has long since lifted and I'm cloaked in sweat. One last push around Dolphin Point and past the sombre bronze linked figures that form the memorial to the Bali bomb victims takes me into the welcoming arms of Coogee. And now, a decision: do I run back, walk, or wimp-out and get the bus? There's only one real answer to that – it's too good a trail not to trot twice. Although perhaps I'll take it easy on the return leg, stopping to absorb the artwork along the way. **PK**

ORIENTATION

Start // Ben Buckler Point
Finish // Coogee Beach
Distance // 4.3 miles (7km) one way
Getting there // The train from Town Hall to Bondi Junction takes 11 minutes. Numerous buses take you to the beach.
When to go // Sydney is pleasant year-round. Sculpture by the Sea takes place late October to early November.
Where to stay // Bronte, Clovelly and Coogee all offer arguably better beaches than Bondi, with accommodation near the ocean and a little less boisterousness.
More info // www.sculpturebythesea.com
Things to know // If you're in Sydney in August consider joining 80,000 runners on the City to Surf run from Hyde Park in the CBD to Bondi Beach.

MORE LIKE THIS
SYDNEY'S SUBURBS

MAROUBRA TO MALABAR

The Bondi-to-Coogee route is a classic coastal run when done at dawn, but at other times it can be frustratingly busy. This route, slightly further south, provides a much less travelled but every bit as beautiful alternative. Start from the southern end of Maroubra Beach and simply keep the Southern Ocean on your left, while running bush-lined trails that trace the dramatic headland cliffs past Magic Point. Carry on around Boora Point and into Long Bay, before hitting another belter of a beach at Malabar. For a longer run, continue on to La Perouse and Unesco World Heritage-listed Bare Island in Botany Bay, via Little Bay, Cape Banks, Henry Head and Little Congwong Beach.
Start // Maroubra Beach
End // Malabar Beach (or La Perouse for the longer option)
Distance // 2.8 miles (4.5km)
More info // www.nationalparks.nsw. gov.au

ROYAL BOTANIC GARDEN TO BARANGAROO RESERVE

Sydney might boast most of Australia's oldest and most recognisable structures, but it's a city in a constant state of evolution, making it all the more fascinating to explore on the hoof. This linear run begins in the beautiful Royal Botanic Garden and skirts along the shoreline overlooking Woolloomooloo to Mrs Macquarie's Chair, an exposed sandstone pew poking into Sydney Harbour. Views of the Harbour Bridge are superb. But carry on around Circular Quay and past the famous Opera House to get even closer to the iconic span. Continue through The Rocks, the city's oldest quarter, to Barangaroo Reserve, a fantastic foreshore park that opened in 2015.
Start // Corner of St Mary's and Prince Albert roads
End // Barangaroo Reserve
Distance // 3 miles (5km)
More info // www.barangaroo.com

LANE COVE NATIONAL PARK

A world away from the busy eastern suburbs, this national park on Sydney's sensational North Shore offers runners an escape along some quiet and wildlife-rich routes that are as rewarding as they are challenging. A circular off-road foray follows the south bank of Lane Cove River from the Chatswood end of the park along the red gum-lined Riverside Walk to De Burghs Bridge. Here, you can cross the water and return along the opposite bank, taking the Lane Cove Valley and Heritage walking routes. Look and listen out for kookaburras and lorikeets that live among the eucalypts, caves and rocky outcrops. A 10km sealed-surface option out-and-back along Riverside Rd might appeal to road runners, but the elevation is brutal.
Start // Delhi Rd bridge
End // Chatswood
Distance // 7 miles (11.2km)
More info // www.nationalparks.nsw. gov.au

From top: Sydney's Royal Botanic Garden; Barangaroo Reserve, with Harbour Bridge in the background

ULTRA-TRAIL AUSTRALIA

Formerly known as the North Face 100, this gorgeous tour of the Blue Mountains remains the most famous long-distance race in the southern hemisphere.

T en kilometres,' they said. 'You'll only need to run the final
10 kilometres.' I had been assigned to write a profile of Dean
Karnazes, one of the most famous ultramarathon runners in
the world. The venue for our interview would be the Ultra-
Trail Australia trail-running festival (back then called The
North Face 100). It's the biggest trail ultra on the continent and
one of the biggest in the world.

Karnazes was, of course, planning on running all 100km.
Whereas the longest run I had done in any one stretch in my
entire life was 8 miles (12km). So when organisers told me I could
be dropped a mere six miles (10km) from the finish line I believed
them. And that's how I ended up running my first ultra, by accident.

As I headed towards the undulating Blue Mountains World
Heritage Wilderness, east of Sydney, I couldn't help but second-
guess my training regimen. When it comes to the UTA, they say
you should train for uphills, downhills and stairs. And regardless

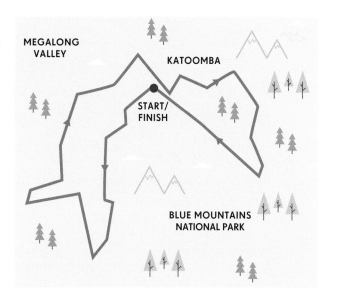

MEGALONG
VALLEY

KATOOMBA

START/
FINISH

BLUE MOUNTAINS
NATIONAL PARK

© Pete Seaward | Lonely Planet

of whether you've entered the 13.6-mile (22km) distance or the ultra distances of 31 or 62 miles (50/100km), they all require preparation.

I, however, didn't think I had to train, boldly calculating that a measly 10kms could be 'cheated' by a mid-thirties Average Joe like me who was in reasonably good shape. I did a total of two 5km outings in the two weeks prior and figured that should do the trick. And it might have, had the race organisers not accidentally dropped me off at the halfway mark of the full 62-mile (100km) distance.

But I still had a job to do. Thankfully, as I met up with Karnazes, he immediately began to relay anecdote after anecdote about a life of adventure running, providing great fodder for my article. And the landscape was truly magnificent. The towering cliffs and rock formations of 'The Blueys' attract 6000 participants from all over the world, many of whom flock to the event year after year, hydropacks, grippy shoes and grittier determination at the ready.

Like Karnazes, they are attracted not just by the glitz of the biggest showpiece of trail-running Down Under, but by the sheer beauty of the trails that crawl up, down and along soaring cliff-lines, ridges and escarpments with alluring names such as Narrow Neck, Iron Pot Ridge, Honeymoon Lookout and the aptly named Sublime Point. The 4500-plus metres of ascent includes brutal climbs up Golden Stairs, Taros Ladder and, of course, Furber Steps – 998 stairs ascending approximately 650ft (200m) at the final stretch.

It's not just the climbing that takes one's breath away. The

"I made a pact with Karnazes: if he kept going, I would, too, and try to complete my first ever ultramarathon"

Megalong Valley is remote and bucolic. The Six Foot Track section is quintessential Australian bush running, and the course passes waterfalls in the eastern ramparts. The Grand Clifftop Track demarks the cafe-packed villages and quiet residences of the Blue Mountains while passing through the deep and dramatic wilderness of the national park and Jameson Valley, 2000ft (600m) below.

Trying to pretend I could somehow keep up with a man best known for running 50 marathons in 50 states in 50 days, I walked gingerly backwards up a steep mountain in the Megalong Valley. I was now an unofficial participant in Australia's biggest trail-running ultra. The denial was powerful as I simply focused on the few feet in front of me, and on prying more great material from Karnazes.

It turned out he had had a shockingly bad first half of the race and, by the time I joined him, was contemplating dropping out. That's when I did something that, to this day, I can't quite understand: I made a pact with him that if he kept going then, in return, I would try to complete my first ever ultramarathon off the back of zero training. Unfortunately, he agreed.

After about 18 miles (29km), no pretty name or postcard-worthy

AUSSIE ELITES

During the 2010 UTA, Australians Stuart Gibson and Andrew Lee finished in a dead heat (in a time of nine hours, 31 minutes and 11 seconds), after going toe-to-toe for the last dozen miles. They crossed the line holding hands, something the pair are now often teased about. In 2014, Gibson again tied for first, this time alongside Andrew Tuckey. They didn't hold hands.

From left: surrounded by eucalyptus in Blue Mountains National Park; prepare to climb a lot of stairs. Previous page: the Three Sisters rock formation above Jamison Valley

view could numb the fatigue. Even worse was the pain and dread of the final push as I looked up at twinkling lights blinking through the treeline high above, signalling the far-away finish line. But as I edged closer to the base of the final cliff, I could hear the crowd roaring for those runners who were already crossing the line. It sounded so close it fooled me into thinking I was about to complete my first ultra. But then I spotted a trail-side sign indicating six miles to go. My hopes were dashed. My legs suddenly felt like jelly and my stomach dropped at the thought of the climb ahead.

Mr Ultramarathon Man, Dean Karnazes, had the good wisdom to cut me loose long before, sprinting off not long after our final checkpoint. And once he felt the pull of the finish he did what any elite runner would do and picked up the pace for a respectable finish time of 14 hours and 42 minutes. He did say before leaving me in the dust that this was one of the toughest he'd done. I concurred.

I, on the other hand, ended up finishing a slice before midnight – a full three hours behind Karnazes. But I finished. I had unintentionally run my first ultra – the first of what is now 30 and counting. Admittedly, I have yet to officially enter the full 62-mile (100km) main event at Ultra-Trail Australia. But having now run both of the shorter distances several times each, including large sections of the longer ultra course, it's officially on my bucket list. And I'll probably train for it when I do it. **CO**

ORIENTATION

Start/End // Scenic World, Katoomba, Greater Blue Mountains World Heritage Area
Distance // 62, 31 or 13.6 miles (100, 50 or 22km)
Getting there // Katoomba is roughly 2 hours' drive west of Sydney.
When to go // The trail-running festival happens every May (though trails are open all year round).
Where to stay // There are hotels, motels, B&Bs and hostels in Katoomba, Leura and Wentworth Falls.
More info // www.ultratrailaustralia.com.au
Things to know // UTA is a 'runners' ultra, in that there are long sections of non-technical fire road. Nonetheless, it's unwise not to train for steep terrain and lots of stairs, going up (hamstrings) and down (quads).

Opposite: the running continues long after the sun sets at New Zealand's Tarawera Trail Run ultramarathon

MORE LIKE THIS
ANTIPODEAN TRAIL-RUN FESTS

TARAWERA TRAIL RUN, NEW ZEALAND

Tarawera Ultramarathon is New Zealand's biggest trail-running festival, held annually in February. Part of the much-acclaimed Ultra-Trail World Tour, the event boasts a line-up of 100 mile (162km), 63 mile (102km), 31 mile (50km) and 12.4 mile (20km) distances, exploring the Rotorua wilderness on the North Island. The course runs through places that have deep cultural significance to local Maori people, with natural highlights including seven lakes, thick forests and a myriad of waterfalls. Around 1500 participants compete, including some of the world's best runners. The trails are runnable, scenic and point to point. Every finisher receives a beautiful locally inspired wooden medal (the 100-mile finishers get a pounamu pendant).The two longer distances are both qualification races for the Western States 100 Mile Endurance Run, while the longest is also a qualifier for the Ultra Trail du Mont Blanc (UTMB).
Start/End // Rotorua, New Zealand
Distance // 12.4–100 miles (20–162km)
More info // www.taraweraultra.co.nz

WARBURTON TRAIL FEST, AUSTRALIA

The newest kid on the Australian trail-running festival block, this one's a little different. Sure, spread over three days in mid-March, it boasts a tough 31-mile (50km) mountain range-crossing Lumberjack Ultra – so named in honour of the sawmillers who worked the region in the mid 19th century – a 13.6-mile (22km) up-and-back mountain climb with 3280ft (1000m) of ascent, and a couple of mid-distance races, as well as a 3-mile (5km) fun run. But what marks the Warburton Trail Fest as a little more eccentric than most is the 'Multiday Madness' entry option, whereby participants take on as many of the events as possible, for an overall crown. The finale event is a short 1-mile trail run that then finishes with a 1-mile paddle down a river on lilos. And yes, you have to carry your lilo for the initial run leg! Dress-ups are encouraged.
Start/End // Warburton, Victoria
Distance // 2–31 miles (3–50km)
More info // www.warburtontrailfest.com

GONE NUTS 101, TASMANIA

Named after Tasmania's imposing volcanic plug known as 'the Nut', this two-year-old race held every March has three different distances: 63, 31 and 15 miles (101km, 50km and 25km), which start in Stanley, Rocky Cape National Park and Boat Harbour respectively, and finish in Wynyard. Largely a coastal run, the terrain includes everything from singletrack that travels over windswept bluffs to sand and pebbles underfoot, as runners traverse pristine beaches. But inland stretches bring you deep into the bush along rough 4WD tracks and overgrown trails, with stream crossings across the Millicent Valley. The climbs promise to be challenging but fun, as the undulating terrain never quite destroys you.
Start/End // Stanley, Tasmania
Distance // 15–63 miles (25–101km)
More info // www.gonenuts.com.au

THE GHOST RUN OF WAIHI GORGE

You'll have plenty of companions as you navigate the mine-scarred mountainsides of New Zealand's Waihi Gorge – you just may not be able to see them.

I have run all over New Zealand and still only found one place where I need my headtorch during the day: Waihi Gorge in the North Island. Hugging the sides of a steep narrow cut in the earth, the trail passes through a network of tunnels carved out by gold-mining lust. The mines can be explored during an undulating 6-mile (10km) loop that circumnavigates a canyon dripping with history and unsurpassed natural beauty. And it's the prospect of a supernatural sighting that has always made this run one of my favourites.

The town of Waihi is a two-hour drive south of Auckland, within easy reach of Rotorua and Taupo. Gold was discovered here in the early 1800s and, by 1908, it was the fastest-growing town in New Zealand. Luckily for the trail runners and hikers who converge here these days, the same catastrophic geological upheaval that brought precious minerals closer to the earth's surface also created dramatic mountains and ravines. Most tourists are content with a short stroll around the close to the car park. But one must venture beyond the interpretation panels to really feel the sense of history and, possibly, commune with the gorge's former residents. At one point these ravines were home-and-income to more than 2000 people living in straggly buildings that clung precariously to the sheer rock walls. No one lives here now, and the stillness is haunting.

Meanwhile, Waihi itself is lively, with a plethora of accommodation. Yet, for me, the Department of Conservation campground at Dickey's Flat is always basecamp. Waking up here, I take the luxury of a leisurely breakfast in the warm spring sunshine before donning my running shoes and pack.

The first few hundred yards loosen me up, as I bounce across the first of many single-file wooden suspension bridges along the route.

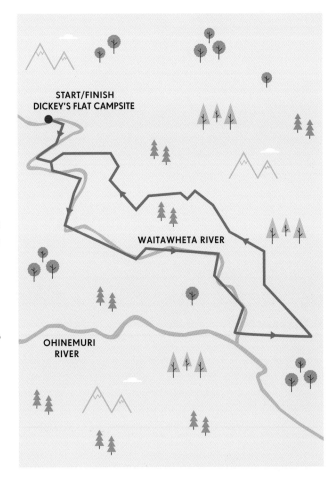

START/FINISH
DICKEY'S FLAT CAMPSITE

WAITAWHETA RIVER

OHINEMURI
RIVER

Crown Track stretches before me, flickering in and out of the sun as patches of cool, damp forest alternate with small clearings of flax and grass. The trail is wide, flat and well-graded, and I relish the sense of flow, as I skim along beside the Waitawheta River.

But sunshine and birdsong quickly disappear as the trail climbs gently above the river, which has now swollen to a deep, fast torrent. The trail is littered with tools and machinery abandoned a century ago. A set of stairs takes me higher above the river and my excitement builds as a tunnel signals the start of the Windows Walk.

Donning my headtorch, I step cautiously into the gloom. What men these were, grubbing at the dank walls for 16 hours a day, inching deeper and deeper into the mountains in search of sparkles in the bleak rock. Miners desperate to escape this hell were known to sever their own thumbs to be relieved of duty, and the Waihi Museum contains rows of human digits preserved in jars.

The rock-strewn tunnel floor makes for slow going and I am beginning to shiver when I see thin rays of natural light seeping

> ## "More tunnels follow, but these are shorter, allowing me to stash my headtorch and forge on in the darkness"

in from the first window. Leaning on the rough-hewn sill, I stare straight down into the thrashing Waitawheta River. I continue, bypassing a handful of windows before popping out into bright sunlight and clear running again. More tunnels follow: these are shorter, allowing me to stash the headtorch and forge on in the darkness. As i jog carefully along a disused tramway, an abandoned railway wagon makes for fun photography.

A short flight of stairs deposits me rather abruptly into a large clearing and a dramatic landscape – the tumultuous confluence of the roaring Waitawheta and Ohinemuri Rivers. At approximately three miles in, this marks the apex of my loop. And to this point the route has not been all that taxing. There are several options in front of me: tracing the right bank of the Ohinemuri River, the Karangahake Historic Walkway extends four miles past Owharoa Falls to the fascinating remains of Victoria Battery. Alternatively, a few hundred metres along the Walkway, a half-mile-long disused railway tunnel and an open double-level truss bridge make for a terrifically fun loop.

Today, however, I long for the trees so decide to follow the western side of the gorge – a very different experience to the relatively easy running of the morning. I brace myself for a sharp climb up through the damp tree-lined Scotsman's Gully. My legs feel fresh and the road hums smoothly by. County Rd slowly ascends Karangahake Mountain and I become conscious of a different age of industry. The Kaimai Ranges were logged heavily in the 1800s for native kauri trees. These forest giants live for well over 600 years, attaining girths up to 5m in diameter.

Gravel soon peters out and I am back on forested single-track.

PUMPHOUSE PRESERVATION

Waihi's Pumphouse was built in 1904 to house steam pumps for the deepening Martha Mine. When electricity rendered the machinery redundant in 1914, the equipment was removed and the building declared a historic monument. In 2004, engineers discovered the ground was too unstable because of the underground mines. So Teflon-coated concrete beams were used to slide the three-storey 1,840 tonne icon 300m to where it currently resides.

Clockwise from top: river crossings made easy; old railway tunnels-turned-footpaths; NZ's famous silver fern. Previous page: nearby Karangahake Gorge

© John Bentley | Alamy Stock Photo

© Paul Abbitt rml | Alamy Stock Photo

The trees touch overhead and birds click and squawk in the canopy. Silver fern is abundant, recognised the world over as the emblem of the New Zealand All Blacks rugby team. As the trail continues to wind around the face of Karangahake Mountain, I catch the occasional vertiginous glimpse down the rock face into the depths of the canyon. It is always surprising how much height is gained on this leg, as the running is smooth and uncomplicated.

But now I have reached the final junction, and excitement bubbles up in me again. The main track continues onwards and upwards towards the mountain's summit. Instead, I break left to access the rollercoaster ride affectionately known as 'Dubbo's'. Dubbo 96 Track is steep and soft, true singletrack at its best. I am grinning inanely as I hurtle downwards, placing faith in my feet to find solid contact at each lunge. Tall broadleaf and podocarps filter out much of the sunlight, creating an atmosphere of delicious mystery. I marvel at how quickly the ascent I worked for is lost.

Bottoming out at a cold, clear stream, the trail climbs sharply over a small quad-destroying ridge before finally spitting me back onto wide, sunny Crown Track, where the journey began. Cooling down on the final flat stretch back to Dickey's Flat, I pause on the last bridge to gaze into the quietly moving river. It has been an evocative jaunt, and I wonder whether the miners and loggers also paused in their trudge back to camp at the end of an arduous day, arrested by the majesty of the mighty Karangahake. I would like to think so. **VW**

ORIENTATION

Start/End // Dickey's Flat Campsite
Distance // 6.25-mile (10km) loop
Getting there // Karangahake Gorge is 140km (a 2-hour drive) south of Auckland; 130km north of Rotorua.
When to go // Year-round, but the tracks may be closed by rockfall or flooding in inclement weather.
Where to stay // Basic camping is available at Dickey's Flat, or there are several motels in Waihi or the nearby resort of Waihi Beach.
More info // www.doc.govt.nz/karangahake
Things to know // Bring a headtorch for the tunnels, light thermals in colder months, and check the Department of Conservation website for track closures before you go.

*Opposite: Wairere Falls tumbles
500ft (153m), with fun running
trails near the top and bottom*

MORE LIKE THIS
NEW ZEALAND TRAIL RUNS

MT PIRONGIA

Lying in slumber just 15 miles (25km) from
the Tasman Sea, Mt Pirongia reclines
gracefully like a sleeping woman. Be
warned, however, this extinct volcano,
with her numerous basalt cones, is
certainly no lady. Rising dramatically
to a height of 3150ft (960m) above the
Waikato plains, the summit is known for
notoriously fickle weather that is prone
to rapid deterioration. There are steep
and treacherous drop-offs, slippery rocks
to clamber over and the trails can be
extremely muddy at any time of year.
Steel yourself for a challenge – plan
and prepare well, take warm and dry
gear, and be prepared to travel slowly at
times. In return, those who run Pirongia
are rewarded with rare flora and fauna,
impressive views and some of the most
technical running to be had in New
Zealand.
**Start/End // Grey Road car park
Distance // 7.4-mile (12km) loop via
Tirohanga and Mahaukura tracks
More info // www.doc.govt.nz/**

THE PINNACLES

Testimony to its appeal, a day-trip to the
Pinnacles is on the official '101 Must-Do' list
for New Zealanders. The main track traces
the original route taken by packhorses
to carry supplies to kauri loggers and
gold-diggers in the early 1900s, climbing
through stunning native forest and
crossing numerous small streams. The trail
continues past the hut before climbing
to the Pinnacles themselves – a good
head for heights and confident footing is
required to make the final climb up these
rocky spires. A popular location to view
sunrise and sunset, the Pinnacles command
panoramic views of the Coromandel
Peninsula, Hauraki Gulf and Kauaeranga
Valley. Escape the crowds by returning via
historic Billygoat Track, dotted with rusting
machinery left abandoned by retreating
loggers and miners.
**Start/End // Kauaeranga Valley road-
end
Distance // 12.4-mile (20km) loop via
Pinnacles and Billygoat tracks
More info // www.wildthings.club/trails/**

WAIRERE FALLS

If hills provide the motivation to get you
out of bed early, the climb to Wairere
Falls is a great way to bank some vertical
miles. Somewhat dramatically, the Wairere
River slides off a wide, rocky shelf at the
southwest end of the Kaimai Ranges to
tumble down 500ft (153m) to the plains of
Te Aroha. The rock shelf is a popular spot
for summer bathers, but extreme care must
be taken during periods of heavy rainfall,
when the Falls can double in volume. This
short out-and-back route delivers 1900ft
(580m) of elevation in just over two miles,
with an equally quad-thrashing descent
– exercise caution on slippery rocks and
wooden stairs. Above the Falls it is possible
to access other trails that lead deeper into
the southern Kaimai Ranges.
**Start/End // Goodwin Rd (off Old Te
Aroha Rd)
Distance // 4.3 miles (7km)
More info // www.wildthings.club/trails/**

A TOUR OF TASMANIA'S FREYCINET PENINSULA

This devilishly delightful trail run covers it all, from the high ground of the Hazards to the pinot grigio-clear waters of Wineglass Bay.

The best runs are often the ones you never intended doing. Whether sublime, unscripted scrambles or even flat out mistakes, it's these accidental adventures that live on in the memory, long after leg muscles have forgotten the extra miles. At least, this is what I told myself as an intended quick loop around one little corner of Tasmania's Freycinet National Park – a sub-seven-miler from Parsons Cove to Wineglass Bay, via Hazards Beach and the Isthmus Track – mistakenly morphed into a nearly 19-mile (30km) circuit around the peninsula.

I'd always wanted to do this route at some point. Although it's rare to see another runner on normal days (we're well outnumbered by walkers), the full Freycinet Circuit is talked about in language of awe by trailhounds who have taken it on. It's even run as a race every July. Neatly knitting together a network of cracking paths to traverse granite peaks, brilliant white beaches and thick coastal forests, it's a route that every visiting runner wants to experience. But it wasn't part of the plan that day – I had a plane to catch.

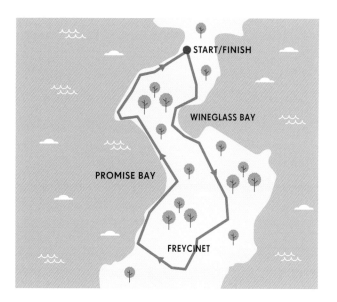

START/FINISH

WINEGLASS BAY

PROMISE BAY

FREYCINET

© Visual Collective | Shutterstock

"At Wineglass Bay it was impossible not to cast off my kit, streak across the squeaky white sand and plunge into the ocean"

I was on Australia's Apple Isle for reasons far removed from running, but the thought of leaving without at least a cursory explorative flit around Freycinet felt criminal. So, setting off from the trailhead at first light, I trotted along the flat Hazards Beach Track, skirted Great Oyster Bay from Parsons Cove and curled around the ankles of Mt Mayson. Mayson is one of four peaks (along with Mt Amos, Mt Dove and Mt Parsons) collectively known as the Hazards, which stand sentinel across the peninsula's delicate neck. Warming to my mission I picked up the pace, as thoughts of Tasmania's past chased me along the path.

For millennia, the indigenous Toorernomairremener people had this place to themselves, leaving middens made from oyster shells as the only enduring evidence of their existence – an existence immediately threatened when European sails appeared on the horizon. A Dutch explorer left his mark on the map in the naming of Freycinet, but it was the Brits who first found a use for this faraway land.

It seems utterly inconceivable now, but this stunning spot was once a dumping ground for Georgian society's undesirables – a place where unimaginable horrors were inflicted on hundreds of unwanted humans. Infamous penal colonies were established nearby, at Port Arthur and Maria Island, and convict labour was used to develop Freycinet, a delicate finger of land pointing into the Tasman Sea. Ironically, thousands of Poms now pay good money to come here.

Rising over a spur, a sudden movement shook me back to the present. I whispered an apology to the red-necked wallaby I'd rudely disturbed. A joey lay awkwardly in her pouch, legs and arms jutting out either side of a cheeky head, as it nonchalantly nibbled dewy grass at the track's edge.

The Hazards' peaks protected me from the glare of the rapidly rising sun, casting the trail in cool shadow. No need to worry about stepping on any sleepy tiger snakes just yet, they were all busy breakfasting in the bush between the she-oaks, and wouldn't start sunbathing on the tracks until later in the day.

Passing Fleurieu Point and Lemana Lookout, where the view is full of Promise Bay, I hit the golden ground of Hazards Beach about 2.5 miles (4km) into the run. I instinctively veered towards the hard-packed sand left behind by the retreating tide, and it was here, bamboozled by the beauty of the beach, that I ran right past the sand ladder leading up to the track that shortcuts across the isthmus to the northern end of Wineglass Bay.

I only realised my mistake on reaching Lagunta Creek, at the end of the 2-mile-long beach. But my leg muscles were well warmed and I decided to crack on through the eucalypt forest towards Cooks Beach. By now I was fully committed. My map indicated it would almost be as far to run back as it would be to carry on, and a desire to keep exploring blinded me to the contour lines that revealed a big climb just ahead.

BLOODY PAST

Besides its horrible convict-era history, the deceptively beautiful beaches and coves around Freycinet were once-upon-a-time fouled by blood-and-gut waste, products of a whaling and fishing industry, which attracted sharks in the same way that the peninsula now pulls in travellers. In fact, the Hazards are named after Captain Richard 'Black' Hazard, an African-American whaler.

From left: Hazards Beach treasures; Great Oyster Bay; a female red-necked wallaby with her precious cargo. Previous page: Tasmania's famous Wineglass Bay

The track then veered inland, rounding Mt Freycinet. Refilling my hydration pack from Botanical Creek, I ascended the flanks of 1900ft (579m) Mt Graham. Crossing East Freycinet saddle, now nearly 10 miles (16km) into the run, and with my quads quarrelling with my brain, I climbed the spine of the peninsula, picking a route through boulders as I battled a crosswind.

The view and the cool breeze easily compensated for the climb. Wonderful Wineglass Bay winked from below; beyond that, the cliffs of Mt Dove dove down into an azure ocean. Scrambling onwards, I crossed a woody plateau and dropped through a gully towards Graham Creek, then traced Lone Rock Ridge down to the southern end of Wineglass Bay, where a crescent of bright white sand cups the translucent Tasman Sea. Confronted by the most beautiful beach I've ever set foot on, completely devoid of human company, it was impossible not to cast off my kit, streak across the squeaky-fine sand and plunge into the ocean. Still dripping, I traced the track back to the trailhead, crossing the saddle between Mt Mayson and Mt Amos to Parsons Cove.

The drive to Launceston airport was nervy, but I made the plane. Just. I pitied the poor person sat beside me, though. Unshowered, my skin was streaked white with salt from sweat and Wineglass Bay brine and, with a head fizzing with post-adventure adrenaline, fuelled by fear of almost missing my flight, I couldn't stop babbling on about the best run I never should have done. **PK**

ORIENTATION

Start/End // Parsons Cove
Distance // 18.6 miles (30km)
Getting there // Coles Bay is 115 miles (186km) northeast of Hobart; 104 miles (167km) southeast of Launceston. From there, continue to Parsons Cove along Honeymoon Bay.
When to go // This trail is doable all year, but conditions on the higher part can be very cold and potentially treacherous in winter (June to August).
Where to stay // The Freycinet Lodge offers 4-star cabins in a stunning location. There's basic, cheap walk-in camping on the shores of Wineglass Bay.
More info // www.parks.tas.gov.au
Things to know // Runners, like walkers, are urged to tackle the track anti-clockwise, to help halt the spread of a deadly plant pathogen, Phytophthora (root rot).

Opposite: as part of England's South West Coast Path, the Purbeck peninsula has plenty of great trail-running

MORE LIKE THIS
PENINSULA LOOPS

ISLE OF PURBECK, ENGLAND, UK

Not an island, but a pretty peninsula pointing into the English Channel, Purbeck is part of the Unesco World Heritage-listed Jurassic Coast, which runs along the crumbly cliffs and beautiful beaches of Dorset and Devon. It's also on the South West Coast Path, Britain's biggest long-distance route, which provides sublime running conditions for people wanting to explore features such as Durdle Door sea arch and Lulworth Cove. The place oozes history, from Neolithic settlements to Napoleonic forts, via old smugglers' paths and WWII bunkers. For a 20-mile loop, leave the famous Square and Compass pub, prance to Dancing Ledge and trace the coast to Old Harry Rocks overlooking Swanage. Follow the Purbeck Way to Corfe Castle before returning across the common.

Start/End // Worth Matravers
Distance // 20 miles (12.4km)
More info // www.southwestcoastpath. org.uk

WILSON'S PROMONTORY, AUSTRALIA

Mainland Australia's most southerly point, 143 miles (230km) south of Melbourne, is a popular destination. Beyond the busy Tidal River campsite, however, trails tiptoeing into the bush transport runners into a landscape that's remained unchanged for millennia, where wombats and rock wallabies are commonly encountered, kookaburras cackle and secluded bluewater bays and secret beaches, reachable only by foot or boat, offer respite from the heat of the day. The sensational Southern Circuit via the lighthouse is a 37-mile (60km) epic, suitable only for the hardiest of trail runners. However, a brilliant marathon-distance option can be done by following the inland track between Waterloo Bay and Oberon Bay, which cuts out the southern half of the peninsula, but still takes in the best beaches.

Start/End // Tidal River
Distance // 26.2–37 miles (42km–60km)
More info // www.parkweb.vic.gov.au

SHEEP'S HEAD, IRELAND

The slenderest of the three fingers that point into the Atlantic from West Cork's craggy coastline, Sheep's Head is a picturesque peninsula, complete with pretty villages (Kilcrohane, Ahakista and Durrus), and dramatic ocean views. Ultra runners might be tempted by the 54-mile (88km) circular route from Bantry to the evocative sight of the lonely lighthouse at the extreme tip, before returning along the south side of the peninsula. But several smaller circuits are imminently doable for more modest runners, including the Poet's Way Loop, a 7.7-mile (12.5km) waymarked route named after local wordsmith Denis M Cronin. This sets off in a southwesterly direction from Tooreen, skirts Dunmanus Bay and passes Lough Akeen en route to the Sheep's Head lighthouse, before returning on the Bantry Bay side.

Start/End // Bantry Bay or Tooreen
Distance // 7.7 miles (12.5km)
More info // www.thesheepsheadway.ie

INDEX

Managing Director, Publishing Piers Pickard
Associate Publisher Robin Barton
Commissioning Editor Will Cockrell
Art Director Daniel Di Paolo
Designer Ben Brannan
Image Research Ceri James
Editors Will Cockrell, Nick Mee, Yolanda Zappatera
Print Production Nigel Longuet

August 2019
Published by Lonely Planet Global Limited
CRN 554153
www.lonelyplanet.com
20 19 18 17 16 15 14 13 12 11 10 9 8
Printed in Malaysia
ISBN 978 17886 8126 1
© Lonely Planet 2019
© photographers as indicated 2019

Lonely Planet Office

Ireland
Digital Depot,
Roe Lane (off Thomas St),
Digital Hub, Dublin 8, D08 TCV4

STAY IN TOUCH lonelyplanet.com/contact

Authors Richard Askwith (**RA**) is author of Today We Die A Little: Emil Zátopek, Olympic Legend to Cold War Hero (Yellow Jersey); Greg Benchwick (**GB**) has paced friends at the Leadville 100, run one marathon in Big Sur, and jogged across the globe – @gregbenchwick; Joe Bindloss (**JBS**); John Branch (**JB**) is the author of the Dipsea story from The New York Times June 17 © 2018 The New York Times. All rights reserved. Used by permission and protected by the copyright laws of the United States. The printing, copying, redistribution, or retransmission of this Content without express permission is prohibited. Kate Carter (**KC**); Stephanie Case (**SC**) is @runningcase on Twitter and www.ultrarunnergirl.com; Jayne D'Arcy's (**JD**) latest attempts of extreme wellness feature on www.jaynedarcy.com.au; Charlie Engle (**CE**) – learn more about 5.8, his biggest adventure yet, at www.charlieengle.com; Adharanand Finn (**AF**) is the author of Running with the Kenyans and The Rise of the Ultra Runners; follow him @adharanand. Damian Hall (**DH**) is an outdoor journalist, author, record-breaking ultra runner, public speaker and tea guzzler – www.damianhall.info. Patrick Kinsella (**PK**) is a journalist and author who specialises in tales about trails (and, often, ales) – @paddy_kinsella. Rachel Levin (**RL**) is a journalist and the author of LOOK BIG: And Other Tips for Surviving Animal Encounters of All Kinds (Ten Speed, 2018) – byrachellevin.com (Reprinted with permission of The Wall Street Journal, Copyright © 2019 Dow Jones & Company, Inc. All Rights Reserved Worldwide). Brian Metzler (**BM**) is a Boulder-based journalist who has run in 30 countries and authored several books – brianmetzler.com. Gabi Mocatta (**GM**); Sebastian Neylan (**SN**) is based in Melbourne after half a decade in London working with Lonely Planet – @swobba. Etain O'Carroll (**EO**) has been writing for Lonely Planet for more than 15 years and running all her life – Etaino.co.uk. Chris Ord (**CO**) is the editor of www.trailrunmag.com, a race director, and guides trail run holidays (www.tourdetrails.com). Matt Phillips' (**MP**) latest exploits include racing up London's 52-storey Cheesegrater for charity – @Go2MattPhillips; Piers Pickard (**PP**); Alicia Raeburn (**AR**) – www.mileslesstraveled.com; Mark Remy (**MR**) is the author of Runners of North America – A Definitive Guide to the Species and creator of www.DumbRunner.com. Brendan Sainsbury (**BS**) has authored over 50 Lonely Planet guides and run thousands of miles in the process. Sarah Stirling (**SS**) is an adventure writer based in Snowdonia – SarahStirling.com; @sarah_stirling. Regis St. Louis (**RS**); Michael Wardian (**MW**) is a professional runner with many national championships and first place finishes – @mikewardian; Vicki Woolley (**VW**); Karla Zimmerman (**KZ**) lives in Chicago; follow her @karlazimmerman. **Cover and illustrations** by Ross Murray (www.rossmurray.com)